High Growth Enterprises

The Role of
Founder Characteristics
and Venture Policies

High Growth Enterprises

The Role of Founder Characteristics and Venture Policies

Mathew J. Manimala

World Scientific

NEW JERSEY · LONDON · SINGAPORE · BEIJING · SHANGHAI · HONG KONG · TAIPEI · CHENNAI · TOKYO

Published by

World Scientific Publishing Co. Pte. Ltd.
5 Toh Tuck Link, Singapore 596224
USA office: 27 Warren Street, Suite 401-402, Hackensack, NJ 07601
UK office: 57 Shelton Street, Covent Garden, London WC2H 9HE

Library of Congress Cataloging-in-Publication Data
Names: Manimala, Mathew J., 1950–   author.
Title: High growth enterprises : the role of founder characteristics and
    venture policies / Mathew J. Manimala.
Description: New Jersey : World Scientific, [2023] |
    Includes bibliographical references and index.
Identifiers: LCCN 2022034415 | ISBN 9789811265365 (hardcover) |
    ISBN 9789811265372 (ebook) | ISBN 9789811265389 (ebook other)
Subjects: LCSH: Entrepreneurship. | New business enterprises. | Industrial policy.
Classification: LCC HB615 .M357 2023 | DDC 658.4/21--dc23/eng/20220902
LC record available at https://lccn.loc.gov/2022034415

British Library Cataloguing-in-Publication Data
A catalogue record for this book is available from the British Library.

For any available supplementary material, please visit
https://www.worldscientific.com/worldscibooks/10.1142/13115#t=suppl

Desk Editors: Aanand Jayaraman/Sandhya Venkatesh

Typeset by Stallion Press
Email: enquiries@stallionpress.com

To
My beloved Mother,
Marykutty James Manimala,
who left us for her heavenly abode on 8th August 2021,
with fond memories of her loving care
for our nourishment and growth.

Foreword

This new book by Mathew Manimala, a profound scholar of entrepreneurship, offers us another and unprecedented view of the entrepreneurial landscape. The setting is mountainous. In order to scale the high and rugged peaks of entrepreneurial growth, one must first address the reasons for the reluctance to grow. Then, the different stages of the ascent and the strategies to be adopted must be defined. Equally important are the personal traits that characterize entrepreneurial climbers. With writing that is as precise as it is fluid, Manimala introduces us to that landscape. Walking through it, the reader is led to ask questions about the future of entrepreneurship in the times that we live in. This is the time of the knowledge economy in the digital age, a time to face optimism by equipping ourselves with good mental and physical health and acting so that other living species and nature can enjoy the same good health.

Thanks to the author's excavations, we can imagine new combinations of knowledge and ideas. We will then think about growth without neglecting the quality of progress, with a generation of restless business creators who want to keep moving because "I have never heard of anyone stumbling over anything while sitting down. The wandering dog always finds a bone". This thought of Charles Kettering, the renowned US automotive engineer, can only be appreciated and translated into action by transformative enterprises whose independent judgment points them in the direction of the road less traveled. They use wind power to move the blades of the opportunity mills.

Like the Japanese author Yasunari Kawabata's (2013) *Master of Go,* the transformative enterprise disposes off quibbling rules in the name of rationality and relies on mutual appreciation among all players in the socio-economic field. It shifts the attention and available resources from solving problems inherited from behavior conforming to the standard vision of exploiting the opportunities arising from a new vision that makes it listen to nature and recognize its relevance. The transformative enterprise realizes that its business depends on the value generated by natural ecosystems. According to US environmentalist Peter Barnes (2021), "the supply of fresh water, soil formation, nutrient cycling, waste treatment, pollination, raw materials and climate regulation are worth between 25 and 87 trillion dollars a year", as compared with a gross world product in nominal terms of about 94 trillion dollars in May 2021. Consequently, the transformative enterprise takes on the task of protecting the wealth bestowed by nature on all living beings and future generations. It does so with durable programs that deliver a transformational shift toward well-being instead of temporary programs lighting hay fires that are smoke and mirrors.

In keeping with this line of thought, transformative enterprises recalibrate profit and question GDP measures of production that neglect individual and social well-being. Such an enterprise does not aspire solely to create a financial return for itself and its shareholders, as its profits, aligned with investment and personnel costs, are used first to sustain and renew itself and then return the money to shareholders. Humanity needs transformative enterprises whose development is attractive because they do not forget the general good of getting the most out of their mobilized resources to safeguard their interests.

Mathew Manimala's book has the virtue of immersing those who enter his entrepreneurial landscape in an appreciation of growth that ensures the highest degree of prosperity for all, not as a ceaseless accumulation of material wealth. Growth aims to enrich the culture and work of the mind and spirit to live in a better world. Life allows us to safeguard nature and enjoy the gifts it offers us. I am sure that, in view of the findings of the research reported here — which has identified socially desirable qualities such as the pursuit of excellence, people orientation, and reality contact as characteristics of high-growth entrepreneurs — this book will contribute its share toward the development of a balanced and inclusive perspective of enterprise growth with due consideration of societal and environmental concerns among academics, practitioners, and policymakers.

References

Barnes, P. (2021). Capitalism's most grievous flaws are, at root, problems of property rights and must be addressed at that level. *EVONOMICS*, October 24.

Kawabata, Y. (2013). *The Master of Go*. New York: Vintage Books. (First published in serial form in 1951).

Piero Formica
Professor of Entrepreneurship &
Senior Research Fellow,
Innovation Value Institute,
National University of Ireland,
Maynooth, Ireland

Preface

In 1990, when I was at Manchester Business School (MBS) on a faculty exchange program supported by the European Foundation for Management Development (EFMD), I had the opportunity to listen to Dame Stephanie Shirley, one of Britain's greatest female entrepreneurs. She was at MBS to deliver the Silver Anniversary Lecture. In a thought-provoking and inspiring address, which was partly autobiographical, she explained the issues related to entrepreneurial start-up and growth. During the informal interactions after the lecture, in response to a query about the impediments to venture growth, she remarked that the biggest barrier to her own firm's growth at that stage was herself. While this appeared to be rather strange to me at that time, a detailed study of entrepreneurial stories (including hers) showed that there were many stages in the growth of ventures, and many entrepreneurs would hesitate to go further at different stages. Many are the reasons for such hesitation, which are discussed in this book. In the case of Shirley, many of her innovations (such as the use of freelancers working from home and panel members in place of employees), which significantly reduced her overheads and employee costs and thereby contributed to the initial success of the venture, had to be abandoned at the growth stage. Naturally, it is stressful for any entrepreneur to repudiate their own innovations.

Another issue that is commonly mentioned in this regard is the entrepreneurs' desire to retain control within the family, whereas in many cases, family members may not be interested in or competent in taking the business forward. This was a real problem for Shirley too, as her only son was autistic and died at the age of 35. But the lack of successors within the family did not deter her from expanding and growing her business. On the contrary, she professionalized the business and 'let it go' out of her control. Subsequently, when the study reported in this book was conducted, it was found that this loosening of control was a key characteristic of growth-oriented entrepreneurs. Although it may not always involve the relinquishing of full control, as was the case with Shirley, there is a change in the control orientation of the growth-oriented entrepreneur. I describe this as a change from 'property orientation' to 'entity orientation' (the latter being the way one would deal with a son or daughter, as opposed to one's property). Since the case study of Dame Stephanie Shirley illustrates the changes required of the entrepreneur and the enterprise at different stages of the enterprise growth process, it is included as Appendix 1 in this book.

It was this meeting with Dame Stephanie Shirley that prompted me to revisit the theories on entrepreneurship, especially the phenomenon of enterprise growth. It is true that a single case cannot be used as proof for a theory, but it can generate hypotheses that can be tested empirically through further research in order to modify that theory. While considering the story of Shirley, one obvious theory that comes to mind is Everitt Hagen's theory that 'status-withdrawal', associated with disadvantaged and marginalized groups like refugees, is the cause of entrepreneurship. While the rise of Stephanie Shirley (née Vera Buchthal) from her refugee status to entrepreneurial excellence aptly illustrates the validity of Hagen's theory, it may be pointed out that the theory does not hold in her older sister Natale's case. Although Natale also came to the UK from Nazi Germany as a refugee, she didn't become an entrepreneur but further migrated to Australia and settled there. Her status as a 'double refugee' (to the UK and later to Australia) did not make her an entrepreneur. The empirical researcher's responsibility, therefore, is to show that there is a greater proportion of entrepreneurs among refugees than among the general population, which will provide some support to the 'status-withdrawal' theory. However, if all refugees do not become entrepreneurs, there will still be a question as to what else is required to convert a refugee into an entrepreneur. It is in this context that researchers turn their attention to the personal characteristics (motives, traits, policies, etc.) of the individual.

A similar logic would apply to the empirical research on enterprise growth. It is possible that enterprise growth could be facilitated by several factors, in which case one should look for the critical factor. There are theories linking firm growth with firm profitability on the one hand and industry growth on the other, which are but common sense and need to be tested empirically. Similarly, cases like that of Dame Shirley suggest that the characteristics of the entrepreneur may have a major role in deciding the growth or stagnation of a venture. Prior research studies are, therefore, reviewed in order to assess the extent of support for the influence of these variables on enterprise growth. Based on the findings of this review, a study was designed for assessing the extent to which the relevant variables are present for high- and low-growth ventures and their founders. The variables measured (as may be seen in the Questionnaire reproduced in Appendix 2) were as follows: (1) Venture characteristics (which included the assessment of firm profitability, firm growth parameters, and industry growth, among others); (2) Management practices of the venture; (3) Personal policies of the principal promoter; (4) Work motives of the principal promoter; and (5) Background and early experiences of the principal promoter. The scores for these variables were then used for computing the growth index and the interlinkages among the variables. Based on the relationships identified through the analysis of the above data, a model for the emergence of growth ventures is developed in this book.

Although a few research papers were published based on this work in the UK and the subsequent work done in India, the idea of a book came up when I became associated with the Global Entrepreneurship Monitor (GEM) project for two years as the leader of the India team. Being a consortium of researchers from different countries, the GEM project had more than 30 country teams working with it at that time and had a fair representation from all the major countries. One of the interesting (but at the same time, disappointing) findings about the global entrepreneurial scenario was that the growth expectations of entrepreneurs were abysmally low. The proportion of entrepreneurs expecting to create at least 20 jobs in five years was less than 1%. The Indian scenario was even more depressing; a large majority of start-ups were zero-employee ventures, with the average number of employees being 0.08, while the average number of employees expected by a start-up in five years was less than 2 (1.42, to be precise). Such low expectations for enterprise growth, especially when India had one of the highest TEA (Total Entrepreneurial Activity) Index scores (as of 2002), second only to Thailand, and had average or above average scores on many of the Entrepreneurial Framework Conditions (EFCs), could naturally be interpreted as some kind of 'growth unwillingness' on the part of entrepreneurs. The same was true for most other countries involved in the GEM studies.

A review of the research literature showed that 'growth unwillingness' is widely prevalent among entrepreneurs and that the reasons for it are based on the personal characteristics and preferences of the entrepreneurs. Hence, the focus of this book on the relationship between personality/background variables and enterprise growth is justified. As is explained in the book, the data from Indian entrepreneurs could not be used for this analysis because many of them were unwilling to reveal data on their financial performance for a few successive years, and so the growth index could not be computed for them. The present analysis, therefore, is exclusively based on the British data. Interrelationships among the variables may not change with the change in the countries or time periods of data collection. For example, a relationship established between the height and weight of individuals will be more or less the same with data from different countries or time periods. It is, therefore, with this confidence that the results of this study are presented to the community of researchers, academics, practitioners, and policymakers. It is hoped that this book will stimulate their thought processes, guide their actions, and initiate such studies in different contexts, as required.

About the Author

 **Mathew J Manimala** (MBA-Cochin, MBSc-Manchester, Fellow-IIMA) retired in 2018 after serving a term as Director of Xavier Institute of Management and Entrepreneurship (XIME), Bangalore. Prior to that, during 2001-15, he worked as Professor at the Indian Institute of Management Bangalore (IIMB), where he has also served as the Jamuna Raghavan Chair Professor of Entrepreneurship, as the Chairperson of N S Raghavan Centre for Entrepreneurial Learning (NSRCEL), and as the Chairperson of OB-HRM Area. His earlier academic positions were as Senior Faculty and Chairperson-HR Area at the Administrative Staff College of India (ASCI), Hyderabad, and as Lecturer at Cochin University of Science and Technology (CUSAT), Kochi. He is a recipient of a few prestigious research fellowships (such as: EFMD Fellowship at Manchester Business School, UK; and the Shastri Indo-Canadian Fellowship at the University of Calgary, Canada) and academic awards including the Heizer Award of the Academy of Management for "Outstanding Research in the Field of New Enterprise Development". He has published/presented about 100 research papers/case-studies (mostly in international journals, edited volumes and conferences) and 11 books in the areas of Entrepreneurship and Organizational Behavior. He is the Editor (since 1999) of *South Asian Journal of Management*, published by AMDISA.

Acknowledgments

On the occasion of publishing this book on high-growth enterprises, the help and guidance received from several individuals and agencies are gratefully acknowledged.

- European Foundation for Management Development (EFMD) for the fellowship offered by them, which made it possible for me to work for a year at Manchester Business School (MBS) and carry out this research in the UK.
- The late Professor Alan W Pearson, Founder Director of R&D Management Unit at MBS, and the Editor of the *R&D Management* journal, who was my academic partner, supporting my research work at MBS.
- The late Professor Douglas Wood, who provided the administrative support for the work at MBS.
- Professor Pradip N. Khandwalla, Former Professor & Director, Indian Institute of Management Ahmedabad (IIMA), who helped with the design of the research instrument.
- Professor Shailendra Vyakarnam, then at Cranfield School of Management, who helped with part of the data collection.
- Mr John Stuart and the five anonymous reviewers of WSPC, whose comments and suggestions were helpful in revising the manuscript.
- Professor Piero Formica, an internationally renowned scholar and author in the fields of knowledge economics, entrepreneurship, and innovation, and the Winner of the Innovation Luminary Award 2017, who blessed this book with an inspirational and insightful Foreword.

- Colleagues and administrators of my employer institutions, Administrative Staff College of India (ASCI), Hyderabad, and Indian Institute of Management Bangalore (IIMB).
- Messrs K. Sadanand, T. Ganeshwara Rao, P. Sridhar, and Mrs R. Gowri, who provided secretarial assistance at various stages.
- Mr John Stuart and his team of editors (especially Ms Sandhya Venkatesh and Mr Aanand Jayaraman) at World Scientific Publishing Co., who were prompt and meticulous in carrying out the editorial work on the manuscript and in publishing this book expeditiously.

I wholeheartedly thank all of them and the many others who could not be mentioned here by name. Their contributions in enriching the content and enhancing the readability of this book are greatly appreciated.

Contents

Chapter 1

Growth: The Sour Grapes of Entrepreneurship

A Sequel to the Fox and the Sour Grapes Story

Entrepreneurs are generally action-oriented individuals, with very few of them having academic/philosophical inclinations. They usually do not worry about building theories about their behavior, leaving that to 'idle' academic observers. However, there are a few exceptions to this rule. One such entrepreneur who presided over a fast-growing innovative Indian enterprise was interviewed by the correspondent of a business magazine (Kapur, 1985) on why some entrepreneurs take to a path of high growth while many others prefer to stay where they are. He narrated the following story, which is a sequel to the well-known fable of the *Fox and the Grapes*. When the fox returned to his friends after his unsuccessful attempts to bite off a bunch of grapes and told his friends that he did not try seriously to get at the grapes because he knew they were sour, his friends started teasing him as they saw through his game. He took this as a challenge and began the regular practice of jumping and climbing, while others enjoyed their life, relaxing, playing or eating fat chicken. At last, the fox managed to reach the grapes only to find out that they were really sour. It was, however, too damaging for his ego to admit that the fruit of this several days of grueling toil was inedible. So, he went on eating them and finally died of gastric ulcers.

Business growth, it appears, is prompted primarily by the entrepreneur's need to satisfy his/her own ego. The motives commonly attributed to an entrepreneur's desire for business growth are not without their

1

disincentives. Take, for example, the profit motive. It is true that growth may bring more profits (although, in some cases, losses are accepted in the short run for sustaining growth), but very little of these are available for the entrepreneur's personal use. One part of the profit is given away as taxes, and the other part is re-invested for further growth. Besides, the 'paper profits' may often attract wealth taxes and estate duties. It is also argued that business growth brings recognition to the entrepreneur, which acts as a motivator. However, the fact is that there is no unmixed recognition for the entrepreneur. He or she is often criticized as a monopolist, a capitalist, a tax-evader, and an exploiter of the poor. A third reason for an entrepreneur wishing to embrace growth is that a growing organization can retain good talent. But if one decides not to grow, there is no pressing need for good talent. If growth involves tensions, anxieties, loss of personal control of one's enterprise, and exposure to various financial and social risks, why should an entrepreneur decide to grow, if not to satisfy his/her ego? This notion is reinforced by the fact that the conventionally attributed reasons for enterprise growth do not provide any unmixed benefits to entrepreneurs.

Taking a cue from the existentialist school of philosophy which believes that the purpose of life is living, not happiness today or salvation thereafter, the entrepreneur in the *Fox and the Grapes* story explains to the correspondent that the purpose of business is being in business, not profits today or security tomorrow. If the act of being in business has the compulsion within it to grow, then one grows. One has to flow with the currents, not passively, but through active cooperation with the forces of growth. A similar view has been expressed by the founder of a fast-growing British enterprise, who is of the opinion that beyond a certain stage, the growth of an enterprise does not depend on the entrepreneur, but on the compulsions and exigencies of its internal and external environment. All that the entrepreneur has to do is not to do anything that would deliberately restrict the growth of his/her enterprise. In fact, this entrepreneur goes on to suggest that at the most critical stage of an enterprise's transition into growth, the most serious impediment to the process is the entrepreneur himself/herself (Shirley, 1991: see the details of this case in Appendix-1), implying that the primary reason for the growth or otherwise of an enterprise is the entrepreneur's attitudes and strategic orientation. The findings of the Global Entrepreneurship Monitor (GEM) studies (Reynolds *et al.*, 2002; Manimala, 2002a) show that less than 1% of start-ups globally (the figure is much lower for Indian start-ups) have aspirations for high growth, which is indicative of some kind of 'growth unwillingness' among entrepreneurial ventures.

Growth Unwillingness

It may sound rather strange that entrepreneurs have to be admonished not to deliberately restrict the growth of their enterprises. Do they really want to restrict enterprise growth? The growing volume of literature on the growth unwillingness of 'entrepreneurial ventures' suggests that willingness to let the enterprise grow is far less common than generally believed. Many entrepreneurs are not comfortable with, and are unable to cope with, the growth of their enterprises. The reasons may be different in different cases. An entrepreneur who successfully developed and commercialized the T-disc Oil Skimmer was planning to sell off his business when it was doing very well in the national as well as international markets. The reason given by him was that from this stage onwards there was very little design work involved and that the entrepreneur had to spend most of his time in meetings, making telephone calls, and writing letters. He also mentioned that even though his enterprise was making money, very little of it was available to him for his personal use. Besides, the growth venture was also eating into his personal time (Manimala & Pearson, 1991).

Similar cases of the inability or unwillingness of entrepreneurs to manage the diverse types of functions required through the growth stage of their businesses have been reported by others. Davis (1987), for example, cites the cases of Steve Jobs of Apple Computers and H. Ross Perot of Electronic Data Systems. It is sometimes pointed out that as these companies are large, their problems may not be representative of the problems of SME entrepreneurs. The proponents of this view forget that these huge corporations were also small when they started and have gone through similar processes of growth. In a lighter vein, one can explain this phenomenon by stating that even the strongest of men were born as helpless babies! Another related issue is that the size of the start-up may not indicate the size or longevity of the future organization. To take an analogy from the plant ecosystem, the size of the seed may not indicate the future size or longevity of the plant. The coconut may be larger than the acorn, but the full-grown coconut tree is much smaller than the mature oak tree and has a much shorter lifespan of 60–70 years, compared to the lifespan of more than 1,000 years for an oak tree! The same is the case for business start-ups. Some of the present-day giants, referred to in this book, began their lives as home-based start-ups, often with single-person/ zero-employee operations and make-shift arrangements.

When Steve Jobs started Apple Computers in 1976 in partnership with Steve Wozniak, the 'manufacturing' was done in Jobs' garage, which was made available for the work by the sale of his van to raise the initial investment funds. Supplementary funds were raised by selling Wozniak's scientific calculator. So, this new venture was even smaller than a typical 'small business' and grew gradually but not without setbacks. In the wake of a huge slump in the sale of Apple-Mac computers in 1985, Apple's Board voted out Jobs — its founder — as they thought he was too tech-focused to be able to manage the commercial functions required at the growth stage. They paid him compensation of USD 150 million, with which he started another small company (NeXT) with capital of USD 7 million. He returned to Apple in 1997 when the company needed a revamp of its products and technology, a task that was admirably accomplished by Jobs through the creation of technologically sophisticated products like the iMac, iPad, iPod, iPhone, iTunes, MacBook Air, etc. (Biography.com, 2014).

In the case of Perot too, the start-up (Electronic Data Systems) was originally quite small, with an initial investment of USD 1,000 borrowed from his wife, Margot. The initial years were hard. Even with his credentials as a former salesperson of IBM, Perot had to make 77 calls in person or over the phone before he could get his first customer, Collins Radio. As he could not afford to have regular employees, he engaged two computer experts to moonlight for him after they had finished their full-time jobs with Collins Radio. The company had a gradual growth and was later bought out by General Motors, who initially retained Perot, but later found him unacceptable for the kind of work needed at that stage and discharged him with compensation of USD 700 million (Davis, 1987; Womack, 2019). The return of Steve Jobs to Apple at a later stage of development illustrates that growth *per se* is not the problem, but the kind of tasks to be performed by the entrepreneur in the growth stage are. There has to be a fit between the person's interests/competencies and the type of tasks to be performed. Many entrepreneurs, especially those dealing with technology-based products and services, may not be inclined to perform the predominantly administrative, financial, marketing, and HR-related tasks required at the growth stage.

The above cases illustrate the unwillingness and/or inability of some entrepreneurs to perform certain kinds of tasks that are necessary at different stages in the growth of the enterprise. In such cases, the enterprise can grow if the entrepreneur brings in partners/managers with the required competencies. A celebrated partnership of this kind is that between Soichiro Honda, a hard-core technologist who focused on developing new designs, and Takeo Fujisawa, who looked after the financial and marketing operations of the Honda Motor Company (Britannica, 1998). In some cases, the entrepreneur voluntarily quits the scene or is removed/replaced by other individuals or agencies that are comfortable with performing the growth-related work. However, a majority of enterprises stagnate at this level, beyond which their promoters are unwilling or incapable to deal with the complexities of enterprise growth. This is not necessarily because there are no opportunities for growth. In a study by the Swedish Small Business Federation, it was found that more than 50% of their sample believed that there was scope for expansion but did not intend to pursue these opportunities (Davidsson, 1989). There must be something more than mere economics and opportunity considerations in deciding whether to grow or not. According to economists, a firm under perfect competition would grow until it reaches the size where the long-run marginal cost is equal to the price of its products (Mansfield, 1979). However, cost function studies have shown that profitable firms of widely differing sizes can and do co-exist within the same industry (Mansfield, 1979; Kumar, 1984). This may be due to the fact that perfect competition is just an ideal and not a reality. There are, therefore, no economic compulsions for an enterprise to grow to a particular size. It appears that entrepreneurs can, to a large extent, choose the size of their firms. Growth, therefore, can be a function of the entrepreneur's willingness and desire rather than the economic considerations and/or the availability of opportunities.

The stagnation of new ventures, especially in the small and medium sectors, has often been mentioned as a vexing problem for developing economies. Statistics, however, show that developed countries also experience similar problems. In the US, for example, 74% of new jobs created are by new entrants, and only 26% are by expansion. Besides, for every three new jobs created, two are destroyed. The share of small and medium enterprises (having less than 500 employees) in job creation is estimated to be 55% of entry jobs and 57% of expansion jobs (Kirchhoff & Phillips, 1988). Similar findings were obtained in a later study by Kane (2010), who analyzed longitudinal data about US companies from Business Dynamics Statistics (BDS), which are authentic data collected and supplied by Federal Statistical Research Data Centers. It was observed that, while the start-ups are job-creators (creating about 3 million jobs every year), the established firms (including the ones in their first year of start-up as well as those in existence for over two centuries) are job-destroyers (making a loss of about 1 million jobs every year).

Even though more than 55% of job creation is attributable to the smaller sector, these figures are somewhat misleading because of the very low proportion of jobs created due to expansion and growth, the destruction of two existing jobs for every three new jobs created, and the high limit of 500 employees for a small enterprise. Besides, according to another estimate, 12–15% of small firms are responsible for 75% of the jobs created by small firms (Birch & McCracken, 1982). This may provide a rough estimation of the percentage of firms that grow. Needless to say, it presents a very dismal picture. While it may be argued that these findings were obtained a few decades ago and so may not be valid under the prevailing scenario of the explosive growth of technology-based firms, newer studies are also coming up with similar findings. In a recent study of what the authors called the 'brutal facts' of UK business demography, it was observed that 75% of firms which start small stay small and, over a decade, around 75–80% of new firms will close (Anyadike-Danes *et al.*, 2015). Another estimate from the UK (Lee, 2014) suggests that high-growth firms (HGFs) constitute less than 5% of the total number of new firms. This study also identified the main problems that HGFs have encountered in their growth paths, which are in six areas: attracting and recruiting the right talent, skill shortages, obtaining finance, cash-flow management, shortage of managerial skills, and finding suitable premises. On closer scrutiny, these six areas can be reduced to two: talent and finance; and if the right talent is in place, they will be able to find the money to finance the business. It could therefore be stated that the growth of the enterprise is primarily a function of the entrepreneurial/managerial competencies of the promoter(s) and/or their ability and willingness to find the right talent and delegate the tasks to them.

The global scenario is less encouraging, as revealed by the Global Entrepreneurship Monitor (GEM) studies involving more than 30 countries (Reynolds *et al.*, 2002; Manimala, 2002a). While about 12% of the adult population was engaged in start-up activities, only 1% of them expected to have at least 20 employees in 5 years. Expectations in India were far more subdued, where the average number of employees expected by start-ups (constituting 17.9% of the adult population) in 5 years was as low as 1.42. It seems that a certain degree of growth unwillingness is endemic to start-ups in the small- and medium-sized sectors.

Reasons for Growth Unwillingness

There is a growing body of recent research literature on why some firms are unwilling to grow. These reasons are briefly discussed below:

1. 'Income-Sufficiency' Feeling

Some businesses merely function as instruments to provide an income. The primary motive of their owners in starting them is to have a regular income that they would otherwise have sought from employment. These owners are satisfied as long as their businesses help them in maintaining a certain standard of living and, therefore, have no desire to make their businesses grow (Birch, 1987). Similar observations have been made by Carland *et al.* (1984) who distinguished between 'entrepreneurs' and 'small business owners' on the basis of the presence or intent of open-ended growth in their enterprises. In a study of 400 small Swedish firms, Davidsson (1989) observed that about 40% of his sample was not moti-vated by the economic incentives for growth. They felt that they were making enough money and did not want their enterprises to grow any further. Similar observations have been made by Wiklund *et al.* (2003) and Lewis (2008) on the dominance of non-economic motivations for entrepreneurs. Considerations of the possible downsides of growth, espe-cially on one's quality of life, can be a deterrent to the active pursuit of business growth.

2. Desire for Full Control

One of the major implications of enterprise growth is that it necessitates changes not only in the facilities, systems, structures, and procedures but also in the ownership and control (Manimala, 1988a, 1999). The need for the latter kinds of changes may be traced to economic reasons (Jensen & Meckling, 1976), as further capital required to sustain growth may neces-sitate changes in the ownership structure. Similarly, as operations become larger, it becomes impossible for the owners to control all the aspects of the business. Powers have to be delegated to professional managers. A good number of entrepreneurs are unwilling to do this. They seek to maintain what the author has called elsewhere a 'property orientation' toward their enterprises, rather than an 'entity orientation', which is essential for letting the organization grow in its own way (Manimala, 1992c). An 'entity orientation' refers to the ability of entrepreneurs to treat their enterprises as autonomous entities with the right to choose their own destiny. This is somewhat similar to bringing up a son or a daughter who needs a lot of guidance and instructions from the parents during childhood but has to be given the freedom to choose for himself or herself later in life. In the case of an enterprise, this would mean that the organization should be permitted to grow and develop according to its internal and external 'compulsions'. In other words, the entrepreneur has to help the organization evolve its growth strategy, taking into consideration the relevant factors in the external environment, including the market and the special capabilities and needs of all its stakeholders. However, for most entrepreneurs, the desire to retain absolute control over their enterprises actively restricts growth. Even an enlightened entrepreneur such as Steve Shirley, who declared that beyond a certain level of growth the entrepreneur should have very little say over matters of enterprise growth, admitted that it took her more than 25 years to realize this (Shirley, 1991)! In fact, she made a very candid admission that beyond a certain phase of growth, the biggest impediment to the growth of an enterprise is the entrepreneur himself or herself. The 'let-it-go' philosophy of growth implemented by Steve Shirley in her firm is discussed in detail in the case study in Appendix 1 of this book. Later studies have also shown that 'growth-averseness' is a characteristic especially typical of micro-enterprises (Gherhes *et al.*, 2016). A major reason for this is identified as the fear of losing control, with the acquisition of external resources and an increasing number of stakeholders. As a result, there are a large number of entrepreneurs who deliberately restrict the growth of their enterprises because of their desire to retain absolute control over their ventures.

3. Fear of Additional Work

It is obvious that growing an enterprise will involve additional work for the founder. Many entrepreneurs feel discomfort with such demands because of the anticipation of a heavier workload, unfamiliar work, and the need for constant vigilance on how to tackle emerging situations. Davidsson (1989) reported that some entrepreneurs restrict the growth of their enterprises because of their fears of a heavier workload. However, there is more to this anxiety than a mere increase in the volume of work; there is also the fear of having to take on unfamiliar tasks. As Sadler and Barry (1970) have observed, owner-managers prefer to perform tasks which they like or are familiar with rather than the ones where they have little expertise, but those may be priority activities necessary for ensuring the survival and growth of their businesses. Although many entrepreneurs restrict the growth of their enterprises in order to avoid the additional and different types of tasks necessary for managing growth, a few (who may be characterized as the 'growth-oriented') adopt a strategy of building partnerships with people who can perform these necessary tasks, so that the entrepreneurs can focus on their strengths and areas of interest. In order to illustrate this point, one may cite the celebrated examples of complementary teams such as Bill Gates and Paul Allen at Microsoft, Steve Jobs and Steve Wozniak at Apple, and Soichiro Honda and Takeo Fujisawa of Honda Motor Company. Though it may be argued that these are large multi-national companies and so their strategies may not be applicable to small start-ups, it should be noted that they were also once small start-ups and struggled with growth issues. While such partnerships are an effective way of managing additional and different types of tasks and thereby helping the founder entrepreneur to stay focused on his/her areas of interest, very few founders adopt this strategy, as they are apprehensive about losing control over the business. Moreover, even after forging such partnerships, it is obvious that the entrepreneur presiding over a growing business has to be constantly vigilant. As Henry Ford has rightly pointed out, "...if to grow is success, then one must wake up anew each morning and keep awake all day" (Davis, 1987, p. 4). Eternal vigilance is the price of growth, and many entrepreneurs are not willing to pay this price.

4. Fear of Losing the Personal Touch

Many entrepreneurs adopt a style of managing the enterprise through personal interactions with their employees rather than through well laid out systems and procedures. This is the most appropriate style during the early stages when the enterprise is relatively small. Entrepreneurs often fall in love with their personalized style and do not want to change it. They also feel that their employees would be unhappy if they were to distance themselves from them and initiate management through systems, procedures, and rules. An Indian entrepreneur who used to visit his shop floor every day and hold daily discussions with his employees found it disturbing that with growth he could not continue to manage in this style. "So far we have been a close-knit group", he said, "...and people have grown with us. It upsets me that with growth we may be losing some of this personal touch" (Ravindranath, 1984). The British entrepreneur, Steve Shirley (1991) also found it difficult to retain the image of a 'caring company' as the growth process began. Quoting other studies on enterprise growth, Davidsson (1989) stated that fear of reduced job satisfaction among employees and concern about losing the unique small-firm atmosphere are among the major factors in making entrepreneurs decide against enterprise growth, a finding that was also reaffirmed by a related study conducted later (Wiklund *et al.*, 2003). It was observed by Matlay (1999) that employee relations in small firms tend to be personalized and informal. Obviously, this is not suitable for managing a large organization. Entrepreneurs who are comfortable with the personalized and informal style and have made it a way of life in their small organizations may not be willing to change it in the name of growth. A related issue pointed out by Hamm (2002) is the entrepreneur's affinity to employees and comrades from the start-up phase, which could make him/her give a greater priority to their concerns over those of the enterprise.

5. Lack of Managerial Resources

It has often been observed that many entrepreneurs lack managerial skills, and this is a major cause of their problems, including the stagnation of their enterprises. One reason for the lack of managerial skills among SME entrepreneurs is that many of them start as craft-based businesses, whose founders come with sound technical knowledge but with very little managerial knowledge or experience (Beresford & Saunders, 2005). Such ventures are likely to live with their managerial deficiencies when they are young and small, as they do not have the financial or organizational clout to attract managerial talent from outside to compensate for their own deficiencies.

Entrepreneurs need support from professional managers, especially in the growth stages of their enterprises. A growing business needs specialized expertise in several areas such as accounting, finance, legal, technology, operations, marketing, analytics, HRM, and organizational design. Obviously, it is not possible for a single individual to have expertise in all of these and many other functional areas of management, and hence it is necessary for entrepreneurs to engage professionals to assist them in expanding their business activities. However, many entrepreneurs hesitate to engage professionals, as they believe that their business is too small and cannot afford to pay for such services. This leads to a vicious cycle of small businesses not professionalizing for want of finance and therefore making less money in the future and thus becoming smaller and weaker.

Stevenson and Gumpert (1985) have observed that while entrepreneurs have special skills in the pursuit of opportunities, creation and mobilization of resources, and liaising with external agencies and individuals, they are not as good in the management of already acquired resources. It is for this latter aspect of enterprise management, critical during the growth phase, that entrepreneurs need assistance from professional managers. In another study, Smith and Cooper (1988) found that entrepreneurs were less 'comprehensive' in decision-making behavior than professional managers. The former were seen as less interested in using rational models, gathering systematic information from within and outside the organization, doing formal analyses, optimization, systematically assigning responsibilities to lower levels, and spending time and resources to arrive at the best possible decisions. Professional managers would place great emphasis on these processes whereas entrepreneurs tend to make decisions based on their own hunches, intuitions, and gut feelings, which alone cannot promote and support growth. The heuristics that help them make effective decisions in the start-up phase (Manimala, 1992c) may not be as useful in the growth phase. This is because growth brings with it problems and issues such as the need for producing adequate volumes according to the required schedule, attracting and developing the required talent, evolving new planning and control processes, altering reward systems, and ensuring an adequate flow of cash through the proper management of finances (Kazanjian, 1988), all of which require a good deal of professional knowledge and competencies. This is why Gibb and Dyson (1984) observed that the shortage of resources experienced by small firms, especially during the growth stage, is not only financial but also managerial. Kotter and Sathe (1978) expressed similar views, observing that growing firms experience an insufficiency of resources, a lack of trained staff, and non-coherent systems and structures. Later studies, as pointed out in a comprehensive review of the literature by Dwyer and Kotey (2016), confirmed all of these points and added a few more, suggesting that the growth process is complex and management-intensive, all of which makes it a rather uncomfortable path for entrepreneurs on their journey toward their growth goals. It is no wonder that many entrepreneurs generally prefer to avoid such discomfort by restricting the growth of their businesses.

A related issue is the non-availability of 'entrepreneurial individuals' in the business family, who are ready to take the business forward in the next generation. The serious problem of succession in the small- and medium-sized business sectors (Kamei & Dana, 2012) is either because the entrepreneur does not have children or because the children are not interested in carrying on with the business. While this is a problem for SMEs in general, especially in developed countries where the younger members have many other opportunities, growth-oriented entrepreneurs create professional systems to manage succession if there are no children to succeed them in the business. The case study of FI Group Plc, presented in Appendix 1 of this book, aptly demonstrates this process. The founder of this company, Dame Stephanie Shirley, had only one son. He was autistic, and died at the age of 35, so there was no family member to succeed her in the business. She therefore engaged professionals to manage the venture and facilitate its growth. The theoretical perspective involved in this process is explained by this author as an 'entity orientation' (as opposed to a 'property orientation') on the part of the growth-oriented entrepreneurs. That is, the growth-oriented entrepreneur will treat the venture not as a property over which they have absolute control but as an entity that has its own life. The difference is like in the way one deals with a son or daughter, as compared to dealing with a property. The non-availability of family members for succession purposes need not be an impediment to enterprise growth.

6. Lack of Strategic Thinking Orientation

One of the direct consequences of not having adequate managerial resources is that entrepreneurs will have to spend most of their time on routine matters. This is why Penrose (1959) observed that growth depends on the extent to which the owner-manager builds a management team, delegates routine jobs, and creates some free time for strategic thinking. Professional managers not only enable entrepreneurs to get such thinking space, but more importantly, they bring with them expertise for environment scanning, information analysis, and evaluation of new ideas for growth (Wild & Swan, 1973; McGivern & Overton, 1980; Churchill & Lewis, 1983). They may also compensate for the entrepreneur's lack of experience outside the enterprise.

While the lack of time and expertise is the most frequently cited reason for entrepreneurs not having a strategic orientation, there are other reasons as well. Prominent among these are the entrepreneur's hesitation to make a 'new' beginning, his/her mistrust of outside consultants (Krentzman & Samaras, 1960; Robinson & Pearce, 1984), and the restrictive influences of family members (Gibb & Dyson, 1984). There are many cases where the entrepreneur has to accommodate almost all the members of his/her family in the business, irrespective of the number of people required, their interests, competencies and/or professional qualifications. The business then becomes overstaffed, and 'grows' around the limited skills and narrow perspectives of these people. The enterprise obviously cannot afford to employ professionals, as it is already overstaffed with the many family 'partners' involved. Besides, these partners may impose 'ideological' as well as financial restrictions against employing outsiders. Most of these entrepreneurial ventures, therefore, are neither inclined nor equipped for strategic thinking. Consequently, very few of them are able to systematically exploit growth opportunities. An effective way of controlling the influx and interference of family members in the business is demonstrated by Ford Motor Company, where family members are required to apply for specific vacancies in the company based on their qualifications, expertise and interests, and work their way up in the hierarchy, so that their performance is the only criterion for their inclusion in the business (Ramsey, 2019). Most businesses, however, fail to adopt such policies and thereby get bogged down by the burden of unqualified family members and get derailed from the growth path by their unwanted influence and interference.

It has been observed that even the few companies that adopt successful growth strategies are reacting to external pressures rather than proactively planning for growth (Starbuck, 1965). The reason for the subsequent stagnation of a large number of enterprises that were quite entrepreneurial during their start-up period (Stevenson & Jarillo, 1986) may also be traced to their failure to develop strategic thinking and planning. A similar conclusion was reached by the Advisory Council on Science and Technology (ACOST), UK, whose study (1990) identified the small and medium enterprises' lack of strategic management thinking as a major inhibitor to their innovativeness and growth.

Stages of Small Business Growth

Examination of the causes of enterprise stagnation naturally leads to a 'stage-theory' of enterprise growth. It has been suggested that different stages of growth require different kinds of strategies (Greiner, 1972;

Dunkelberg & Cooper, 1982; Churchill & Lewis, 1983; Hanks *et al.*, 1993; McMahon, 1998). In the early stages, the concern of the entrepreneur is primarily on product definition and positioning, convincing financiers and acquiring resources, building production capacity and establishing one's presence in the market (Block & MacMillan, 1985; Galbraith, 1982; Gilmore & Kazanjian, 1989). Later, during the growth stage, the entrepreneur will have to worry about mass/volume production, standardization of products and processes, building and maintaining market share, and so on. In the maturity stage, the emphasis will be on cost control, profitability, building reserves and surpluses, and the search for further opportunities for growth (Gilmore & Kazanjian, 1989). Entrepreneurial strategies, as well as the decision-making styles, will have to be adapted according to changes in the dominant concerns of the enterprise. A few such changes observed in high-growth enterprises by Smallbone *et al.* (1995) include the following: from production orientation to market-development orientation; from the production focus to the productivity focus; and, from an operational focus to a strategic focus at the top level. According to these authors, the last one is particularly important, as enterprise growth depends more on the entrepreneur's characteristics than on the enterprise characteristics. Some entrepreneurs may find it uncomfortable to cope with such changes and may decide not to grow beyond a particular stage. An understanding of the 'stage-theory' would therefore be of help in providing insights into the phenomenon of enterprise growth.

One of the early theories about the growth of organizations suggested that this is the result of a series of crises (Lippitt & Schmidt, 1967; Greiner, 1972). Greiner, for example, observed that a crisis may be resolved through evolution or revolution depending on the manner in which it is tackled. If the crisis is anticipated and proactively dealt with, the organization would evolve smoothly into the next stage of its development. If not, a revolutionary change would occur. The common pattern, however, is that every stage of growth is preceded by a crisis and is resolved by both evolution and revolution. According to Greiner (1972), the following sequence is an appropriate description of a typical growth process: growth through creativity, crisis of leadership; growth through direction, crisis of autonomy; growth through delegation, crisis of control; growth through co-ordination, crisis of red tape; growth through collaboration, crisis of complicity, and so on; (the last crisis was left undefined by Greiner and has been added by the present author).

Other theories on growth stages are based on the product mix and structure, or on the dominant concerns and functions of the entrepreneur from time to time. Maidique (1980), for example, has identified three stages of enterprise growth based on the complexity of their structure. The three stages are termed small, integrated, and diversified, the primary criterion for the classification being the number and nature of products. A similar classification was proposed by Christensen and Scott (1964), where they talk about one-unit enterprises with no specialized functions, one-unit enterprises with specialized functions such as marketing and finance, and enterprises with multiple operating units. A majority of the stage theories, however, are based on the dominant concerns and functions of the entrepreneur at particular times. In a study by Kazanjian (1988), it was found that there are four distinct stages in the development of an enterprise. In stage one, the major concern of the entrepreneur will be resource acquisition and technology development. This may be called the 'conception' stage. The second stage is that of 'commercialization' where production-related start-up problems dominate. During the third stage, which may be designated as the 'growth' stage, the dominant problems are those related to sales, market share, and organizational issues. The final stage, namely, that of stability, is dominated by the issues of maintaining profitability, implementing internal controls, and planning/preparing for future growth. It is apparent that the model closely follows the life-cycle concept. As far as the problems associated with the different stages, empirical support for them was partial.

A variant of the life-cycle model is the economic model proposed by McGuire (1963) following Rostow's model of the stages of macro-economic development. The 'traditional small company' (which is the first stage) passes through the stages of planning for growth, departure from existing conditions (take-off), professional management, and finally the stable stage of mass production. This last stage is marked by a broadening of the objectives to make them more inclusive, so as to evince an interest in the welfare of the society at large. Along with the financial growth of the firm, a change in the style of management is also indicated in this model, signifying the changing needs of an enterprise at different stages of growth. Steinmetz's (1969) model is based on the manner in which the leader controls the organization. Accordingly, there are four stages: direct supervision, supervised supervision, indirect control, and divisional organization.

Churchill and Lewis (1983) proposed a comprehensive model of enterprise growth, integrating many features of previous models. In testing their model empirically, they found that there were five stages in enterprise growth, with the third stage having two sub-stages. The stages are as follows: (1) existence, (2) survival, (3a) success-disengagement, (3b) success-growth, (4) take-off, and (5) resource maturity. An important observation made by these authors is that the 'grow-or-fail' hypothesis implicit in many prior models was not valid in all cases. Enterprises can stagnate at any of the above stages, just as they can fail, sell themselves, merge with other units, or move forward. Stagnation is quite common between the success-D and success-G stages because of the need for the renewed and vigorous involvement of the owner in the enterprise once again at this stage, which some owners are unwilling to do. During the initial stages of existence and survival, the enterprise goals are the same as the owner's goals, and it is the owner's ability to do things that makes or breaks the business. At the early phase of the success stage, however, the owner should be able to disengage himself/herself from the business, delegate tasks to professional managers, and use the 'free time' for pursuing strategic interests, including the start-up of other businesses. Alternatively, the owner might get involved in the business once again more vigorously and bring the business to the take-off stage. It is this decision, which depends on a host of personal, organizational, and environmental factors, that makes the difference for the enterprise in terms of its future growth. It would therefore imply that the growth of an enterprise largely depends on the entrepreneur and his/her decision about a more vigorous second involvement in the affairs of his/her venture. As noted above, the proposers of stage theories generally believe that there are specific and different functions of management, which would assume importance at different stages. However, some other studies (e.g., Kazanjian, 1988) have found only partial support for the varying importance of different functions at different stages of growth. Birley and Westhead (1990) also posited that the stage theory was not applicable to all firms in the same way; while they admitted that firms do change, they added that the stages need not follow the same pattern or sequence for all businesses.

Theories of Small Firm Growth

The discussion in the section above on the stage theories of enterprise growth has helped to highlight empirical support for the hypothesis that firms may stop growing at different stages. However, there is no intention to suggest that this is the only theory on firm growth. According to O'Farrell and Hitchens (1988), there are four groups of theories on firm growth. In addition to stage theory, the other three are (1) the industrial economics theory, (2) the stochastic theory, and (3) the strategic choice theory.

As in the case of stage theory, none of the other theories are monolithic. There are various hues and shades within each group. For example, within the industrial economics group, there are 'conflicting' views about why small enterprises exist, grow, and/or stagnate (Pedersen, 1991). The 'modernization' theorists believe that small enterprises are a stage in the process of industrial development and will disappear from the economy as it reaches the full development stage. The 'dependency' theorists, on the other hand, believe that small units are the result of economic authoritarianism and exploitation by the larger units operating from developed countries. According to these theorists, global business is controlled by a few large units and their subsidiaries, with smaller units allowed to operate only in so far as they serve the interests of the larger ones, as subcontractors, suppliers, etc. These theories have been questioned of late, as there are many successful smaller enterprises even in the most developed countries of the world. Therefore, economists are looking for new explanations for the existence of small enterprises. Pedersen (1991), for example, explains the existence of a large number of enterprises of varying sizes as a network created in response to the varying scales of economies for different kinds of work and the need for specialization.

The present author, however, would like to compare the industrial ecosystem to the biological ecosystem, where every plant or animal (big or small) serves a purpose and so need not replace its features with those of others. In other words, grass serves a purpose that an oak cannot. If all plants became oaks, that would create a dysfunctional ecosystem. Collaboration among the different units in an industrial ecosystem requires them to have different competencies, implying differences in their features, faculties, and functions. This, in fact, provides the philosophical legitimacy for having organizations of different types, sizes, and activities. For the same philosophical reason, it is not necessary that all businesses grow. On the contrary, considering the very low rate of survival and growth of the seeds and seedlings produced by nature, it might even offer a philosophical explanation of why the survival rate of start-ups is quite low. According to a survey reported by *smallbiztrends.com*, about 50% of US start-ups close down by their 5th year (Mansfield, 2019).

Another report states that the long-term survival rate of start-ups in the US is less than 10% (Bryant, 2020). The Indian situation is similar, if not worse. Quoting a report by the IBM Institute for Business Value and Oxford Economics, an article on *moneycontrol.com* states that over 90% of Indian start-ups fail within the first five years (MoneyControl, 2018b). No wonder then that Indian high-growth firms (HGFs) are relatively few in number. The comparison with the biological ecosystem would offer a philosophical-level explanation for the behavior of the industrial ecosystem, as both of them ensure 'quality through quantity', based on the principle of the 'survival of the fittest'.

While the industrial economic theories are based on macro-economic factors, stage theories primarily focus on the differential patterns of how enterprises respond to their internal and external environment. The stochastic and strategic choice theoretical models are apparently the opposites of each other. The former believes that survival and growth are a matter purely of chance or are determined by the environment in which the unit happens to exist and operate, while the latter believes that enterprise growth can be managed and manipulated by the strategic choices of the individuals at the top. This issue was empirically tested by the present author with reference to the emergence of innovative entrepreneurs under various environmental conditions (Manimala, 1992b), where it was found that innovators emerge in very different and even contrasting types of task environments (comprising institutions that facilitate the immediate tasks of business, such as financial institutions, industry-specific infrastructure, educational institutions, government agencies, and training and consultancy agencies). On the other hand, the general environment (comprising family socialization, early-stage education, socio-cultural norms, economic/legal/political environment, general infrastructure, etc.) has a role in shaping the entrepreneurial attitudes of individuals, who then go about implementing their innovative ideas, with or without the help of the task environment (see Fig. 1.1). As will be explained below, the findings of this analysis assign a role to the environment as well as to strategic choice. The distinction made between the general and task environments is critical to the understanding of this phenomenon.

The model implies that the facilitation of the task environment may not create the desired impact unless there are entrepreneurial individuals in the society who can take advantage of such facilities. However, if the general environment of a country is conducive to the development of entrepreneurial individuals, such individuals will create new ventures

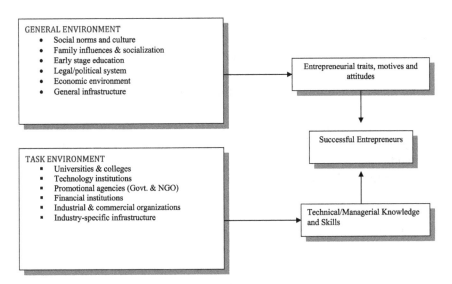

Fig. 1.1.   The role of the general and task environments in new venture creation and growth.

Source: Reproduced from Manimala (2008).

even if the task environment is not favorable. They would use the available facilities and also create those that are not provided by the government or public authorities. This would therefore mean that the critical factor in the creation of new ventures is the existence of the entrepreneurial individual who can then create the required task environment or adapt available facilities/resources to suit their requirements. The same model would apply to enterprise growth, which depends largely on the drive and innovative actions of the entrepreneurial individual rather than extrinsic factors such as the nature of the industry or the availability of resources.

Against this background, it appears that a dominant theory in management — the resource-based view (RBV) — has limited applicability to entrepreneurship in general and enterprise growth in particular. According to the RBV model, firm performance is a function of the resources that it possesses and the characteristics of these resources, which are represented by the 'Valuable, Rare, Imperfectly Imitable, and Non-substitutable (VRIN) model (Wernerfelt, 1984; Barney, 1991). This model was later modified to the VRIO model, where the 'O' stands for the organization's ability to capitalize on these resources. While RBV provides basic insights into the way firms can capitalize on their internal resources to improve their performance, the entrepreneur's concern is about how to create or acquire the resources required. This is because entrepreneurs start from scratch and initially have very few internal resources to rely on, discouraging many of them from moving forward to the growth path. The high-growth entrepreneur, on the other hand, sees the lack of resources as a challenge and explores all possible ways of acquiring them. It may not be inappropriate to compare the passion that they have for their businesses to the addiction of an alcoholic. The present author recalls a conversation with a friend who was an alcoholic, while traveling to an Indian state where alcohol was prohibited. When asked how he would satisfy his daily requirements, he casually replied "I am not particular about drinking; if it is available, I will drink, but if it is not available I will make it available, and drink". High-growth entrepreneurs can be described as having a similar mindset. If resources and facilities are available, they would use them to their advantage; if they are not, they would make them available, carry on with their work, and achieve their goals.

Some examples from the business field illustrate the predominant role of the entrepreneurial individual in the management of enterprise growth. To most people, a restaurant is a business with limited possibilities for expansion and growth. It is therefore quite amazing how McDonald's (a small-time burger shop established in California in 1940 by the brothers, Richard and Maurice McDonald) has grown to become a dominant global company, McDonald's Corporation, which serves over 69 million customers in more than 100 countries, and is the world's second-largest private employer with 1.7 million employees and over USD 21 million in revenues. The fast growth of McDonald's is attributed to the franchise strategy adopted and vigorously implemented by Ray Kroc, the aggressive salesman and business strategist who joined the company in 1954 as a franchisee and later acquired it in 1961 (Britannica, 2020). This case demonstrates how the physical and human resources needed for the expansion of a restaurant chain could be created without any cost to the company while retaining and enhancing the brand image and reputation. The creation of resources through the franchise strategy is not only a 'no-cost option' but also a source of continuous flow of revenues for the franchisers. While the environment was similar for all restaurants, it was this innovative idea and its passionate implementation by an entrepreneurial individual that created such inexpensive resources to support the phenomenal growth of this venture.

To take an Indian example, the contrasting performances of the companies managed by the two Ambani brothers (Mukesh and Anil) are quite illustrative of the role of the entrepreneur in promoting enterprise growth (Deccan Herald, 2020; BBC News, 2019). Both of these individuals started with similar resources, support systems, and net worth after the partition of the family's businesses in 2005. In fact, the net worth of Anil was about Rs 550 crore more than that of Mukesh in 2006 (ET Now Digital, 2020). However, by 2020, Mukesh was ranked as the richest person in Asia, whereas Anil had to declare in a UK court that: "My net worth is zero after taking into account my liabilities. In summary, I do not hold any meaningful assets which can be liquidated for the purposes of these proceedings" (The Economic Times, 2020). His flagship company, Reliance Communications Ltd, has become insolvent and is being closed down. Paradoxically, in the same telecom industry where Anil failed (and even corporate giants like the Tatas had failed earlier), Mukesh started his company (Reliance Jio Infocomm Ltd) in 2016, and in less than 5 years made it the largest wireless carrier in India, forging ahead of the established players like Vodafone and Airtel. Today, at a time when the economy is in severe crisis due to the Covid pandemic, Reliance Jio has managed to attract six big global tech investors, including Facebook and General Atlantic, offering a total stake of over 16% to them (NDTV, 2020). The contrasting performance of these two brothers in the same industry cannot be attributed to the differences in the nature of the industry (because both were in the same industry) or to the availability of resources (because both inherited similar and significant amounts of resources), but to the differences in the nature of the individuals. Ironically, it appears that even an MBA degree may not be of help in overcoming the limitations imposed by the attitudes and behavioral/strategic orientations of the individual. While Anil has an MBA from Wharton, Mukesh had to withdraw from the Stanford MBA program in order to help his father with the execution of a large project (the construction of a polyester filament yarn plant). Apparently, learning by doing is more effective for entrepreneurship than learning in the classroom! Incidentally, their father and founder of the Reliance Group of companies, Dhirubhai Ambani, was not educated beyond matriculation. This and the other well-known cases of great entrepreneurs (such as Bill Gates, Michael Dell, Steve Jobs, and others) who were college dropouts or had low levels of formal education, support the hypothesis that the personal competencies and attitudes of entrepreneurs play a critical role in the start-up and growth phases of enterprises.

The same phenomenon is observable in the case of managing ventures in extremely adverse circumstances such as those we are now experiencing with COVID-19. An example from the personal experience of this author with a young entrepreneur in the event management business illustrates this point. When all the other players in this field closed down their operations and laid off their employees due to the Covid-induced lockdowns and restrictions, this entrepreneur retained all his employees, paid them their full salaries, and worked with them (in the 'work-from-home' format) to develop new ideas and activities for keeping the business alive and even profitable. One idea that was implemented immediately was that of supplying safety kits to the employees of essential service providers. These kits looked like executive briefcases and contained safety equipment items like masks, goggles, gloves, sanitizers, gowns, shoe covers, etc. Branded as 'We Care', these kits were purchased by many organizations for their employees. Another innovative idea was the creation of a 'Virtual Conference Hall', which had all the features (including the stage and furniture) of a real hall and allowed participants to be present and interact in the hall through the technique of holoportation (that is, an augmented reality experience created by the teleportation of high-quality 3D images of people interacting in real time). With these and other such innovations, this innovative entrepreneur sustained his business without much disruption, while competitors complained of Covid restrictions and closed down their operations. The most amazing part of this story is that he managed such high-tech operations without recruiting any IT experts. His employees were so motivated by his gesture of avoiding lay-offs and continuing to pay full salaries that they took the initiative of learning new technologies from friends, colleagues, and through the Internet. The contrasting courses of action taken by different players in the event-management industry during the Covid crisis show that the most critical factors influencing the fate of an enterprise (be it in a crisis situation or a growth phase) are the personal characteristics, policies, and strategies of the entrepreneurial leader.

The theory that emerges from the above discussion can be characterized as 'behavioral', as the critical factor in bringing about enterprise growth is the behavior of the entrepreneur. However, it is slightly different from the 'behavioral theory of the firm' proposed by Cyert and March

(1992, originally published in 1963). The main argument of the behaviorists is that the decision maker's rationality is constrained by limits on the availability of information, the person's preferences/prejudices, and the level of computational capabilities (Simon, 1955). While these limitations are also applicable to entrepreneurial individuals, the constraints imposed by the 'bounded rationality' and 'limited search' by multiple stakeholders of the large firm are not of much relevance in the case of entrepreneurs. This is because the entrepreneurial firm (unlike the large firm) has fewer stakeholders and the entrepreneur has greater flexibility in changing other stakeholders (including partners and investors). Based on the Schumpeterian theory of macro-economic growth through creative destruction (Schumpeter, 1942), it was argued by Aghion and Howitt (1992, 1998) that macro-economic growth is more a function of endogenous factors than exogenous ones. A similar argument may be proffered for micro-level (firm-level) growth that it is mostly a function of the dynamism and innovativeness of the entrepreneurial individual (Schumpeter, 1934). In view of the above, it was decided that this work should be conducted under the strategic choice paradigm, where our objective will be to identify the strategies, policies, and personality characteristics of entrepreneurs that may be associated with enterprise growth. The inter-relationships among these variables will also be examined.

Growth Strategies

There are very few studies on the growth strategies of entrepreneurial ventures. The apparent lack of research focus on the topic may be explained by the fact that these strategies are not the exclusive preserve of new ventures in their growth stage; some are also applicable to the survival stage of new ventures. Moreover, many of these strategies are common to business organizations in general, and therefore are not 'growth strategies' exclusively pursued by entrepreneurial ventures. Some of the strategies commonly associated with business ventures, that have been investigated by growth venture researchers, are briefly described as follows.

1. Cost Leadership/Low-Price Strategy
Cost leadership, popularized by Michael Porter (1980), and the low-price strategy sometimes associated with it are often pursued by entrepreneurs as an entry strategy. With an increase in the volume of operations, such

firms find it difficult to maintain cost efficiencies and may have to adopt different strategies during their growth stage. This may be why a study by Chaganti *et al.* (1989), on the profitability of small business strategies, found that cost leadership was not associated with profitability under low- or high-intensity price/promotion competition. Needless to say, there is no growth without prior profits. It is therefore unlikely that cost leadership or a low-price strategy would be strongly associated with high-growth ventures. It is basically a survival strategy, as was observed by Hall (1980) in his study of 64 companies. According to him, survival in a hostile environment is achieved either by cost leadership or product differentiation. It is interesting to note that firms following a cost leadership strategy are observed to possess the following characteristics (Schuler & MacMillan, 1984): (1) low risk-taking, (2) strong controls, (3) highly bureaucratic systems and procedures, (4) low levels of staff skills, (5) formalized appraisals, and (6) low developmental activities. The picture painted by these characteristics does not look like that of an aggressive and fast-growing enterprise.

Although there are many enterprises that have used 'cost leadership' as an entry strategy and later migrated to other strategies at the growth stage, it cannot be denied that some of the fastest-growing enterprises of the present times (such as Walmart, McDonald's, Amazon, and IKEA) have very effectively utilized this strategy to support their fast growth. According to the Fortune 500 listings of 2019, Walmart was the world's largest company by revenue with over USD 514 billion, and the world's largest private employer with over 2.2 million employees spread over 27 countries (Wikipedia, 2021). Sam Walton, the founder of Walmart, is a pioneer and leader in the use of cost-leadership strategy for growth. His strategies for reducing cost and thereby keeping the promise made to his customers of 'everyday low prices' were mainly in the following four areas (Hyde, 2019): (1) low-price/high-volume operations; (2) efficient management of the supply chain; (3) minimizing overheads and operational costs; and (4) leveraging one's clout to bargain with suppliers for reduced prices. Even after achieving the highest levels of growth, Walmart continued to adhere strictly to cost-leadership strategies so as to help their customers live according to the company's slogan: 'Save money, Live better'. In fact, there now does not seem to be another option for them, as they have to continue to compete against newer market entrants with similar strategies, especially online retailers such as Amazon.

Another example of a company making effective use of the cost-leadership strategy to support its growth is that of IKEA, the Swedish furniture business now headquartered in the Netherlands, which derived its name from the initials of its founder, Ingvar Kamprad, Elmtaryd (the founder's family farm), and Agunnaryd (the founder's hometown). Founded in 1943 to sell miscellaneous articles, the company started the furniture business in 1958. The growth of IKEA as a global operator with a revenue of 38.8 billion Euros (2018) from over 12,000 products sold through 424 stores in 52 different countries is attributed mainly to the innovative cost-reduction strategies adopted by the founder, such as follows: (1) the flat-pack system, offered with a DIY (Do It Yourself) kit for assembling the furniture at home, which reduced the cost of transportation; (2) the use of hybrid materials like fiberboards, laminates and recycled materials, which reduced the cost and weight of materials; (3) the use of CNC (Computer Numerical Control) machines, which could be operated even by unskilled workers with some training and thus eliminated the need for expert carpenters and thereby reduced labor costs; (4) the redesigning of products based on regular feedback from customers, which reduced the accumulation of 'unwanted' stock; (5) private franchising (with a 3% commission on sales), which was a quick and 'low/no-cost' way of setting up an IKEA store in a new location; (6) direct delivery from the supplier to the customer, which is a cost-effective way of serving the customer in the areas where there are no IKEA stores (Nawal, 2019). The examples of IKEA and Walmart cited above (as well as many other similar companies) show that 'cost-leadership' can be used very effectively for supporting enterprise growth.

2. Product Differentiation/Innovation

Product differentiation is often the result of product innovations, and so researchers often use the two terms interchangeably. Differentiation can be partial or total. The former, involving modifications to existing products, is far more common than the latter, which involves the introduction of totally new products. It is commonly believed that the more innovative the firm, the more likely it will experience faster growth. While several case studies offer evidence in support of this hypothesis, the findings from some empirical studies are ambivalent. Colombelli *et al.* (2013), for example, found that innovative firms grow faster than non-innovative ones. Similar results were reported by Roper (1997) in an earlier study of small enterprises in the UK, Ireland, and Germany, where it was observed that the output of innovative small firms grew significantly faster than that of non-innovators. On the other hand, earlier researchers like Romano (1990) found that both low-growth as well as high-growth ventures innovate. The difference, however, is that the low-growth firms' innovation is primarily in response to customer reactions, while that of the high-growth firms is prompted by changes in technology, results of in-house R&D work, competition in the market, changes in the market, product life cycle, customer reactions, and so on. Similar conclusions were reached by Manimala (1988a, 1992c, 1999) in relation to innovative entrepreneurs' strategies for new idea management. Two other empirical studies, however, found that innovation is not related to growth performance. In a study of the growth performance of high-tech ventures, Eisenhardt and Schoonhoven (1990) found that technological innovation, enterprise strategy, and market competition were not related to growth, but the characteristics of the founding top management team and the market stage of the enterprise's products were related. Similarly, Chaganti *et al.* (1989) found a mild negative correlation between innovativeness and profitability. The negative relationship is probably because of the excessive preoccupation of the entrepreneur/firm with product modifications to the neglect of other functions like marketing, which are critical for sustaining growth. It has also been observed by later researchers (e.g., Demirel & Mazzucato, 2012) that a combination of other factors is required for product innovation to bring about firm growth.

Fombrun and Wally (1989) investigated the relative importance of these different factors in their study of 95 fast-growing small firms in the US. The factors that emerged as important were the strategic orientation of the firm and product diversity, whereas quality, cost, and innovation appeared to gain importance selectively, depending on the situation. In an earlier study by this author (Manimala, 1988a, 1999), it was observed that entrepreneurs resorted to product innovation or differentiation primarily as a means to avoid competition. Apparently, those firms that would avoid competition rather than fight it may be averse to aggressive business practices and so may shy away from growth. Several cases of entrepreneurs who started businesses through the 'new/innovative-product' route illustrate this point (e.g., Manimala & Pearson, 1991; Piramal & Herdeck, 1985; Ross, 1975). According to a taxonomy developed by this author (Manimala, 1988a, 1996a, 1999), many of these innovative entrepreneurs are primarily inventors and tinkerers, and it was only incidental that some of the inventions and modifications made by them had commercial value and thus offered an entrepreneurial opportunity to the inventors. Therefore, when the business grows to a stage where the need for commercial expansion and diversification overshadows the need for invention, tinkering, and modification, some of these inventor-turned entrepreneurs prefer to dispose of the business, others withdraw into a 'corner', and still others oppose the pressures for growth. This could be a reason why in some cases the growth process only starts with the second or third generation of a business (Calori & Bonany, 1989).

One example (in the Indian context) for the phenomenon of the focus on growth developing in subsequent generations of a business is found in the story of the inventor-turned entrepreneur, Lakshamanrao Kirloskar (MoneyControl.com, 2018a). Although he started his career as a teacher of drawing/painting at Sir J. J. School of Art in Bombay, he had to leave that job because he was partially color-blind. Since he was also talented with machines and liked to tinker with mechanical gadgets, he started a cycle repair shop in Belgaum (the district headquarters of his native village, Gurlahosur) and used his spare time to 'invent' gadgets useful for the farming community around him. Two of his inventions during this period were a chaff cutter and an iron plough. When he was forced to close down his cycle shop because the municipality acquired his place for developmental work, he had to look for a new workspace. Fortunately for him, the ruler of Aundh gifted him a vast stretch (32 acres) of barren land by the side of a railway line. With no settlements in the nearby area, this place was not suitable for the cycle shop, and so he decided to set up an industrial township (Kirloskarvadi) housing 25 workers on the site (modeled on those in European countries, which he had read about), where he set up a small firm (Kirloskar Brothers) in 1910 in partnership with his brother, Ramuanna, to manufacture iron ploughs, an innovative product designed by him to facilitate the work of local farmers. The business was tough, as it was difficult to convince the farmers to replace their wooden ploughs with the iron ploughs, as traditional farmers saw these as being harmful to the soil. It took him two years to make his first sale. The company was not making much progress with the iron plough business, and the business could only be launched into the high-growth track with the entry of his son, Shantanurao (popularly known as S. L. Kirloskar), who joined the business in 1945 (at the age of 22) on his return from Massachusetts Institute of Technology (MIT), US, with a Bachelor of

Science degree in Mechanical Engineering. While he respected the innovative products developed by his father, he also recognized the need for more sophisticated products to launch the company into the growth trajectory. Similarly, he felt that the location of the units should be within the city to facilitate the movement of goods and people. Accordingly, he set up two companies in 1946, one in Bangalore (Kirloskar Electric Company) and the other in Pune (Kirloskar Oil Engines Limited). The latter company (KOEL) was in partnership with Associated British Oil Engines Export Ltd, UK. These were followed by a series of other start-ups, resulting in about 30 companies in this group by the time S. L. Kirloskar retired. Between 1950 and 1991, the group recorded a growth in assets of over 32,401%, which is one of the highest growth rates in Indian business history.

Similar to the findings on the role of new products in promoting growth, there are also some surprising observations and findings about the role of strategy. For example, Eisenhardt and Schoonhoven (1990) stated that growth was not related to strategy. Somewhat surprisingly, this finding has also been supported by some innovative entrepreneurs. Steve Shirley (1991), an innovative entrepreneur from the UK (whose detailed case study is presented in Appendix 1 of this book), stated that beyond a certain level, the growth of the venture does not depend on the entrepreneur or his/her strategies, but on the internal or external pressures on the venture; all that the entrepreneur needs to do, according to her, is to 'let it go'. Paradoxically, this is also an entrepreneurial action arising from the 'entity orientation' (as opposed to the 'property orientation') identified in this study as a characteristic of high-growth entrepreneurs. The overall picture that emerges from the various studies is that product innovations or differentiations in themselves may not automatically promote growth unless they are combined with some other types of innovation, especially those in managing the boundary (Manimala, 1988a, 1992a, 1999). Besides, there also have to be corresponding changes in the design and policies of the organization, which should be characterized by greater autonomy, risk-taking, high quality of products, customized service, market research, advertising, and the creation of a high-profile external image (Dess & Davis, 1984; Schuler & MacMillan, 1984; Fombrun & Walley, 1989). This is especially because product innovation is often associated with technological leadership in the field, which requires a large number of specialist staff who can be attracted and retained only by adopting the designs and policies specified above (Maidique & Hayes, 1984).

3. Product Range/Diversification Strategies
While product differentiation indicates a qualitative difference in the company's products vis-à-vis those of its competitors, product range strategies refer to the number of products and services being offered by the company. These products need not be different from those of competitors. The strategy here is to attract customers not because of the uniqueness of one's products and services, but because of the wide range of products and services provided. The attraction for the customer is that it is like a 'package deal' covering related products and services or like shopping in a supermarket where the customer gets most of what he or she wants under one roof. Once the dependability of the producer is established, the customer will have partly solved his or her choice problems. This may be the reason why the strategy of offering a wide range of products and services is quite popular with growth ventures. From the point of view of the enterprise, this is an effective way of spreading risks and absorbing the fluctuations in the fortunes of individual products and services and thereby ensuring steady growth for the enterprise. Empirical studies have identified the strategy of product diversity to be associated with fast-growing enterprises (Chaganti *et al.*, 1989; Fombrun & Wally, 1989; Boag, 1988). Although this relationship was found to be valid by subsequent researchers, a few have suggested modifications to it. Kang *et al.* (2020) observed that this relationship is valid only for diversified product portfolios based on specialized knowledge. In another study (Kim *et al.*, 2016), it was found that this relationship is curvilinear (with an inverted U-shape), suggesting that maximum firm growth happens at moderate levels of product/technological diversification.

The two methods for achieving product diversity are well known. Much has been written about related and unrelated (or conglomerate) diversification. The overall finding of these numerous researchers is that related diversification would lead to high performance in the long run. One of the strongest expressions of this finding is the prescription offered by Peters and Waterman (1982) that in order to be 'excellent', organizations should "stick to their knitting". The trend was set by earlier studies (Chandler, 1962; Rumelt, 1974) and has been confirmed by later studies (Roberts & Berry, 1985). In the latter study, performance was measured in terms of growth, and the authors reported that fast-growing firms concentrated on one key technological area and introduced product enhancements related to it. Conversely, it was observed that the poorest performers in terms of growth were those who moved into unrelated areas. However, a few cases of fast-growing enterprises (Manimala, 1988a, 1999) show that they take the route of conglomerate diversification. This is particularly true of firms in mature industries where growth opportunities in the same industry/technology are limited. An obvious way out of this cul-de-sac is to diversify into young industries with newer technologies (Smith & Cooper, 1988). Thus, it may be noted that while related diversification is sought for the synergies of operations, conglomerate diversification is undertaken to provide opportunities for growth in different directions. In the context of the research finding by Eisenhardt and Schoonhoven (1990), barring the founding top management's will, the market stage is the single most important factor affecting growth; it is not surprising that for enterprises in mature industries, conglomerate diversification is perhaps the only feasible strategy for growth. What is critical is not whether the firm diversifies into related or unrelated areas but how the 'conglomerate' is subsequently managed. In a study of Hitachi's diversification and growth, Bowonder and Miyake (1992a) observed that the firm's new products were by and large unrelated to the existing ones and that the internal coherence and synergies within the organization were maintained through the design of appropriate structures, systems, and procedures rather than through the relatedness of products. Moreover, there could also be synergies among apparently unrelated products that may not be obvious to external observers but are quickly grasped by insiders (Manimala, 1996b). When a steel maker gets into electronics/software, the synergies come through the 'process-control' route; on the other hand, if a ceramics manufacturer gets into electronics, the synergies come through the 'materials' route. When a cigarette manufacturer diversifies into edible oils, the synergies are through the supplier segment of agricultural products. For the textile company diversifying into textile machinery, the source of synergy is the knowledge of the market. These synergies can come through several routes, and so the external observer, to whom these routes are not obvious, may interpret such diversifications as unrelated. But the entrepreneur's definition of related diversification may be much broader. In other words, there can be different types of relatedness in diversification, as implied by Markides and Williamson (1994) when distinguishing between 'strategic' and 'market' relatedness.

4. Premium Product/Pricing Strategy

There are two elements in the premium product strategy, namely, high quality and high price. An orientation toward quality is apparently a strategy for slow but steady growth and is not generally associated with high profits except in a situation of promotion competition (Chaganti *et al.*, 1989). Similarly, high prices can rarely be sustained unless they are associated with high quality. The strategy of skimming the market using high prices is usually adopted in the initial stages of market growth when competition is relatively low. The premium product strategy, therefore, will not be the most preferred strategy for growth-seeking companies, even though it will be widely used in the initial stages to create a quality image among the customers.

Notwithstanding the research findings about the non-sustainability of the 'premium product/pricing strategy' as a long-term strategy for supporting enterprise growth, there are many organizations that have effectively used this strategy and achieved significantly high levels of growth. The most celebrated example of the effective use of this strategy is that of Apple (Nielson, 2014; Pradhan, 2020). Their strategy is based on the following four principles: (1) offer only a small number of products; (2) focus on the high-end or premium products; (3) give priority to profits over market share; (4) create a halo effect that makes customers crave for and eagerly await the arrival of new products from the company (Nielson, 2014). In essence, the strategy is that of maintaining an image of high quality by periodically introducing innovative features in the new versions of the product and charging correspondingly high prices, so that customers perceive it as a prestigious acquisition. For this reason, the strategy of premium pricing is also called 'image pricing' and 'prestige pricing'. The company actively manages the 'rumor-mill' about the new features of the next version of its products so as to keep the customer-expectations high. Similarly, they keep the prices high mainly through a strategy of selling through their own stores (the Apple Store). In India too, there are companies successfully using the strategy of having exclusive showrooms for their products, such as Bata and Reliance Textiles (the latter through the brand, Only Vimal), although the latter has now been sold off to a Chinese company (Jagannathan, 2014). If and when they sell through dealers, these companies minimize the commission, so that dealers are unable to give any discounts. In addition, they also enforce a condition of 'Minimum Advertised Price' (MAP) on dealers (Pradhan, 2020). Such strategies for preventing discounts are intended to maintain the luxury image of the product. While the 'premium product/pricing strategy' has worked very well for Apple and contributed to its growth for quite some time, it appears that the strategy cannot be stretched too far, as evidenced by the recent price cuts by the company (Banerjee, 2019). As the competition grows stronger and stronger, the premium product/pricing strategy becomes less and less sustainable.

5. Market Breadth and Penetration Strategy

Market breadth and penetration can be described as the opposite of premium product strategy. The latter is a specialist strategy and the sales target is restricted to one or a few segments of the market. The generalist breadth and penetration strategy, on the other hand, is based on a product that is required by most segments of the market. Extensive distribution covering a wide range of regions and relatively low pricing for intensive penetration into the various segments of the market are the other characteristics of the generalist strategy. It has been observed by Romanelli (1989) that the specialist strategy is more appropriate during the early phases when the enterprise is struggling for survival or when industry sales are declining. Generalists fare better when industry sales are increasing or when the organization starts growing. This, coupled with the finding of Eisenhardt and Schoonhoven (1990) that enterprise growth depends primarily on industry growth, suggests that generalist strategies have a greater role in enterprise growth. This hypothesis is strengthened by the observations of Boag (1988) whose study on the growth strategies of electronic companies showed that diversified firms following 'market-breadth strategies' needed lesser marketing efforts to sustain their growth compared to those following product/market-focused strategies. A later study (Stam & Wennberg, 2009) on the R&D activities of new firms showed that among high-tech firms, R&D activities helped in product development but not in firm growth, except for a limited number of firms. On the other hand, for low-tech firms, R&D had no impact on firm growth, which was largely driven by the growth ambitions of the founding entrepreneur. As low-tech firms are not active in R&D, they do not have innovative/premium products, for which they can charge premium prices. Naturally, they have to resort to 'market-breadth/penetration' strategies, which is why these strategies are observed to be associated with 'generalist' entrepreneurs.

6. Strategic Use of External Resources

It is well known that there are two types of enterprise growth. One of these is a slow and steady pattern using internally generated resources, which this author has called 'organic growth' (Manimala, 1992c). In contrast to such 'growth from within', there is another type that may be described as growth through the strategic use of external resources (Birley, 1985; Jarillo, 1988, 1989; Lorenzoni & Ornati, 1988; Maidique, 1980; Morgan, 1988; Thorelli, 1986). The use of external resources can vary in degrees. Forming a wider network of friends and associates and making appropriate use of them as required (Birley, 1985; Jarillo, 1988; Manimala, 1998; Thorelli, 1986) are perhaps the lowest degree of the use of external resources for growth. Such networks may comprise strong or weak ties (Granovetter, 1973), where the former would be operated in an ego-centric manner and the latter in a socio-centric manner (Lechner & Dowling, 2003). According to these latter authors, firm growth can be facilitated by any of these four types of network ties. However, the findings of a few other researchers on this issue are more ambivalent. Havnes and Senneseth (2001), for example, found no relationship between networking and firm growth, except in the case of a geographic extension of markets, whereas Luo and Child (2015) proposed a "composition-based view (CBV) of firm growth", which involves the creative use of ordinary resources for generating extra-ordinary results, although they further observed that the CBV effect will be temporary and is often restricted to the 'imitative' or 'catch-up' stage of the firm's growth.

The second level consists of more intensive networking with the specific objective of using the resources of others (Jarillo, 1989; Lorenzoni & Ornati, 1988). The firm therefore deliberately refrains from creating certain facilities, which it proposes to 'borrow' from others. This is an easy way of increasing one's turnover and profits without increasing investment and employment costs. This is accomplished generally by the formation of relatively permanent 'constellations' (Lorenzoni & Ornati, 1988) of firms that co-operate with each other. The success of such constellations depends on various factors such as the choice of the field, the methods adopted for controlling the external resources, the ability to retain high visibility in spite of acting as part of a constellation, the selection and promotion of partnerships, and the mechanisms to develop and monitor inter-firm relationships. The relationships within such constella-tions may be mutual as in the case of the joint development of products and sharing of benefits, or it may be unidirectional as in subcontracting or ancillarization. While there are studies (e.g., Giunta *et al.*, 2012) that have found a positive relationship between sub-contracting and firm growth, researchers have also observed that the relationship is not linear, which calls for the judicious use of such strategies. Research on the impact of sub-contracting and supply-chain partnerships on firm growth is also rather ambivalent. On the one hand, studies such as Wynarczyk and Watson (2005) found that firms with supply-chain partnerships experi-enced significantly higher growth rates and, on the other, work by researchers such as Park *et al.* (2010) found no positive impact of sub-contracting on firm growth but only on survival; however, they found that networking as a consequence of clustering had a positive impact on both survival and growth. In general, the impact of sub-contracting seems to be conditional, as is evident from the findings of Kumar and Balasubrahmanya (2010), where it was observed that if the sub-contracting is with a transnational company, it would lead to technological innova-tions and better performance.

The use of external resources in the growth phase increases the flex-ibility of the enterprise in addition to reducing investments and lowering risks. This may be why this strategy is seen to be very popular with growth-seeking ventures. Jarillo (1989) found that fast-growing firms make much more (about 64% more) use of external resources than the average firm. Needless to say, during the growth phase, when organiza-tions need to assemble relatively large amounts of resources in a very short period, it is a very convenient strategy to make maximum use of external resources. However, a major problem in continuing with this strategy is the difficulty in controlling the external resources, over which the firm in question has very little direct authority. A natural extension of this strategy, therefore, is to acquire controlling rights over the external resources. Enterprise growth by acquisition is a popular strategy with growth-seeking ventures. However, academics have questioned the long-term viability of such growth, particularly because of the difficulties associated with the integration of non-compatible cultures. In fact, it was observed in a study of a large panel of UK firms (Dickerson *et al.*, 1997) that acquisitions have a detrimental effect on firm performance and that growth through internal investment yielded better returns than growth through acquisitions. These findings are in sharp contrast with the findings of an earlier study of British enterprises by Morgan (1988), where it was found that several firms have effectively used acquisition as a strategy for rapid growth.

7. Strategic Alliances

A strategic alliance is also a way of making use of external resources. Subtle differences, however, have been made between the constellations discussed above and strategic alliances. Constellations revolve around a dominant firm in the group and have several participating firms, whereas strategic alliances reflect equal partnerships among a few firms with regard to specific issues. The idea is primarily to avoid wasteful competition and duplication of efforts and exploit the synergies resulting from joint action. It is therefore not surprising that this strategy has become increasingly popular with growth-seeking companies (Bertodo, 1990; Hamel & Prahalad, 1990; Harrigan, 1989; Lewis, 1990), especially with large corporations that have already established themselves in their core competence (Hamel & Prahalad, 1990). For smaller enterprises, on the other hand, collaborations most often would involve a dependency relationship. It is also observed that the success of this strategy is moderated by the market and resource conditions — that is, in volatile markets, it is the resource-rich organizations that will be successful, whereas in stable markets, resource-poor businesses would also gain by pursuing it (Park *et al.*, 2002).

8. Exploiting the Special Situations of Other Organizations

While small firms are generally unable to develop and utilize constellations and strategic alliances, there are several ways in which they can exploit the special needs, lethargy, bureaucracy, and failures of large organizations (Drucker, 1985; Manimala, 1998). Some of these ways are very common, while the others are exceptional. They include: working as ancillaries, subcontractors, and suppliers of raw materials and components; further processing of the large firm's finished goods; making better use of the skills and resources developed in the vicinity by large firms; and exploiting the myopia, the lethargy, and the failures of large organizations, through what Drucker (1985) calls 'creative imitation' and 'entrepreneurial judo'. The traditional view about the relationship between small and large firms is that it is a dependency relationship and so is to the disadvantage of the small firms (Wilson & Gort, 1983). It appears that while 'ordinary' small firms would find it difficult to overcome the dependency relationship, the growth-seeking firms are able to switch to the exploitative relationship quickly.

It is not only the large commercial organizations that have idle resources and by-products that are amenable to 'exploitation' by growth-seeking entrepreneurial firms. The issue of new-product development by entrepreneurial firms is a case in point. It is indeed a paradoxical phenomenon that many new products are developed by small firms that lack the resources to set up R&D facilities. In a comprehensive review of the literature on the 'R&D work' in new firms, the present author has found that these growth-seeking new firms cleverly exploit the resources of other commercial and non-commercial organizations for this purpose (Manimala, 2002b). The most commonly used network resources for this purpose are as follows: (a) large corporates who have a need for externalizing some of their activities which do not strictly fit in with their core business or are too small for their scale of operation; (b) smaller units of the same nature who have similar or complementary interests but are unable or unwilling to bear the full risk and therefore are interested in sharing the load, as well as the risk and returns; (c) research institutions who periodically come up with potentially useful ideas but consider it to be a distraction to spend their valuable time on the mundane activities involved in the commercialization of their work or are not competent for such work; (d) funding agencies interested in high returns and therefore prepared to take high risks; and (e) government and public agencies who are interested in the development of their domains, for which they consider the innovative entrepreneur as one of the most effective instruments. It is therefore obvious that each of these agencies is motivated by self-interest (not philanthropy) and thus can provide opportunities for meaningful and productive partnerships for the entrepreneur.

Characteristics of Growth-Seeking Entrepreneurs

The search for personality characteristics that would distinguish between entrepreneurs and non-entrepreneurs, successful entrepreneurs and unsuccessful ones, etc. has been largely infructuous. A detailed review of the literature on the traits-and-motives research covering the period up to the last decade of the 20th century is available in Manimala (1992c, 1999), the conclusion of which was that there is no agreement among researchers on the critical traits or motives of entrepreneurs. A subsequent review (Busenitz *et al.*, 2014) that extended into the first decade of the

21st century pointed out that there were four main themes around which entrepreneurship research was being carried out. While the theme of 'entrepreneurial individuals and teams' still remained a favorite theme for a few researchers, there were many more papers on other themes such as entrepreneurial opportunities, environments, and modes of organizing. The disillusionment with the traits-and-motives research has led to three different approaches in recent research on entrepreneurship, namely, (1) the study of environmental factors promoting entrepreneurship; (2) the study of the interaction among individual, organizational, procedural, and environmental factors; and (3) the classification of ventures/entrepreneurs into different groups and the comparative study of the characteristics of each group. The present study may be classified under the third approach. The attempt here is to find out whether there are significant differences between high-growth and low-growth ventures in terms of their strategy preferences, policy orientations, and the personality characteristics of their founders. Research on the strategy preferences of growth ventures has been discussed in the previous section. As for personality characteristics, the scenario is hardly different from the research on the traits of entrepreneurs in general. There is no conclusive evidence in support of one trait or another. This is why the primary focus of this study is on the strategic/policy orientations of growth ventures, and not the traits and motives of entrepreneurs. However, as the study proposes to investigate the relationship, if any, between the policies/strategies of the venture and the personality characteristics and background of entrepreneurs, a brief summary of the prior research on the latter two sets of variables (namely, background variables, and traits and motives) is presented as follows.

1. Background Variables

There are several theories about the 'ideal' background from which entrepreneurs are likely to emerge. Weber (1930) talked about the religious ideology of Protestantism, McClelland (1961) about the child-rearing practices in the family, and Hagen (1962) about the physical and social displacement and refugee status of an earlier generation. These theories have not been able to get unmixed support from subsequent studies. Moreover, theories associating entrepreneurship with physical/social displacement, material/psychological deprivation, and refugee status may often deal with subsistence entrepreneurship. This is probably why among growth-venture research studies, there are very few studies focusing on background variables.

The focus of the few available studies linking the background variables and enterprise growth is on the age and previous experience of the owner-manager rather than on upbringing, childhood experiences, and ancestral history. One of these studies (Cragg & King, 1988) found that younger firms with younger owners had greater chances of growth. These findings contradict the thesis (commonly known as Gibrat's law) of the French economist Robert Gibrat (1931) that firm growth is a stochastic process and is independent of firm size. Subsequent studies have shown that this theory is not valid for firm growth, in either the manufacturing or service sector (Audretsch *et al.*, 2004). Older firms may become less and less innovative/growth-oriented, as they become conditioned by their previous successful practices and develop a sense of complacency and inertia. This may be why some later researchers have even found a negative correlation between the age of the firm and their growth (e.g., Zhou & de Wit, 2009). Similar findings were obtained by a Japanese study (Honjo, 2004), where it was observed that younger and small-sized firms are more likely to grow than older ones.

While the focus of the above research was on the age of the firm, other studies like Belenzon *et al.* (2019) focused on the age of the CEO rather than on the age of the firm. They found that when the CEO of a closely held firm (which is the case with most start-ups) grows older, he/she become more risk-averse and prefer to focus on survival rather than on risky investments for profitability and growth. Such perceptions about the relatively high propensity of the young for developing novel ideas and taking risks to implement them are prevalent among the general public and are popularized by young achievers, as pointed out by Azoulay *et al.* (2020). In the introductory part of their paper on the subject (pp. 65–66), they have reproduced the comments of a few great entrepreneurs, namely, Mark Zuckerberg, the founder of Facebook ("Young people are just smarter."); Paul Graham, the venture capitalist and founder of Y Combinator ("The cutoff in investors' heads is 32…after 32, they start to be a little skeptical."); and Vinod Khosla, the co-founder of Sun Microsystems and venture capitalist ("People under 35 are the people who make change happen, …people over forty-five basically die in terms of new ideas."). However, the findings of the study by Azoulay *et al.* (2020), based on an analysis of the administrative data at the US Census Bureau, did not support the 'young-founder hypothesis' for high-growth firms. The average age of the founders of the fastest-growing firms at the time of founding was observed to be 45. In other words, the founders were middle-aged, not young. The reason for this may be that older entrepreneurs may have greater access to the human, social, and/or financial capital required for supporting firm growth.

Notwithstanding such research findings, one should not ignore the possibility of having extreme cases, especially those in the older age-groups. For the enthusiastic entrepreneur, age is just a number, as may be inferred from the cases of some well-known entrepreneurs, who started their high-growth businesses at a ripe old age. One such celebrated case is that of Colonel Harland Sanders who started his business, KFC (Kentucky Fried Chicken), at the age of 65 and was rejected 1009 times by restaurants before someone agreed to sell his special-recipe chicken cooked under high pressure with numerous herbs and spices, subsequently promoted as "Finger Lickin' Good" (Singh, 2012). By 1971, less than two decades after its inception, KFC had become a global brand with over 3,500 franchises in different countries, generating annual revenues of more than USD 700 million (Britannica, 2021). Another case of an 'old-age' start-up of a high-growth venture is that of a luxury hotel chain in India (Hotel Leelaventure Ltd, now renamed HLV Ltd) by Captain C. P. Krishnan Nair, who launched his first 5-star hotel near the international airport in Bombay (now Mumbai) in 1986 when he was 64 years of age. Three decades later, this company had created about 10 luxury hotels in the major cities and tourist destinations of India, many of which are in partnership with reputed international hotel chains (HLV Ltd, 2021). Besides the Hotel Division, the Leela Group has more than a dozen other divisions in the areas of Resorts, Real Estate/Housing, Fashion, IT/Software, Techno-parks/Business parks, etc. (The Leela Group, 2021). Since the assets for the hotels were created through debt funds, there were financial strains on the Group, and so they have recently changed their strategy from being an 'asset-heavy' ownership company to an 'asset-light' management company by selling their assets to a Canadian real estate management company, Brookfield Asset Management (Baggonkar, 2019).

The two examples cited above show that high-growth firms can be created by entrepreneurs of any age, but their success depends on the kind of strategies adopted for achieving fast growth. Moreover, the efficacy of these strategies depends on the context. For example, the debt-supported 'asset-heavy' strategy may be successful when the business is booming, but become a burden under recessionary conditions. While the passion for creating a high-growth venture may exist in any age group depending on the personality characteristics of the individuals involved, the relative advantage of older entrepreneurs may be derived from their prior work experiences. In the case of Captain Krishnan Nair, the idea of starting a luxury hotel in India occurred to him when he was traveling abroad and staying in such hotels for his previous business of textile export. He realized that there were very few such facilities in India where he could entertain his customers when they made business trips to India. Similarly, he connected with his future international partners through the networks created with his previous business. These connections were also useful for building his contacts and credibility with potential lending agencies. Thus, prior work experience (be it as an employee or an entrepreneur) can help the individual in developing different types of 'capital' (such as ideas' capital, human capital, social capital, and financial capital) required for creating new ventures, especially high-growth ventures. There are many cases where potential entrepreneurs perceive gaps in the market and identify market-relevant ideas for business start-ups based on their work experiences. By this process, they 'accumulate' the ideas capital required for their future business. Similarly, they are able to acquire human, social, and finance capital as they develop and gain credibility with business contacts who may become potential customers, suppliers, partners, employees, lenders, and investors. Prior work may also help in building cash reserves that can serve as the seed capital for the new start-up. It is for these reasons that the prior experience of the entrepreneurial individual assumes importance to researchers.

As pointed out above, there are two aspects of the entrepreneur's prior work experience that are relevant for performance; one is the prior employment experience of the entrepreneur, and the second is their prior experience in owning and managing enterprises. In a comparison between 39 high-growth and 39 low-growth enterprises selected from the *Inc.* listing, Feeser and Willard (1989) observed that the founders of high-growth firms had prior experience in related areas and had worked in larger, especially publicly held, companies. Such large, resource-rich organizations can serve as 'god-fathers' for the potential entrepreneurs that work with them. This process could be compared to that of a father training his son in the family's trade/occupation in a traditional society. For example, in the traditional caste-based economy of India, a barber's son would be trained to become a barber. While training, it would be difficult and risky for him to cut the hair of a real customer. Under this situation, the father may 'magnanimously' offer his own head for the training. In the same way, large organizations with enough slack resources may not mind their enterprising employees experimenting with new ideas. Some employees make good use of this opportunity and get trained by this 'god-father' for their future entrepreneurial initiatives. As for the prior experience in owning and managing enterprises, the 'experienced' entrepreneur is found to be more successful and growth-oriented. The importance of getting experience in 'related areas' is also highlighted in a later study (Jo & Lee, 1996), where a positive relationship between prior experience in related areas and firm growth was found, as well as a negative impact on growth if the prior experience of the entrepreneur was in unrelated areas.

An explanation for the consistently observed linkage between the entrepreneur's prior work experience and firm performance is offered by Ronstadt (1988) through what he calls the 'corridor principle', which means that the early ventures of an entrepreneur serve as a corridor through which further opportunities become visible. In other words, an entrepreneur's ability to see and exploit business opportunities substantially increases because of his being in business, and therefore entrepreneurs with prior entrepreneurial experience are likely to exhibit a greater urge for high performance and growth. Similarly, Duchesneau and Gartner (1990) found that high-growth entrepreneurs opted for broader business types and had prior start-up experience. They also found that such entrepreneurs had 'entrepreneurial parents', suggesting their upbringing also had an influence. It appears that venture growth is primarily a function of the entrepreneur's *prior experience* and *motivation*, as is observed by Laguir and Besten (2016), who investigated the role of six different aspects of the entrepreneur's background: education, work experience, gender, motivations, nationality, and age, in promoting innovation and growth, but did not find any impact on firm growth for the other four variables. While there is general agreement among researchers about the benefits of prior work experience for entrepreneurship, this is not the case with the several studies on the traits and motives of entrepreneurs (which are discussed in the following sub-section).

2. Traits and Motives
Research on entrepreneurship has not had much success in identifying the traits and motives that could predict entrepreneurial success. Among those proposed are risk-taking ability (Knight, 1921), desire for autonomy (Collins & Moore, 1970; Sexton & Bowman, 1985), tolerance of ambiguity (Schere, 1982; Sexton & Bowman, 1985), perseverance (Kourilsky,

1980), achievement motive (McClelland, 1961), and so on. A later study (Brandstätter, 1997) attempted to compare the traits of founding owners with those of inheriting owners and showed that founders were emotionally more stable and self-assertive (independent) than inheritors. While most of these researchers have focused on identifying one or two critical traits/motives responsible for entrepreneurial initiatives, an 11 country study by Scheinberg and MacMillan (1988) came up with five: (1) Need for Approval; (2) Need for Independence; (3) Need for Personal Development; (4) Welfare Considerations; and (5) Perceived Instrumentality of Wealth. With the progress in research on entrepreneurial motivation, further additions can be made to this list, such as the 'Desire to Follow Role-Models' (Dubini, 1988) and the 'Desire to get Tax Reductions and Indirect Benefits' (Birley & Westhead, 1994). Based on a cluster analysis of 23 motives for business start-ups, Birley and Westhead (1994) identified seven generalized types of owner-managers: the insecure, the followers, the status avoiders, the confused, the tax avoiders, the community-oriented, and the unfocused. Surprisingly, however, there was no relationship between these motivational types and the subsequent growth of their firms in terms of sales or employment. While the motives of the entrepreneurial individual influence the start-up activities, the growth of the venture may depend more on the organizational characteristics such as goals, efficacy, and communicated vision (Baum & Locke, 2004).

In a study of the psychological characteristics associated with entrepreneurial performance, Begley and Boyd (1987) examined the relevance of five characteristics: (1) need for achievement; (2) locus of control; (3) propensity to take risk; (4) tolerance of ambiguity; and (5) Type-A behavior. They found that there were very few associations between psychological characteristics and growth performance. Some of these associations were difficult to explain. For example, having an internal locus of control was associated with a low liquidity ratio, whereas a high need for achievement was associated with a high liquidity ratio. According to a curvilinearity analysis, it was found that for variables like having a propensity for risk-taking and tolerance of ambiguity, there was a 'threshold effect', implying that the trait was associated with high performance up to a certain level, beyond which performance decreased. This is not surprising, especially because prior studies by McClelland (1961) had shown that moderate risk-taking was a characteristic of high achievers. Such moderation in one's ambition for achievement seems to be 'common-sense', as suggested by the Shakespearean analogy, where he compares ambition to the act of mounting a horse; if you jump too high, you fall on the other side! While McClelland's (1961) prescription was about moderate risk-taking as a component of achievement motivation, a later study by Roberts (1989) found that such 'moderation' is applicable even to achievement motivation itself! In his study of high-performing technical entrepreneurs, he found that not all of them ranked highly on achievement motivation. In fact, the profile of an average technical entrepreneur was characterized by a moderate need for achievement, a moderate need for power, and a low need for affiliation. Their need for financial gain is relatively low, but they have a high need for autonomy and independence (similar to the findings of Brandstätter, 1997), and are continuously in search for newer and bolder challenges.

Smith (1967) undertook a study of the entrepreneurial characteristics associated with enterprise growth and classified entrepreneurs into two groups. The 'opportunistic' entrepreneurs were characterized by having breadth in education and training, high social awareness and involvement, confidence in their ability to deal with the business environment, and future orientation. The firms started by this group grew about nine times faster than those started by 'craftsman' entrepreneurs who had the opposite characteristics. Though a subsequent study by Smith and Miner (1983) found further support for these findings, other studies have failed to corroborate them. For example, Bracker *et al.* (1988) found no significant difference between opportunistic and craftsman entrepreneurs with regard to their success in financial performance. A different scheme of classifying individuals, namely, the Myers and Briggs Type Indicator (MBTI), was used by Ginn and Sexton (1990) to ascertain the differences, if any, between fast-growth and slow-growth entrepreneurs. Out of the four MBTI dimensions of Extroversion-Introversion, Sensation-Intuition, Thinking-Feeling, and Judgment-Perception, two dimensions showed significant differences in a group of 143 founders/CEOs of *Inc.* fast-growth companies, as compared to the founders/CEOs of 150 slow-growth companies. The former (the fast-growth group) were more 'intuitive' and 'thinking' in their approaches. In other words, they were more concerned about considering future possibilities while gathering information and adopted a planned and organized approach to implementing new ideas. It may also be noted that this author reported a similar finding in his study of innovative entrepreneurs (Manimala, 1999). This work found that the more innovative entrepreneurs were more comfortable with their own hunches and gut feelings than their less innovative counterparts, even though the former were also careful to collect systematic information so as to be able to manage the risk better.

It is obvious that the traits-and-motives research on growth venture entrepreneurs has not produced any conclusive results. The complexity, variety, and 'non-conclusive' nature of trait research can be best seen from the disillusionment of the master-researcher of the field, David McClelland. In 1961 McClelland proposed that achievement motivation was the critical trait of entrepreneurs. By 1976, there was a change in his theory in favor of a 'three-dimensional profile' constituted by a high need for power, a low need for affiliation, and a high capacity to discipline oneself (McClelland & Burnham, 1976). Later, McClelland, in association with McBer and Company, felt that there was once again a need to start from scratch and adopted a new method of research called Behavioral Event Interviewing (Boyatzis, 1982) to identify the critical traits of entrepreneurs, some of which were initiative, assertiveness, efficiency orientation, systematic planning, and commitment to work (McClelland, 1986). Reviewing the status of trait research at a luncheon meeting during the *Third Creativity, Innovation and Entrepreneurship Symposium*, McClelland (1987) stated that there were as many as 42 different entrepreneurial characteristics mentioned by at least two sources and many more identified in other studies. The most frequently mentioned traits were identified as confidence, perseverance, energy, diligence, resourcefulness, creativity, foresight, initiative, versatility, knowledge of product and market, intelligence, perceptiveness, and so on. One might wonder what has happened to achievement, power, and other motives. A more important question is whether it would serve any useful purpose if one were to explain the phenomenon of entrepreneurship (if one can) with the help of 42 or more variables! It appears that in the case of growth venture research, one cannot expect much from the long history of investigation into personality traits and motives, as the findings sometimes veer into unexpected directions. In one such study (Zhou & de Wit, 2009), it was found that entrepreneurs having a strong need for achievement are less likely to promote firm growth, which is rather like 'dethroning' a princely concept of entrepreneurship research (*n-Ach*) from growth-venture research.

Based on a comprehensive review of the literature on firm growth, Coad (2007) reinforced the 'inconclusiveness' of firm growth research and stated that none of the parameters traditionally being associated with entrepreneurial performance (such as innovation, productivity, and financial performance) could predict firm growth. In fact, the R-square in the regression analyses of growth with various performance parameters was in the low range of 4–10%. According to him, it is difficult to find support for any one of the three major theories of enterprise growth, namely, (1) the classical theory of Penrose (1959), where firm growth is viewed as an end in itself and as a process of utilizing the learning and resources accumulated within the firm; (2) the neo-classical theory, where firm growth is viewed as a means to achieve some other end, often stated as that of reaching an 'optimal size'; (3) the population-ecology theory, where firm growth is seen as an outcome of the environmental push.

While it is possible for entrepreneurs to overcome the constraints posed by the environment, a distinction made by this author (Manimala, 1992b) between two types of environments (the general environment and the task environment) with respect to their role in promoting innovation may be applicable to firm growth as well. It was observed that changes in the task environment (comprising educational/training facilities, business incubators, industrial estates, financial institutions, etc.) may not bring about any significant increase in innovation unless there are entrepreneurial individuals capable of effectively utilizing such task facilitation. Development and supply of entrepreneurial individuals in society, on the other hand, is a function of the general environment in the country (comprising the legal-political, social, cultural, and economic institutions). Growth-oriented attitudes and behaviors among entrepreneurial individuals are the necessary prerequisites for identifying the resources available in the environment and utilizing them effectively in support of firm growth. Not surprisingly, some of the prior studies on this issue have found a significant association between firm growth and a firm's entrepreneurial behavior (Stevenson & Jarillo, 1990; Brown *et al.*, 2001). While acknowledging the importance of entrepreneurial behavior at the firm level, it should be pointed out that the behavior of the firm is dependent on the attitudes and behavior of those who own and manage it, and hence it is legitimate to take another look at the traits, motives and organizational policies of the entrepreneur.

Objectives of this Study

There is some evidence from the literature that enterprise characteristics, especially the strategies employed, of fast-growth ventures might be different from those of slow-growth ones. The major objective of the research reported in this book is to investigate these differences with a view to developing a profile of high-growth ventures based on founder characteristics and enterprise policies/strategies. When the study was being designed, the author had an opportunity to do research in the UK, on account of a fellowship from the European Foundation for Management Development (EFMD). Hence, the data collection was started in the UK and was subsequently continued in India. As the Indian sample was reluctant to give information on their financial performance, they could not be classified into high- and low-growth groups, and so were excluded from the growth-venture policy analysis, for which the study was originally designed. However, the data from the Indian sample on founder characteristics and their enterprise policies helped in extending the analysis to include a cross-cultural comparison of these variables. It was also possible to use these data along with the British data for an analysis of the inter-relationships among these variables. Thus, the objectives of the original study were slightly extended and can be summarized as follows:

1. Identification of the strategies and policies of high-growth ventures as compared to their low-growth counterparts.
2. Identification of the personality traits (personal policies) of growth-seeking entrepreneurs.
3. Identification of the dominant motives of growth-seeking entrepreneurs.
4. Identification of the background and early experiences of growth-seeking entrepreneurs.
5. Comparing the changes, if any, in the motives, traits, and the strategy/policy variables between the start-up and subsequent stages of the venture.
6. Examining the explanatory and discriminatory powers of the above variables vis-à-vis high-growth and low-growth ventures.
7. Making a cross-cultural comparison of British and Indian enterprises in terms of their policies and founder characteristics. (As the focus of this book is on enterprise growth, the discussion on this issue will not be covered here.)
8. Establishing the inter-relationships, if any, among the above variables; that is, how background, traits, motives, strategies, and performance influence one another.

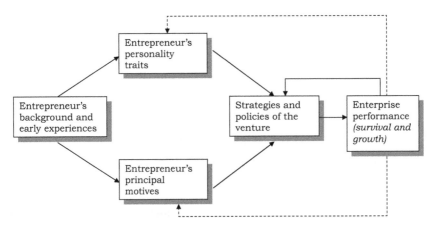

Fig. 1.2.   The theoretical model.

Note: Dotted lines indicate long term effects.

Hypotheses

Our major hypothesis is implied in item 8 above and presented in Fig. 1.2.

Although the study was initially designed with the objective of identifying growth venture policies and strategies, it cannot be denied that the policies and strategies of the enterprise could be the result of other influences, including the background, traits, and motives of the entrepreneur. Hence, this book has included these variables and made an attempt to build a theory around their inter-relationships.

As for the minor hypotheses, they may be briefly stated as follows:

1. It is likely that growth-seeking entrepreneurs come from different backgrounds than those of their stagnating counterparts. As the literature on entrepreneurs' background has not produced any consistent evidence on this issue — with one group of researchers asserting that entrepreneurs are socially and psychologically marginalized people suffering from displacement and deprivation and having limited support in terms of education and training, and another group stating that they are people with broader education, experience, and involvement in the larger concerns of the society — it may be safer for us not to make any specific hypothesis about the background but wait for the outcome of the study.

2. The case of personality traits is similar. Again, the literature does not support any specific hypothesis. It is likely, however, that the traits are different for the two groups.
3. As for the motives, it is likely that the growth-seeking entrepreneurs are motivated primarily by the higher-order motives. Conversely, low-growth entrepreneurs are likely to be motivated by lower-order motives.
4. Strategy/policy is the variable in which one would expect the largest number of differences between the high-growth and low-growth enterprises. The following strategies/policies may be preferred by the high-growth group:
    *   Continuous search for new ideas and efforts for technology improvement;
    *   Market breadth and penetration strategies;
    *   Diversification, including into unrelated areas;
    *   Strategic use of external resources, including strategic alliances and networking.
5. It is also hypothesized that the differences identified between the two groups in terms of the above variables would enable discrimination between the two groups and so could be used in exercises involving the identification and prediction of growth-seeking entrepreneurs.
6. As far as the differences between the British and Indian entrepreneurs are concerned, it is expected that the differences will be more with reference to the culturally determined personality characteristics rather than the enterprise policies. In fact, the differences in enterprise policies are also likely to be more in those areas that are susceptible to influence by culture and personal style. (However, this issue is not discussed in this book, for reasons explained earlier).
7. The questionnaire used in the study is also designed to measure the strength of the traits and motives and enterprise policies at two different phases of the enterprise, the start-up period and the later period. It is expected that there may be some differences between the two phases, especially in terms of enterprise policies.

Organization of the Book

In addition to this introductory chapter, which contains the review of literature on growth venture research and some cross-cultural perspectives on entrepreneurship as well as sets out the objectives of the book and the hypotheses, there are five other chapters. Chapter 2 covers the design of the study, including the general methodology, sample selection, data collection, data analysis, etc., along with a discussion on the limitations of this methodology. Chapters 3–5, which explain the findings on growth ventures, are based only on the British data. Indian data could not be used for this analysis because of the respondents' reluctance to reveal financial data on the performance of their enterprises. It was therefore not possible to compute the growth index and classify the ventures into high- and low-growth groups. Hence this part of the analysis was performed using only the British data.

Chapter 3 discusses the basic findings on high- and low-growth enterprises. Computation of the growth index, correlations among enterprise growth, profitability and industry growth, and the identification (through *t*-tests) of the distinguishing variables with respect to high- and low-growth ventures are discussed in Chapter 3. The next chapter is devoted to the identification of the major dimensions of the four groups of variables revealed by the factor analysis. Chapter 5 discusses the explanatory and discriminatory powers of these variables, and their inter-relationships, along with the findings on the changes in the strengths of the variables over a period of time after the start-up. For the reasons explained above on the limitations of the Indian data (absence of financial data and the limited number of responses received during the relevant period), the entire analysis presented in this book is based on the British data only. While it was possible to use the Indian data for cross-cultural comparisons on entrepreneurial background, traits, motives and enterprise policies, that analysis is not included in this book, as it is not directly relevant for the discussion on the theme of enterprise growth.

Chapter 6 then provides a discussion on the findings of the study, highlighting its contributions, implications for theory and practice, along with the limitations of the study, and indicating directions for further research. This chapter is followed by two Appendices. Appendix 1 provides a case study of a British entrepreneur whose growth story illustrates the validity of a few theories on entrepreneurship as well as some of the findings of this study. Appendix 2 is the questionnaire used for this study and provides the details of the variables (background, policies, traits, and motives of the entrepreneur and the policies of venture) that were investigated.

Chapter 2

Research Design and Methodology

During an earlier study of entrepreneurial policies by the present author (Manimala, 1988a, 1999), it was found that entrepreneurs' policies, especially the start-up policies, are generally not stated or articulated clearly by the promoters for enforcement in their firms. There were cases where entrepreneurs were not even aware of their policies, or professed different policies than what they practiced. An incident from the researcher's experience of interacting with entrepreneurs in connection with the previous study would illustrate this phenomenon. The conversation (as part of the pilot study) was with an entrepreneur who was in the growth-stage of his venture and has set up two additional units in two different states of the country. Reports in the business-media stated that the expansion of operations to two other states was a strategy for spreading risk, as his home-state had occasional problems of power-shortage and trade-union-activism. It was, therefore, obvious that this entrepreneur was following the 'heuristic' expressed in a commonly used business-proverb, "Don't put all your eggs in one basket". As this proverb could express the 'risk-spreading heuristic' very well, this was used in the conversation to explain the implied heuristic. The response of the entrepreneur, however, was rather surprising. Nodding his head in disagreement, he said: "This is what the merchants would do, but I do what the hen does. If she puts her eggs in different baskets and shifts from one basket to another by turns, none of the eggs will hatch". While his statement made a lot of sense about the heuristic/ policy he would prefer to follow in the start-up stage, he was actually following a different one at the growth-stage, although without acknowledging it. Content analysis of cases, where the judgment is made based on the

51

actions (rather than the statements) of the protagonists is a better way of capturing the policies actually being practiced by start-up entrepreneurs. Moreover, it offers an opportunity to generate such data from the biographical information about the start-up stage policies of great entrepreneurs, from whom it is not possible to get questionnaires filled up.

The divergence, as pointed out above, between the 'espoused theory' and the 'theory-in-use' (Argyris & Schon, 1974) was particularly evident in the case of startup/nascent entrepreneurs. It was, therefore, decided that entrepreneurial 'heuristics' (unstated, and often unenforced, policies) could be more effectively identified and studied using the 'case-survey method', which involved the analyses of decisions reported in undisguised published cases and the inference of heuristics from them (Manimala, 1988b). As explained above, this method was found to be more effective than the conventional method of questionnaire survey, for the purpose of studying heuristics/unarticulated policies.

In the present study, however, the questionnaire method was adopted, even though the major focus of the study was policies. The reasons for this choice for the present study are as follows:

(a) Since the prior study has already identified the major heuristics/policies, the questionnaire could be constructed on the basis of those findings. Such 'research support' was not available for the earlier study, which made the questionnaire survey more difficult at that time.

(b) The policies investigated in this study are the ones in force during the growth stage, as opposed to those at the start-up stage in the previous study. The enterprise has been in operation for some time and the policies are likely to have evolved and got articulated in the organization by then. Hence, it would be easier for the entrepreneur to respond to the questionnaire.

(c) The purpose of the present study is to compare the policies of high-growth ventures with those of low-growth ventures. A case-survey method would not be feasible, as it would be difficult to get enough number of published stories about low-growth ventures. Hence, a questionnaire study was adopted, which could also generate data from a control group of low-growth ventures.

(d) The case-survey method adopted in the earlier study had a limitation that the cases did not provide uniformly adequate information on all variables, with the result that the researcher could not make finer judgment of degrees. It was, therefore, a three-point scale (*absent–doubtful–present*) that was used in the earlier study. Hence, it was felt that the results should be tested once again using measures on a finer scale, for which a questionnaire study was thought to be more appropriate.

(e) Finally, an important objective of the present study was to establish the relationships, if any, between enterprise policies and the other traditionally researched variables such as the background, traits and motives of the entrepreneur, for which data on all variables are required. Cases rarely provide information on traits and motives and therefore a questionnaire survey was required for collecting such data.

It is true that a self-report-based instrument like a mailed questionnaire filled up by the respondents has a few limitations such as improper understanding of questions, hurried and sometimes careless furnishing of data, volunteer bias, social desirability bias, and so on. Such problems are more pronounced in online surveys. The impact of some of these can be reduced by proper design, pretesting and analysis. Others will have to be tolerated as limitations of social science research. We shall deal with these issues later. In spite of the above limitations, it was found that for the present study a questionnaire survey was appropriate. Mail survey was preferred to email/online survey, as the latter were not very well developed at the time when the survey was conducted.

Design of the Questionnaire

The major input for the design of the questionnaire came from the author's earlier study on entrepreneurial heuristics, and the literature on entrepreneurial traits, motives and background. The questionnaire (see Appendix 2) was divided into five sections. The first section is about the performance characteristics of the organization, mainly for the purpose of computing an index for growth. Two questions at the end of this section on profitability and industry growth were included with a view to finding the correlation, if any, between profitability and enterprise growth, and industry growth and enterprise growth.

The second section titled 'Management Practices' deals with enterprise policies. The items were developed from the author's earlier study. The next three sections are on the personality traits, motives and background of the entrepreneur, respectively. These are based on the findings of prominent studies on these topics. The aim is to identify the important dimensions of these variables and compare them for the two groups of high-growth and low-growth enterprises. It is also proposed to examine the inter-relationships among these variables, so that a theoretical model could be constructed. The respondents were requested to furnish information on the three variables of policies, traits and motives during the start-up period as well. This will be useful for studying changes in these variables, if any, and to make an effort to establish causal relationship among the variables, which would be possible through regression analysis when there is a temporal gap between the measures on these variables.

Sample Selection

Addresses of high-growth enterprises were selected from *Growth Companies Register*, which in two volumes has furnished information on 2000 fastest growing private companies in the UK. The control group of low-growth enterprises were chosen from the FRAME database, which has provided a growth rate for each enterprise based on its sales turnover.

The use of 'external' criteria for sample selection was to ensure that data from high-growth and low-growth ventures are available in the final dataset. It was not the intention to rely exclusively on the growth of turnover for the classification of ventures into high-growth and low-growth ventures. In some cases, growth in turnover may not be an indicator of 'genuine' growth. Increases in turnover growth across different industries may not be comparable. To minimize the effect of 'pseudo-growth', therefore, we have decided to use a combined index for growth in this research, using other variables such as changes in profits, investment, employment, and number of products, along with changes in turnover.

Pre-testing

Before the questionnaires were sent out to the potential respondents, they were pre-tested in a group of 16 entrepreneurs who were participants of an entrepreneurship development programme. It was a testimony to the clarity of the questionnaire that none of these entrepreneurs had to seek clarifications as to the meanings of the questions. One entrepreneur questioned the relevance of seeking information on religion. This was explained to him in terms of Weber's theory of 'Protestant Ethic' (Weber, 1930), which proposed that those who followed the Protestant religion were more entrepreneurial than others. However, this individual felt that there should be a 'no-religion' category as there can be people who do not believe in any religion. This was accepted and was clarified that it could be specified in the 'other' category.

At the time of designing the questionnaire, it was felt that a 16-page questionnaire would take a long time for the respondent to complete, which was proved otherwise in the pre-testing. The time taken varied from 25 to 40 minutes. This was probably due to the fact that the questions were mainly of objective type and required very little writing by the respondents. Added to this was the fact that the questions were clear enough to be understood in the first reading itself. Since there was no need for changing the questionnaire after pre-testing, it was decided that the data collected during pre-testing also could be used in the aggregate analysis.

Data Collection

From the two groups of potential respondents mentioned above, 505 were chosen for the initial mailing of the questionnaire, hoping that about 15–20% would return the completed questionnaires. There were 262 high-growth and 243 low-growth ventures in the mailing list. Of these, 63 questionnaires were returned to the sender as undelivered mail. These were mainly cases of closed down units. 37 completed questionnaires were received by the researcher after one reminder to those who did not respond within 15 days. Since the number of completed questionnaires received was inadequate for statistical processing, another 397 were dispatched in the second phase, of which 52 were returned as undelivered. From this group, 28 completed questionnaires were received. Thus, from a mailed survey of 787 ventures (comprising 442 in the first phase and 345 in the second), 65 completed questionnaires were received, which amounts to a response rate of 8.25%. The number of questionnaires were augmented by another 9 subsequently, which were collected through a survey of Science Park entrepreneurs. Thus, there were 90 responses to questionnaires (65+16+9) for the final analysis.

Most of the questionnaires received were complete in all respects. In fact, there were hardly any omissions in Sections II–IV, which were of the 'objective' type. A few omissions occurred in Section I, probably for the following reasons. Many of the answers in this section had to be written in words and figures, which might have been too much trouble for some entrepreneurs. Some questions in this section were about performance indicators such as profits, turnover, product diversity, employee strength and investment. It is natural that some people have reservations about divulging such information. In a few cases, there was probably a need to refer to company records, failing which the respondent might have opted to leave them blank. Omissions in Section I would adversely affect the process of classifying the ventures into high-growth and low-growth groups, as it reduces the number of enterprises giving information on all five criteria of growth, namely: profits, investment, turnover, employee strength and product diversity. It was decided that this issue could be re-examined at the time of computing the growth-rates on the five variables. If a large number of enterprises are 'silent' on one variable or another, the computation of growth rate has to be done using the variables on which a reasonably large number of enterprises have provided the relevant information. Since the numbers required in the high-growth and low-growth groups are about 30 each, omission of a few data-points is not likely to adversely affect the comparative analysis.

The response rate of 8.25% is relatively low, but can be treated as acceptable. In a survey of entrepreneurship studies by Alpar and Spitzer (1989), it was found that the response rate varied from 8% to 26.5%. These authors, therefore, considered a 20% response rate to be 'normal' even though lower levels also would be acceptable. Though the 'normal' observed range is between 7% and 26.5%, studies have reported response rates as low as 3% (Scheinberg & MacMillan, 1988) and as high as 80% (Foss, 1985). The response rate of 8.25% obtained by the present study is admittedly low, even though it is well within the observed range in similar studies. In this context, it is quite reassuring to note the findings of a recent study (Rutherford *et al.*, 2017) where response rates did not have any meaningful or consistent influence on relationships being investigated in entrepreneurship research.

Data Analysis

The first step in data analysis is to classify ventures into high-growth and low-growth ventures. Traditionally, it is done on the basis of sales-growth in monetary terms. As we have explained above, this can be misleading in some cases, especially if there is no adjustment for inflation. Changes in physical output can be a more reliable measure, but data on these are hard to obtain, and the unit of measurement would not be comparable across industries. We, therefore, have decided to develop a combined index for growth, based on investment, employee strength, and product-diversity along with sales-turnover. Each of these variables also has its limitations. For example, one may invest more in an unwise manner and may not obtain any growth for the enterprise at all. To take another example, it is possible to grow, especially in capital-intensive high-tech areas, without much addition to manpower. Notwithstanding these, it is hoped that the variables may have a moderating effect on one another so that the combined index would be a more reliable index for enterprise growth.

The formula for computing average annual growth rate may be stated in a general form as follows:

$$\left(\frac{\text{Figures for the later period}}{\text{Figures for the earlier period}} - 1 \right) \times \frac{100}{n}$$

where n is the number of years between the two periods.

The differences in the units of measuring the variables (money, numbers, etc.) may not affect the results very much because the comparisons are between ratios. In our data, investment, profits and turnover were measured in monetary terms. Employment and product-diversity, on the other hand, were measured in numbers, that is, the number of employees and the number of distinct products, respectively. The item-omission problem discussed above can come in the way of using all the variables in the index. If a large number of respondents have left out information on one variable, it will be dropped from the index. The remaining growth-rates will be combined using an arithmetic average. An arithmetic average is preferred to a geometric average even though the latter is generally used for averaging ratios, because we do not believe that for a firm to be reckoned as grown, there should be growth in all the four variables listed above. For example, there can be growth through capital/technology intensity without any growth in manpower. If a geometrical average is taken for the above case, the product of the four ratios will become zero because one of the ratios, namely, that of manpower growth, is zero. The implication is that there is no growth unless there is growth in all the four variables, which we do not subscribe to. Therefore, it was decided to use the arithmetic average of the ratios for the purpose of arriving at the combined index of growth.

A frequency distribution of the growth index would enable the classification of ventures into high- and low-growth ventures. A simple thumb rule is to select the bottom one-third as the low-growth ventures and the top one-third as the high-growth ventures. In order that the distinction between the two groups may emerge sharp and clear, it is proposed to leave out the middle group (the moderately growing ventures) from this part of the analysis. The distance, therefore, between the two extreme groups will be large enough to bring out the differences clearly.

Once the growth index is calculated for each enterprise, it is possible for us to establish two important relationships, namely, between profitability and enterprise-growth and between industry-growth and enterprise-growth. These two relationships are especially relevant in view of the two hypotheses, namely, that (a) some profitable enterprises refuse to grow for reasons beyond their economic capabilities; (b) enterprise growth in most cases is dependent mainly on the growth stage of the concerned industry. If the above hypotheses were true, we would expect a low correlation between profitability of the enterprise and its growth, and a high correlation between industry growth and enterprise growth. In other words, in a matrix analysis as given in what follows, we would expect that the points would be scattered throughout the four quadrants in the first case, and concentrated in the low–low and high–high quadrants in the second case.

Enterprise growth

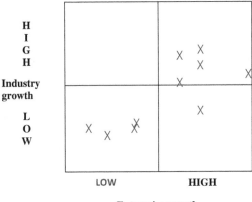

Enterprise growth

In the analysis of Sections II–V, one important task is data-reduction. These sections (on enterprise policies, entrepreneurial traits or personal policies, entrepreneurial motives and the background of the entrepreneur) have 33, 25, 20 and 22 variables, respectively. These are obviously too large for a meaningful and parsimonious explanation of the entrepreneurship phenomenon. It is therefore necessary to do factor analysis on each of these sets with a view to identifying the most important components of these variables.

One of the major conditions for doing a factor analysis is that the number of respondents should be large in relation to the number of variables. A rule of thumb here is that the number of respondents should be at least 3–5 times the number of variables; the more, the better. The 90 completed questionnaires from British ventures can be considered just sufficient for factor analysis, as the largest number of variables for a particular dimension in the questionnaire is 33. However, there is no doubt that it would be better to have more data points. With this in view, data were collected from Indian entrepreneurs later using the same questionnaire, from whom we obtained 64 useable responses. The total number therefore became 154, which were used for factor analysis in the first stage. Subsequently, this analysis was repeated with the data from the British respondents alone. The purpose of these two sets of factor analysis was to check for the difference in the grouping of variables caused by the changes in the number of respondents. Since there were no major differences observed in the two sets of factor analysis, it was concluded that factor analysis with 90 data-points would produce reliable factor groupings. It was therefore decided that the analysis for the purpose of the present study would be done exclusively on the basis of the data collected from 90 British entrepreneurs.

There is another way in which the problem of smaller size of respondents in relation to the number of variables can be tackled. In the method described above, we were trying to increase the number of respondents. The other method is to reduce the number of variables. One way to do this is to find out the standard deviation for each variable and eliminate the ones where the variances are relatively small. Since our sample contains both high-growth and low-growth ventures, we expect differences across these two groups in respect to at least some variables. These variables would naturally show higher degrees of variances. By implication the variables with relatively low variances are unable to discriminate between the high-growth and low-growth ventures, and so would not be of use for the present study. In fact, a low variance can also be due to the influence of 'social desirability', where everyone chooses the socially desirable high or low values. These can, therefore, be eliminated and the factor analysis can be performed using the remaining variables, which would obviously improve the variables-to-respondents ratio. This method may also be tried out during the analysis. A third method in this regard is to identify the distinguishing variables through t-tests and do factor analyses separately for the distinguishing variables. This is perhaps the most practical and meaningful way of doing the analysis in the sense that it would straight away lead to the identification of a set of variables which are characteristic of high-growth ventures, while reducing the number of variables in each group for factor analysis.

Identifying the 'principal dimensions' of the four groups of variables, classifying the ventures into high-growth and low-growth ones, and investigating the relationship of profitability/industry-growth with enterprise growth constitute the first phase of the analysis. The second phase would involve the following:

(a) Factor scores will be computed for the principal components of each of the four variable groups, which will then be the 'variables' for further analysis. The group means of these 'new variables' will be compared for the high-growth and low-growth enterprises through t-tests (if they are not conducted for the variables themselves in the first place). The significantly different ones from among these will indicate the differences between the high-growth and low-growth ventures in terms of

their managerial policies and the background and personality characteristics of their founders. (In the factor analysis of the background variables, we shall leave out the question on religion as it is not measured
on an interval scale). The relationship between religion and enterprise
growth, if any, can be examined separately through a Chi-square analysis of the cross-tabulation of religion and growth categories.

(b) The changes in the variables in course of time after the start-up can be
investigated by conducting *t*-tests for the group means of start-up and
subsequent measures, which are available for the three groups of
variables.

(c) For establishing the relationships among the variables, a regression
analysis would be useful. It can even be used for establishing causal
relationships if it is employed between variables with known time-
sequences. The present study has many such pairs of variables measured with a time-gap between them. Some examples are as follows:

     I. Background variables and start-up traits.
    II. Background variables and start-up motives.
   III. Background variables and start-up policies.
   IV. Start-up traits and later motives.
    V. Start-up traits and later policies.
   VI. Start-up motives and later traits.
  VII. Start-up motives and later policies.
 VIII. Start-up policies and later traits.
   IX. Start-up policies and later motives.
    X. Background variables and growth index.
   XI. Start-up traits and growth index.
  XII. Start-up motives and growth index.
 XIII. Start-up policies and growth index.
 XIV. Background variables and profitability index.
  XV. Start-up policies and profitability index.
 XVI. Start-up traits and profitability index.
XVII. Start-up motives and profitability index.

These relationships will be selectively tested through regression
analysis depending on the theory and the initial findings, especially of
correlations among each of these pairs. In addition, a path analysis
can be done on these variables to bring out the inter-relationships
among them. Thus, the theoretical model proposed in Chapter 1 could
also be tested. Needless to say, such analyses are relevant only if there

are high correlations among the concerned variables, failing which they will be dropped.

(d) It will be of interest to see if some of these variables can discriminate between high-growth and low-growth ventures. A discriminant analysis using the variables that are significantly different for the two groups will reveal the discriminating power of the variables. The findings would be useful for the early identification and selective promotion of growth ventures.

(e) Finally, it should be possible to identify subtypes among ventures based on the policy, trait, motive and background variables. A cluster analysis would reveal this, and would be conducted only if there is sufficient 'prima facie' indications of the presence of clusters among the respondents.

Limitations of the Method

During the discussions above, we have pointed out and examined in detail some of the methodological limitations of the present study. Such limitations are common to all mail surveys and are generally taken for granted. In the following section, we summarize these limitations and discuss their possible impact on the findings of the study, based on the findings of prior research.

a. Low Response Rate

It was noted above that though the response rate of 8.25% was low, it was within the 'acceptance-range' observed in entrepreneurship research (Alpar & Spitzer, 1989; Rutherford *et al.*, 2017). There are several ways in which researchers try to influence potential respondents for a higher response rate. Experiences of researchers with such inducements are not uniformly successful. Some studies on these are reported in the following section, along with the experience of the present researcher. A significant observation made by two researchers on questionnaire response behavior was that most of the 'strategies' are directed toward the respondent, and very little is done by the researcher at the design stage (Yu & Cooper, 1983). Measures directed to the latter are also equally important.

The 'strategies' commonly being adopted are as follows:

i. Contacts through associations.
ii. Taking prior consent of respondents.

iii. Reminders and follow-up.
iv. Address personalization.
v. Declaration of sponsorship and affiliation.
vi. Monetary inducements.
vii. Design features in terms of the nature of topic and the type of questions.

Very often the researcher has little flexibility as far as the topic is concerned, because he/she cannot usually change the subject of his research for the sake of higher response rate. However, there is some flexibility for the researcher regarding the type of questions. We have, for example, designed 'checking type' questions which are found to be more attractive to respondents compared to open-ended and ranking questions (Alpar & Spitzer, 1989; Reja *et al.*, 2003). This was probably one reason why we could manage to get a response rate of 8.25% in spite of the fact that the questionnaire was 16 pages long.

In addition to taking care of some design aspects and the clarity of language, we did adopt other 'strategies' such as declaration of sponsorship and affiliation, address personalization, and reminders and follow-ups. Of these, it was the reminders and follow-ups that had the maximum impact. Evidence from other studies have also shown that follow-ups are one of the most effective ways of increasing response rates (Erdogan & Baker, 2002), whereas address personalization (Wunder & Wynn, 1988) and declaration of sponsorship (Jones & Linda, 1978) had practically no impact on response rates. Although monetary inducements have been found to be effective for consumers (Wotruba, 1966), there are no reports of entrepreneurs having been induced by money to respond to questionnaires. In any case, there was no possibility of offering monetary incentives to respondents in the present study. Taking prior consent was seriously considered, but had to be abandoned because of the shortage of time and money. Contacting respondents through associations was not appropriate in the present study, as there was no assurance that the members of these associations would contain the fastest and slowest growing enterprises.

Even though some of the above-mentioned 'strategies' have been found to be effective in increasing response rates (Alange & Scheinberg, 1988; Foss, 1985; King *et al.*, 2001), we could make use only of the strategy of reminders and follow-ups, which are among the most effective of such strategies (Erdogan & Baker, 2002), and have helped in increasing the responses by another 40% of the responses in the first phase. Finally, if one were to offer an extraneous reason for the relatively low response rate in the UK, it is the severe recession that was suffocating the British enterprises during that time. Obviously, entrepreneurs had more important tasks than filling out questionnaires. The severity of the recession was borne out also by the fact that more than 40% of the mails undelivered due to closure of the units were from among those initially identified as high-growth enterprises. It may also be noted that the response rate in India was substantially higher at about 25%, which was at the upper end of the 'normal' range of 8–26.5% identified by Western researchers for surveys among entrepreneurs (e.g., Alpar & Spitzer, 1989). Although a low response rate can cause biases in the study if it is for identifying the univariate distributions of some demographic characteristics, behaviors and attitudes, there is no evidence of such biases if the attempt is to establish the relationships among variables in a multivariate analysis (Rindfuss *et al.*, 2015). Since the focus of the present study is to identify the relationships, if any, among different sets of variables, one can be reasonably sure to get reliable results from this study, despite the relatively low response rate.

b. Item Omission

The problem of item non-response occurred in the present survey mainly in the first section where performance figures were asked for. There were hardly any omissions in the subsequent sections, which were 'checking questions' related to one's personal background and preferences. Research has shown that item non-response depended mainly on the respondent characteristics, the method of administering the survey (paper/online), and the question types (Ferber, 1966; Craig & McCann, 1978; Denscombe, 2009). There are conflicting reports on the response rate on personal questions. Craig and McCann (1978) observed that personal questions evoked low response. On the other hand, Omura (1983) found that non-response to personal questions is low for respondents with high self-confidence and tendencies toward gregariousness. Our experience was that there was hardly any omission on personal questions. It is likely that entrepreneurs are high on self-confidence and have a tendency toward gregariousness. It is more likely that the 'checking' type of questions made it easier for the respondents to complete the questionnaire without omissions. As we have noted above, checking type of questions are likely to have the highest item response rate. According to one study (Alpar & Spitzer, 1989), item omission rate for ranking questions was 10.9%, for open-ended questions it was 9.7%, and for checking questions it was 3.6%. Even in the first section of our questionnaire, the checking questions on enterprise profitability and industry growth have been answered by almost all the respondents. So, the type of question seems to be the determining factor.

Our 'strategy' for dealing with omissions in the first section has been discussed earlier. We shall use multiple criteria for computing the growth rate, and omit from the comparative analysis a few respondents who have failed to furnish information on at least three criteria. As for the few omissions in Sections II–V, their numbers are so few that it will not make any difference to the aggregate analysis if the blank spaces are filled up by the scale average or the group average.

c. Response Errors

Wrong answers or response errors is a limitation of self-report data, on which the researcher can exercise very little control (McDaniel & Rao, 1980; Mandell & Lundsten, 1978; Peterson & Kerin, 1981; Sjöström *et al.*, 1999). Response errors can arise from any one or more of the following: (a) respondent's inability/difficulty to understand instructions or the meanings of the questions, (b) respondent's lack of time or unwillingness to spend time and the consequent hurry and carelessness, (c) inadequacy of the respondent's knowledge or memory, and (d) deliberate falsification by the respondent for reasons of social desirability, self-aggrandizement, tax avoidance, etc.

Proper understanding of instructions and questions can be ensured by careful reading and editing of the questionnaire with the assistance of a few associates, and by pre-testing it in a group of potential respondents. We took a lot of care at the time of preparing the questionnaire to ensure clarity, so much so that, during the pre-testing, the respondents did not express any difficulty in understanding instructions or questions. As for the effects of social desirability, they influence the group as a whole and can be minimized by eliminating variables having very low variances in the group. In any case, such variables do not contribute much to the comparative analysis on account of their inability to distinguish between individuals or groups. Inadequacies of knowledge and memory may not cause inaccuracies in responding to a questionnaire which primarily seeks to obtain subjective answers. What is important here is the respondent's genuine feelings and impressions. Such impressions of owner-managers, contrary to what is generally believed, closely correspond to what is really happening in the company. According to Dess and Robinson (1984), the judgments of owner-managers contained in self-reports accurately reflected the firm's objective performance. Further support to this proposition was obtained by Wall *et al*. (2004) in their experimental study using both the types of measures in three samples. This may be because what are normally perceived as subjective data spring from a holistic perception of the objective reality by those who are actively involved with the phenomenon (Mintzberg, 1976). Thus, the results of our study may not be adversely affected by the respondents not having factual information. However, we are likely to have distortions due to haste, carelessness and some amount of falsification on the part of the respondents.

d. Sample Size
The sample size of 90 respondents is adequate for many kinds of statistical analysis. With respect to the types of analysis proposed to be performed in the present study, the sample size may be considered inadequate only for factor analysis. We have discussed above our method of testing the adequacy of the numbers with the additional data from Indian entrepreneurs and performing factor analysis using the small as well as the large number of respondents. As the changes in the factor groupings were minor, it is considered to be legitimate for us to do the factor analysis using the smaller sample size of 90, comprising the British respondents only. This would also ensure sufficient homogeneity in the data for subsequent analyses of other kinds. Besides, we would also try to increase the respondents-to-variables ratio by reducing the number of variables using *t*-tests, that is, by choosing only those variables that showed significant differences between high- and low-growth ventures in the *t*-tests.

e. Data as Numbers
Generating data from respondents in the form of numbers has an advantage that the researcher can process them using statistical techniques and arrive at conclusions that are generalizable within certain limits. The disadvantage is that there is very little information on the details of how the strategies, policies, traits and motives translate themselves into reality. It is somewhat like seeing the forest and having very little idea about the individual trees. The contrast is sharp when the present research is compared with the author's previous study (Manimala, 1988), where the method involved a content-analysis of cases, and the numbers generated in that process were used for aggregate analysis, while the case facts provided rich material for understanding and describing specific strategies

and policies. It is the latter component that is missing in the present study, even though we have tried to compensate for it through interviews with a few entrepreneurs.

Concluding Remarks

The most important learning point that emerges from the experiences of this author with various methods of social science research is that each one has its own advantages and disadvantages. One has to choose the most appropriate method depending on the purpose of investigation and the conditions under which the project is undertaken. The present study comes as a 'sequel' to an earlier exploratory study by the author to understand and identify entrepreneurial heuristics. 'Flesh and blood' were more important in the earlier study as the purpose was to explore, experience and identify the policies and strategies. Once this was accomplished, it was important to engage oneself in an exercise of abstract conceptualization, exploration of linkages among variables, and generalizations about high-growth and low-growth ventures; and hence, the present study was taken up. There is greater need for the numbers in this study, as the concern here was to establish relationships and inter-relationships at the micro-level. The questionnaire survey suited very well for it, especially because we required parallel data on several variables for establishing the relationships mentioned above. There are a few limitations for this method, some of which (as noted above) are unlikely to affect the outcomes of this study. The others will have to be accepted as part of the limitations of social science research itself.

Chapter 3

Enterprise Growth, Profitability, Industry Growth and Growth Venture Characteristics

It was noted in the previous chapter that the focus of this study is the comparison between high-growth and low-growth enterprises. Additionally, it was considered important for us to test two major hypotheses about enterprise growth, prevalent among researchers on the topic. One of them is the hypothesis of growth unwillingness of some enterprises (despite being profitable), and the other is that enterprise growth depends primarily on industry growth. As explained earlier, we would test these hypotheses with a simple analysis of two sets of correlations, which will be explained subsequently. The most basic requirement for the above analyses (comparisons and hypotheses testing) is the computation of a growth index for each of the respondent enterprises.

Growth Index

A simple method of computing growth index adopted by some researchers (e.g., Jarillo, 1989) is to compute it on the basis solely of the change in sales over a period. We have considered this option but felt that sales growth in monetary terms can sometimes be misleading. The increase may be due to inflation, which would not be comparable across industries if the rates of inflation in different industries are different. Increases in the physical units of sales may also not be comparable, as the unit sizes and the per unit values may vary widely across different industries. Moreover, a growth in sales may be a temporary phenomenon due to some special circumstances prevailing in the market. It may not, therefore, indicate a stable 'irreversible' movement forward.

What then are the other indicators of enterprise growth? Of course, there are other variables such as changes in investments, profits, employment, and number of products. These too are not without their limitations. Take the case of investments, for example. Growth will often necessitate additional investments. However, some unwise investments may not result in any growth in operations at all. Besides, researchers in recent times (e.g., Lorenzoni & Ornati, 1988) have observed another style of growth whereby companies achieve substantial augmentation of their operations without any additional investments. The strategy is to develop networks and constellations and use their resources instead of creating one's own. This is applicable to human resources as well. A company can increase its operations by subcontracting work and farming out a few activities. Network constellations and alliance arrangements also would enable the company to use the human resources of others. Besides, in some cases, technology can reduce the use of manpower and yet substantially increase the level of operations. We cannot, therefore, rule out the possibility of growth with no or limited, or even negative changes in manpower.

Two other variables mentioned above in this connection are profitability and the number of products. Of these, profitability cannot be included in the computation of growth index for the purpose of this study for theoretical as well as methodological reasons. First of all, an increase in profits may not always be the result of an increased volume of operations or diversity of activities. Profits may arise out of cost reduction, price increases, shortages, etc. Conversely, growth in operations may not ensure higher levels of profits, especially in the initial stages. There may be some time-lag for the new activities to generate steady profits, and hence during the initial stages of growth, an enterprise may even incur losses. Besides, even at the later stages of growth, there can be a situation where profit volume may be large, but the margins are low. In such cases, growth in profitability may not be associated with the growth in operations. Secondly, in view of the hypothesis supported by some empirical studies that enterprise growth is not a function of profits and that entrepreneurs may often restrict the growth of even highly profitable ventures on account of their personal preferences, it was considered expedient not to reckon increases in profits as an indicator of growth. Thirdly, there is a methodological reason for not including profits in the computation of growth index. In order to test the hypothesis that even highly profitable companies would experience restricted growth because of growth unwillingness on the part of the founders, we have proposed to do a correlation analysis between the profitability index and the growth index. If the changes in profits are also included in the computation of growth index, there would be a methodological error of correlating a variable with another one, of which the former is a part, which would yield a high correlation. Therefore, for the purpose of this study, changes in profits will not be used for the computation of the growth index.

Changes in the number of products are an indication of the extent of diversification and, therefore, of growth. The argument, however, against using this variable as an indicator of growth is that it does not give any idea about growth through expansion. A firm with a single product operating in the local market may expand its sales to the national market with a substantial increase in the volume of its business and yet would not be reckoned as a growth company according to the number-of-products criterion. Despite this limitation, there are research studies (e.g., Churchill & Lewis, 1983) which have adopted the growth in the number of products as a major criterion for enterprise growth.

The limitation of this criterion can be partially overcome by combining it with sales growth figures. In the above example of growth through expansion without increasing the number of products, the growth rate will be zero if the change in the number of products alone is considered. However, if the sales growth figures are also considered and an arithmetic average is taken, the overall growth rate would be half that of the figure arrived at using sales data alone, which is more realistic than the zero growth rate that would be obtained if changes in the number of products alone are considered. Extending this logic further, we would argue that a combination of the growth rates computed using changes in the different variables mentioned above would give a more reliable growth rate than the growth rate computed using changes in a single variable. The computation of growth index, therefore, will be based on the changes in four variables, namely, sales, number of products, investment, and employee strength. Profit data will be omitted for the reasons explained above. Other studies that have used multiple criteria for assessing growth have also excluded the profit data. For example, Musso and Schiavo (2008) assessed the firm growth in terms of sales, capital stock, and employment.

The formula for computing the growth rates and the rationale for using the arithmetic average for combining them were explained in the previous chapter on methodology. Combined growth indices for 78 enterprises that have provided data on the relevant variables are given in Table 3.1. Twelve respondents did not give data on some of these variables.

Table 3.1.   Growth index for 78 enterprises computed on the basis of changes in sales, investment, employment, and number of products.

Serial no	Growth index	Serial no	Growth index
1.	5.76	40.	10.85
2.	28.27	41.	4.46
3.	10.67	42.	22.56
4.	18.92	43.	36.35
5.	15.90	44.	34.72
6.	7.39	45.	7.45
7.	37.00	46.	8.24
8.	6.99	47.	21.96
9.	8.45	48.	3.17
10.	6.81	49.	339.91
11.	32.03	50.	43.11
12.	23.17	51.	113.75
13.	8.10	52.	9.56
14.	9.61	53.	9.86
15.	488.03	54.	19.68
16.	60.39	55.	52.71
17.	54.02	56.	2.06
18.	54.02	57.	20.27
19.	34.16	58.	−3.68
20.	159.47	59.	51.32
21.	20.80	60.	87.62
22.	19.06	61.	23.60
23.	35.23	62.	43.28
24.	43.90	63.	−1.68

Table 3.1.   (*Continued*)

Serial no	Growth index	Serial no	Growth index
25.	30.46	64.	2.95
26.	31.61	65.	0.53
27.	19.61	66.	0.00
28.	2.64	67.	1.50
29.	18.92	68.	3.57
30.	−10.30	69.	1.31
31.	3.84	70.	35.84
32.	26.28	71.	30.15
33.	−15.91	72.	25.08
34.	19.75	73.	84.45
35.	18.92	74.	218.37
36.	22.92	75.	15.46
37.	6.68	76.	105.55
38.	8.53	77.	47.58
39.	24.85	78.	54.62

High-growth and Low-growth Ventures

A frequency distribution of growth indices for the respondents showed that the growth rates varied from −15.91% to +488.03% per annum. Thus, the range is wide enough to enable classification of the sample into high-growth and low-growth ventures. The distribution and the classificatory cut-offs are shown in Table 3.2.

In defining low-growth or stagnation, we have chosen a cut-off point of 15% growth rate. In these days of double-digit inflation, a growth rate of 10–15% cannot indicate much growth at all. It is as good or bad as stagnation, even though the figures for employment and the number of products need not be adjusted for inflation. Moreover, we are not talking about 'no growth' but about 'low growth'. Enterprises with up to about 15% growth rate, therefore, can be classified as low-growth ventures. It may be noted that in the distribution of growth indices there is a clear break between 11% and 15% growth rates, which has made it all the more convenient to make the cut-off there, as this point looks like a 'natural cut-off'. The highest rate of growth, therefore, in the low-growth group is 10.85%

Table 3.2.   Growth indices arranged in the descending order and the identification of high-growth and low-growth ventures.

High growth	Moderate growth	Low growth
488.03	24.85	10.85
339.91	23.60	10.67
218.37	23.17	10.67
159.57	22.92	9.86
113.75	22.56	9.61
105.55	21.96	9.56
87.62	20.80	8.53
84.45	20.27	8.45
54.62	19.75	8.24
54.02	19.68	8.10
54.02	19.61	7.45
52.71	19.06	7.39
51.32	18.92	6.99
47.58	18.92	6.81
43.90	18.92	6.68
43.28	15.90	5.76
43.11	15.46	4.46
37.00	--------	3.84
36.35	$N = 17$	3.57
35.84	--------	3.17
35.23		2.95
34.72		2.64
34.16		2.06
32.03		1.50
31.61		1.31
30.46		0.53
30.15		0
28.27		−1.68
26.28		−3.68
25.08		−10.30
--------		−15.91
$N = 30$		--------
--------		$N = 31$
		--------

and the lowest is −15.91%. There are 31 enterprises in this group. The size of the group, therefore, is big enough for parametric statistical analyses.

As for the identification of the high-growth group, one way of doing it is to classify the remaining 47 respondents as high-growth ones. This is legitimate especially because of the clear break of 4% points between these two groups. However, since the parametric analyses can be done with about 30 respondents in the group, it is possible to increase the distance between the two groups and to sharpen their distinguishing features by leaving out a few respondents from the middle of the series, that is, from the lower end of the high-growth group. A rule of thumb for raising the cut-off for the high-growth group is to raise it by 10% points, which would give the lowest growth rate of 25.08% per annum for the high-growth group. 17 enterprises would then be dropped from the high-growth group, reducing the size of this group to 30, which compares well with the 31-strong low-growth group.

As we have noted above, the elimination of a middle segment from the sample was intended to check the influence of borderline cases on the analysis. If, for example, a sample of 100 is divided into two groups of 50 each on some criterion, the difference between the 50th and 51st individual on the criterion will be marginal or nil, but they would be included in two different groups for the purpose of identifying the characteristics of the two groups. Needless to say, this would vitiate the analysis, as the 'distance' between the two groups may not be large enough. Eliminating a middle segment would increase this distance so that the comparisons would really be between the two 'extremes'. By leaving out the middle segment, it is ensured that there is a minimum distance of 14 percent-points between the two groups to be compared, as the lowest growth rate in the high-growth group is 25.08% and the highest in the low-growth group is 10.85%.

Profitability, Industry Growth, and Enterprise Growth

Before we proceed to the identification of the distinguishing features of low-growth and high-growth ventures, it would be worthwhile to examine the two dominant hypotheses on enterprise growth mentioned at the beginning of this chapter. One of them is that all profitable enterprises need not be the growing ones as well, and the other is that industry growth may be a major determinant of enterprise growth. These can be tested through a simple correlation analysis. The three sets of variables required for this analysis, namely, growth index, profitability rating, and industry growth rating for 75 respondents, are given in Table 3.3. Of the 78 respondents for whom the growth rate was calculated, only 75 could be used for the correlation analysis, as three respondents did not furnish data on profitability and/or industry growth.

Table 3.3.   Growth index and the ratings on profitability and industry growth.

Serial no	Growth index	Profitability	Industry growth	Serial no	Growth index	Profitability	Industry growth
1.	5.76	2	1	39	4.46	5	2
2.	28.27	5	3	40	22.56	3	4
3.	10.67	2	4	41	36.35	3	5
4.	18.92	5	3	42	34.72	4	5
5.	15.90	3	5	43	7.45	2	3
6.	7.39	3	4	44	8.24	4	5
7.	37.00	4	5	45	21.96	4	4
8.	6.99	2	1	46	3.17	3	3
9.	8.45	1	5	47	339.91	5	5
10.	32.03	5	4	48	43.1	5	3
11.	23.17	4	4	49	113.75	1	4
12.	8.10	5	1	50	9.56	3	5
13.	9.61	3	4	51	9.86	2	3
14.	488.03	3	5	52	19.68	4	4
15.	60.39	4	5	53	52.71	3	3
16.	54.02	5	5	54	2.06	4	4
17.	54.02	5	5	55	20.27	5	1
18.	34.16	3	2	56	−3.68	1	3
19.	159.47	2	4	57	51.32	4	5
20.	20.80	5	5	58	87.62	4	5
21.	19.06	2	1	59	23.60	5	4
22.	35.23	2	5	60	43.28	3	4
23.	43.90	5	2	61	−1.68	5	4

Table 3.3. (*Continued*)

Serial no	Growth index	Profitability	Industry growth	Serial no	Growth index	Profitability	Industry growth
24.	30.46	3	4	62	2.95	5	5
25.	19.61	3	4	63	0.53	3	1
26.	2.64	5	4	64	0.00	4	4
27.	18.92	3	3	65	1.50	1	5
28.	−10.30	1	4	66	3.57	3	5
29.	3.84	3	3	67	35.84	3	3
30.	26.28	4	5	68	30.15	5	5
31.	−15.91	3	4	69	25.08	5	3
32.	19.75	4	4	70	84.45	2	4
33.	18.92	2	2	71	218.37	5	4
34.	22.92	5	4	72	15.46	5	2
35.	6.68	4	5	73	105.55	3	3
36.	8.53	5	4	74	47.58	3	3
37.	24.85	3	4	75	54.62	5	5
38.	10.85	3	2				

Note: The number of respondents in this table is 75, instead of the 78, for whom the growth index was computed, because three of them did not give their ratings on enterprise profitability and/or industry growth.

As expected, the correlation between profitability and enterprise growth was very low. It was 0.058 ($p \leq 0.310$) and was not significant. On the other hand, the correlation between enterprise growth and industry growth was relatively high. It was 0.221 ($p \leq 0.028$), significant at less than 3%, which means that it is significant at the 5% norm, but not at the 1% norm. As the conventions of statistical analysis accept a significance level up to a maximum of 10%, we can treat this relationship as significant. An incidental result was the lack of correlation between industry growth and enterprise profitability which was 0.10 ($p \leq 0.196$). This non-significant correlation indicates that enterprise profitability is not related to industry growth. On the other hand, the growth of the industry can facilitate the growth of the enterprises. However, as the low values of the correlations and significance level indicate, it may not be possible for everyone to take advantage of a growing industry so as to enhance the

Table 3.4.   Correlation matrix: enterprise growth, profitability, and industry growth.

	Enterprise growth	Profitability	Industry growth
Enterprise growth	1.00	0.058 (0.310)	0.221 (0.028)
Profitability	—	1.00	0.10 (0.196)
Industry growth	—	—	1.00

Note: Figures in brackets are the levels of significance.

profitability or growth of one's venture. The correlation matrix with the three correlations discussed above is given in Table 3.4.

It may be noted that in the pairs correlated above, one is an objective measure and the other is a subjective measure. If both the measures are subjective and the variables have an appearance of relatedness, as in the case of profitability and growth, the respondents may tend to correlate them mentally and give their ratings accordingly, even if the variables are not actually correlated. Such measures would give rise to pseudo-correlations. By measuring one variable (enterprise growth) using objective criteria, we have tried to avoid such a possibility. Besides, since the profitability measure used here is a subjective rating, if the founder of a 'low-growth venture' reports high profitability, we could confidently state that some profitable ventures do not grow even though their founders know very well that theirs is a profitable business. This could be cited as evidence for the hypothesis of growth unwillingness on the part of some entrepreneurs.

The objective realities of performance are not the only reasons for the enterprise growing or not growing. The background and psychological make-up of the founders and the consequent policies and strategies of the venture along with the facilitating and obstructing factors in the environment may have an important influence on enterprise growth, which are worth investigating. Support for this hypothesis was also found in a study by Eisenhardt and Schoonhoven (1990), where they observed strong linkages between firm growth and the founding top team as well as the market stage of the firm. A more recent study in the Eastern context (Singapore) by Tan *et al.* (2007) has also come up with similar findings. According to them, a key element supporting or hindering the growth of a venture is the entrepreneur, whose initiatives in creating intellectual capital, upgrading the technology, and inculcating a participative culture in the organization can greatly facilitate the growth of the enterprise.

The two correlations obtained above have, on the one hand, showed that founder characteristics could be an important influence on enterprise growth and, on the other hand, identified a major factor in the external environment, namely, industry growth, which is apparently a pre-condition for enterprise growth. The correlation of 0.221 is not very high but is significant. It would imply that though there is a relationship between enterprise growth and industry growth, the latter may not be the only variable upon which enterprise growth depends. It is therefore legitimate for us to look for other influences on enterprise growth. A prominent group of variables mentioned in the literature in this regard are the founder characteristics, as we have noted above, especially in the findings of Eisenhardt and Schoonhoven (1990). The next chapter will discuss these variables one by one in detail with special reference to the configurations of the factors involved. In the next section of this chapter, however, we shall provide an overview of the distinguishing features of (the founders of) high-growth ventures in comparison with (the founders of) low-growth ventures.

Distinguishing Features of Growth-Seeking Entrepreneurs/Ventures

Following a theoretical model proposed and discussed by us earlier, the focus of the present investigations is the strategies and policies of enterprises, in terms of which we expect to find differences between high-growth and low-growth ventures. But it is likely that strategies and policies of the enterprise have been influenced by the background, traits, and motives of their founders. So, these should also be investigated. As a first step towards this, we have identified the high-growth and low-growth ventures from our sample. These subsamples have sizes of 30 and 31, respectively, which are adequate for parametric tests. In order to identify the distinguishing features of growth ventures, we have therefore conducted t-tests on all the variables with a view to identifying the ones that are significantly different for the two groups. If the group means for a variable are significantly different for the two groups, that variable is capable of distinguishing between the high-growth and low-growth ventures. It should, however, be noted that the distinguishing variable need not have very high or low values in absolute terms. What is being shown by the *t*-test is only the relative differences which are statistically significant.

The following part of the analysis is organized in four subsections, namely, (a) policies and strategies of the venture, (b) personality traits of the founder, (c) motives of the founder, and (d) background and early experiences of the founder. One of the items on the questionnaire (see Questionnaire, Section V, Item no. 5, in Appendix 2) was not scored on an interval scale. This question, which asks about the respondent's religion, was included for testing the validity of Weber's (1930, originally published in German in 1905) theory on Protestant Ethics as the basis for entrepreneurship and was answered on a nominal scale, for which *t*-test is not appropriate. For this variable, therefore, a Chi-square test was done. The results of the *t*-tests and the Chi-square test are presented in the following subsections of this chapter.

a. Policies and Strategies

Results of the *t*-tests conducted on the 33 policy variables are given in Table 3.5. There are very few policies which are significantly different for the two groups. Listed below are five of them in the order of their significance levels:

1. P-28: Active involvement in public interest activities ($t = 2.68; p \leq 0.01$).
2. P-14: Quality at any cost ($t = 1.85; p \leq 0.07$).
3. P-20: Decentralized setup, and autonomy to the lower levels ($t = 1.80; p \leq 0.076$).
4. P-18: Testing before venturing out ($t = 1.59; p \leq 0.117$).
5. P-21: Collecting systematic information ($t = 1.39; p \leq 0.171$).

It may be noted that only three of the above would satisfy a 90% confidence level cut-off, implying that the dividing line between a stagnating enterprise and a growing enterprise is rather thin. Considering the large number of 'policy variables' that contribute to entrepreneurial performance, it was rather surprising that the difference between the low-growth and high-growth enterprises depends on just three of them. However, when we examine them closely, it would be seen that these few policies have wide-ranging and far-reaching implications for entrepreneurs and their enterprises.

The first and statistically most significant factor is the entrepreneur's conception of the relationship between the enterprise and the society.

Table 3.5. High- and low-growth ventures: *t*-values for policy variables.

Policy variable		Difference				
		Mean	STD ERR	*t*-value	DF	PROB
P1	Tried and tested products	−.421	.490	−.86	56	.394
P2	Own ideas, not borrowed	.012	.376	.03	56	.975
P3	No active search for ideas	−.514	.434	−1.19	56	.241
P4	Changing goals for capturing opportunities	−.333	.451	−.74	56	.463
P5	Continuous search for new ideas	−.081	.239	−.34	56	.736
P6	Knowledge of the technology for oneself	−.090	.294	−.31	56	.760
P7	Recruit the best people	−.152	.270	−.56	56	.575
P8	Partners mainly for capital	−.395	.432	−.92	56	.364
P9	Subcontract the work	−.133	.486	−.27	56	.785
P10	Technical collaboration	−.002	.431	.01	56	.996
P11	Minimize borrowed funds	−.110	.340	.32	56	.749
P12	Avoid competition	−.079	.486	−.16	56	.872
P13	Related diversification	.224	.372	.60	56	.550
P14	Quality at any cost	.643	.348	1.85	56	.070*
P15	Image thro' advertising/publicity	.293	.390	.75	56	.456
P16	Professional systems/techniques/people	.429	.389	1.10	56	.276
P17	Strict rules and procedures	.207	441	.47	56	.640
P18	Test the market before launching	.619	.388	1.59	56	.117
P19	Spread the risks	−.305	.434	−.70	56	.485
P20	Decentralized setup	.771	.427	1.80	56	.076*
P21	Systematic information gathering	.517	.373	1.39	56	.171
P22	Close supervision	−.195	.469	−.42	56	.679
P23	Reward loyalty than performance	.398	.428	.93	56	.356
P24	Aggressive marketing	.317	.517	.61	56	.543
P25	Low-price strategy	−.438	.419	−1.05	56	.300
P26	Industry/professional associations	−.188	.481	−.39	56	.697
P27	Support from friends and relatives	−.007	.443	−.02	56	.987
P28	Sponsor public-interest activities	.881	.328	2.68	56	.010*
P29	Judgmental decisions	.069	.378	.18	56	.856
P30	Profits for owners only	−.202	.518	−.39	56	.698
P31	Confidentiality of information	−.045	.412	−.11	56	.913
P32	Minimize investments	.193	.513	.38	56	.708
P33	Start small/Grow organically	−.219	.397	−.55	56	.583

Notes: '*' indicates a policy that is significantly different at $p \leq 0.10$. The combined sample size was 58, instead of the original 61 (30 + 31), because three respondents did not furnish data on all variables. Hence, the degree of freedom (DF) is 56.

Whatever be the nature of an enterprise's business, growth-seeking entre- preneurs seem to believe that the enterprise has a right to exist only in so far as it serves the interests of the society at large. It may be argued that any enterprise whose products and services are useful to the society and whose operations do not give rise to harmful side effects serves society's interests. The difference, however, is that growth companies deliberately adopt this as a policy and extend their 'society-orientation' beyond the confines of the specific products and services they offer, by taking special interest in matters which are of general concern. Based on the prior work of the author, it is possible to specify how they get involved in socially relevant activities. It may be by sponsoring sports and games, charitable activities, literacy campaigns, environmental protection and development, and so on. Or it may be by setting up socially useful institutions such as educational institutions, hospitals, parks, research centers, etc. Besides, there are those who would like to be actively associated with the projects of the government and the local authorities and to participate in commit- tees, conferences, seminars, publications, and so on. It should be men- tioned that such activities are undertaken not primarily for their altruistic and service values but for the long-term benefit of the enterprise, which is twofold. For one thing, it enhances the company's image among the pub- lic and also gives it a lot of publicity, which in turn would result in an increase in goodwill and sales in the long run. Second, through the above- mentioned activities, the enterprise is able to build a network of influential people and agencies around it, who would, in time of need, help the enter- prise with information and resources required for growth.

The second significant policy relates to quality. The long-term image of an enterprise depends primarily on the quality of its products and ser- vices. It is not surprising therefore that growth-seeking firms take special care to maintain the quality of their products and services consistently at a high level. The reason for the miraculous growth of some Japanese com- panies in recent years is not far to seek. It is nothing but their unswerving loyalty to quality and the emphasis given in these organizations to total quality management. Similar is the case of excellent companies in other parts of the world. It is, therefore, not surprising to see that growth- seeking firms give greater importance to quality.

The third component in the 'package' of growth strategies is a decentralized setup. It is obvious that, as the enterprise grows in size and diversity, a single individual or a 'single-point team' cannot manage it effectively. In fact, this has often been pointed out as a major reason for entrepreneurs restricting the growth of their enterprises. So, those who want their enterprises to grow should decentralize their operations and grant considerable autonomy to the lower levels.

Two other policies listed above, namely, those of testing before venturing out and of collecting systematic information do not qualify for the 90% confidence level. However, they are very close to that. It sounds logical that for identifying and exploiting growth opportunities, it is important that the enterprise has a regular system of continuously collecting information and a system of ascertaining feasibilities through pre-tests. It is also interesting to note that the next in the order of significance is the policy on the use of professional systems, techniques, and people. Needless to say, this is an essential precondition for decentralization, information management, pre-testing, and quality management.

b. Personality Traits
As in the case of policies, there are very few personality traits (which were called personal policies in the questionnaire) that were significantly different for founders of high-growth and low-growth ventures. There are four of them, which are as follows: (i) the desire to excel, (ii) the ability to persuade others, (iii) the habit of generating new alternatives even in familiar situations, and (iv) strict adherence to one's promises. The results of the t-tests are given in Table 3.6, and the four variables which can be accepted as distinguishing traits with a confidence level higher than 90% are listed below, along with the computed statistics.

1. T-22: Desire to be the best in one's field ($t = 2.30$; $p \leq 0.025$).
2. T-14: Preference for using persuasive power rather than authority ($t = 2.17$; $p \leq 0.035$).
3. T-3: Continuous search for new alternatives ($t = 1.92$; $p \leq 0.059$).
4. T-11: Strict adherence to one's promises ($t = 1.79$; $p \leq 0.079$).

It may be noted that the signs of the latter three t-values (variables 3, 11, and 14) were negative in Table 3.6. These were reversed above with appropriate reversals in the wordings of these variables.

The emerging picture of a growth-seeking entrepreneur is deceptively simple. He/she has a strong desire to be the best in his/her field. As for the manner in which this is to be achieved, there is no claim that it is clear in every situation, and so generating alternatives through flexible thinking becomes an important task. For the implementation of the chosen

Table 3.6.   Founders of high-growth and low-growth ventures: *t*-values for trait variables.

Trait variable		Mean	STD ERR	*t*-value	DF	PROB
T1	Everything is fair in business	.114	.441	.26	56	.796
T2	Confidence about one's style of management	−.331	.359	−.92	56	.360
T3	Avoid searching for many options	−.714	.371	−1.92	56	.059*
T4	Close business for a more paying job	−.388	.503	−.77	56	.444
T5	Discomfort with uncertainties	.164	.446	.37	56	.714
T6	Confidence about one's business	.271	.338	.80	56	.425
T7	Failures attributed to external factors	−.214	.339	−.63	56	.530
T8	Successes attributed to one's own actions	−.129	.461	−.28	56	.782
T9	Optimism about the future	.312	.380	.82	56	.415
T10	Conformity to social norms	−.033	.448	−.07	56	.941
T11	Breaking promises for business gains	−.760	.424	−1.79	56	.079*
T12	Feeling overloaded with work in business	−.255	.426	−.60	56	.553
T13	Take the plunge without calculating risks	.267	.506	.53	56	.600
T14	Use authority rather than persuasion	−.717	.331	−2.17	56	.035*
T15	Dislike being told to do things	−.024	.371	−.06	56	.949
T16	Change goals when facing obstacles	−.419	.329	−1.27	56	.208
T17	Avoid failure situations	−.521	.475	−1.10	56	.277
T18	Preference for difficult/challenging tasks	.229	.333	.69	56	.496
T19	Knowledge-sufficiency feeling	−.288	.316	−.91	56	.366
T20	Preference for structured work	−.329	.408	−.81	56	.424
T21	Dissatisfied with status-quo/urge to change	.171	.388	.44	56	.660
T22	Desire to be the best in the field	.843	.367	2.30	56	.025*
T23	Feeling of being misunderstood	−.198	.392	−.50	56	.616
T24	Preference to work alone	−.433	.399	−1.09	56	.282
T25	Feeling unsupported by others	−.352	.441	−.80	56	.427

Notes: '*' indicates a trait that is significantly different at $p \leq 0.10$. The combined sample size was 58, instead of the original 61 (30 + 31), because three respondents did not furnish data on all variables. Hence the degree of freedom (DF) is 56.

alternative, one has to rely on the use of persuasion rather than the exercise of authority. Finally, since the growth-seeker is convinced about the linkage between the enterprise and the society and realizes that no growth is possible without mutual trust among the constituents/stakeholders, he/she takes special care to honor the promises made. Needless to say, most of the promises in business revolve primarily around the quality of products and on-time delivery. For obvious reasons, these are the two most critical factors that determine the success and excellence in the present-day business scenario of competition and globalization.

The results of the above analysis of significant differences have incidentally thrown some light on a methodological issue. We have discussed the social desirability issue above, which might cause some bias in the responses obtained through a self-report questionnaire. One of the statements that we suspected would activate social desirability bias among the respondents was item no. 22 in Section III of the questionnaire: "I want to be the best in my field". Who would not want to be so? Had the social desirability instinct been strong in the sample, there would have been uniformly high scores on this item. On the contrary, it was found that this was the most discriminating item in this section. In addition to identifying a distinguishing personality trait of the growth-seeking entrepreneur, it was possible for us to infer that the social desirability bias was negligible in the present sample. It is likely that entrepreneurs are too independent-minded to be swayed by what is generally considered to be desirable. Whatever be the reason, the fact that the social desirability bias is negligible in the present sample gives greater confidence to the researcher about the validity of the present findings.

c. Motives
As we have noted in Chapter 1, entrepreneurial motives have been thoroughly researched during the past 4–5 decades. Some of the motives identified as important for entrepreneurship are achievement motive, power motive, money motive, and a low need for affiliation. This study was designed to find out, among other things, whether the motives of the growth-seeking entrepreneurs are different from those of their low-growth counterparts. The results of the t-tests are given in Table 3.7. If we use a confidence level of 90%, four motives emerge as significantly different. They are listed below along with the relevant statistics.

1. M-9: Interesting work ($t = 3.48$; $p \leq 0.001$).
2. M-6: Desire for top position in the industry ($t = 2.19$; $p \leq 0.032$).
3. M-8: Desire for better status in society ($t = 1.71$; $p \leq 0.063$).
4. M-7: Desire for power ($t = 1.71$; $p \leq 0.094$).

Even though the questionnaire has generated data on these four motives separately, it is possible that some of these are components of a larger

Table 3.7.   Founders of high-growth and low-growth ventures: *t*-values for motive variables.

| Variable | | Difference | | | | |
		Mean	STD ERR	*t*-value	DF	PROB
M1	Money motive	−.129	.429	−.30	56	.765
M2	Family obligations	.093	.449	.21	56	.837
M3	Social needs	.033	.407	.08	56	.935
M4	Support of higher authorities	−.29	.361	−.63	56	.529
M5	Reputation/Recognition for performance	.105	.312	.34	56	.738
M6	Top position in the industry	.831	.379	2.19	56	.032*
M7	Influence on others (within or outside)	.652	.383	1.71	56	.094*
M8	Social status	.705	.372	1.89	56	.063*
M9	Enjoyment of work	1.195	.344	3.48	56	.001*
M10	Sense of duty/Feeling of obligation	−.329	.471	−.70	56	.488
M11	Developing/utilizing competencies	.455	.300	1.52	56	.135
M12	Achievement of targets	.583	.381	1.53	56	.132
M13	Developing new ideas/innovation	.390	.371	1.05	56	.297
M14	Self-actualization	.348	.492	.71	56	.483
M15	Desire for independence	.010	.347	−.03	56	.978
M16	Desire for involvement	.360	.382	.94	56	.350
M17	Desire for feedback	.102	.311	.33	56	.743
M18	Desire for task variety	.379	.380	1.00	56	.323
M19	Contributions to society	.493	.384	1.28	56	.204
M20	Clean and healthy surroundings	.610	.412	1.48	56	.144

Notes: '*' indicates a motive that is significantly different at $p \leq 0.10$. The combined sample size was 58, instead of the original 61 (30 + 31), because three respondents did not furnish data on all variables. Hence the degree of freedom (DF) is 56.

motive/factor. This will be revealed only through a factor analysis to be performed later. For the time being, the researcher's hunch is that there would be only two motives that distinguish the growth-seeker from ordinary entrepreneurs. The first and most important motive is the enjoyment of one's work. As it was noted in one of the previous studies about innovators by the present author (Manimala, 1998), it is those entrepreneurs who enter the field because of an intrinsic interest in the work involved (and not those who take it up because of extrinsic considerations such as problems with employment, support from others, opportunities for short-term profits, and availability of feasibility studies, project reports, concessional credits, tax benefits, etc.) who would make it big. There is no doubt that the growth-seeker would exploit the external support and opportunities, but these are not the reason why he/she is in the business. It is primarily the love for one's project and the interest in the tasks to be performed for it.

The second important motivator for the growth-seeker is the need for power, which was identified in the mid-seventies by McClelland and Burnham (1976) as a critical motive for entrepreneurship in general, almost as a replacement of the much-touted concept of Achievement Motivation proposed by McClelland (1961) about a decade and a half ago. This study shows that power motive (defined here as the combination of the remaining three variables, M-6/7/8, in the 'significant' list) is significantly high for growth-seeking entrepreneurs. This finding can also be taken as an indication of the need for classifying entrepreneurs before studying their distinctive characteristics. In other words, the power-motive which was identified as a characteristic of entrepreneurs in general, may not be applicable to all types of entrepreneurs in the same way. The same may be true for other traits and motives as well. What is characteristic of one group may not be so with another group. This is why the quest for the uniformly applicable traits and motives has not led to consistent results. In this analysis, we have tentatively defined power motive as a combination of the need to influence, the desire for top position in the industry, and the desire for social status. This assumption has to be validated by a factor analysis, which will be done later. It is possible that the status motive is different from the power motive.

d. Background and Early Experience

It was rather surprising that the background variables, which in many prior studies emerged as critically linked with entrepreneurial performance, did not have much to offer in terms of distinguishing between the low-growth and high-growth groups. The *t*-values are given in Table 3.8. It may be noted that variable no. 5 is on religion, which was not subjected to *t*-test, as it was not measured on an interval scale. All other variables were either in interval or quasi-interval scales.

There are just three variables that are significantly different for the two groups at 90% confidence level. They are:

1. B-21: Institutional support ($t = 1.81$; $p \leq 0.077$).
2. B-6: Ancestral family's level of education ($t = 1.79$; $p \leq 0.08$).
3. B-20: Support of family/relatives, friends and colleagues ($t = 1.67$; $p \leq 0.101$).

Table 3.8.   Founders of high-growth and low-growth ventures: *t*-values for background variables.

Variable		Difference		*t*-value	DF	PROB
		Mean	STD ERR			
B1	Age in years	−2.111	2.394	−.88	51	.382
B2	Number of prior successful ventures	−.177	.275	−.64	51	.524
B3	Number of unsuccessful attempts	.027	.175	.15	51	.878
B4	Practice of religion	−.009	.301	−.03	51	.977
B6	Ancestral family's education	.373	.209	1.79	51	.080*
B7	Ancestral family's profession	.191	.378	.51	51	.615
B8	Level of education (self)	.236	.376	.63	51	.532
B9	Prior experience as employee (years)	.298	.331	.90	51	.373
B10	Nature of employer (levels of industry)	.036	.473	.08	51	.940
B11	Happiness in childhood	−.352	.392	−.90	51	.374
B12	Deprivation/affluence in childhood	−.226	.338	−.67	51	.506
B13	Psychological deprivation in childhood	.309	.515	.60	51	.551
B14	Feeling neglected in childhood	−.074	.477	−.16	51	.877
B15	Family movement from other places	.004	.551	.01	51	.994
B16	Diversity of interests in childhood	.100	.392	.25	51	.800
B17	Number of disappointments in childhood	.132	.409	.32	51	.747
B18	Life-satisfaction up to start-up	.578	.367	1.57	51	.122
B19	Personal success before start-up	.415	.285	1.46	51	.151
B20	Support from family/relatives/friends	.550	.329	1.67	51	.101*
B21	Support from institutions	.717	.396	1.81	51	.077*
B22	Chance/purposeful entry into business	.255	.420	.61	51	.546

Notes: '*' indicates a background variable that is significantly different *at* $p \leq 0.10$. Variable B5 is deleted because it was not measured on an interval scale and therefore was not subjected to *t*-test. The combined sample size for this analysis was 52, instead of 61 (30 + 31), because 9 respondents did not furnish data on all the background variables. Hence, the degree of freedom (DF) is 51.

It seems that growth-seekers and others come from more or less similar backgrounds. One difference for the high-growth group is that they seem to come from families with relatively high levels of education, even though their own educational accomplishments are comparable to those of the low-growth group. The other two variables are about the support received from others. The high-growth group perceives that their families, friends, and relatives as well as the institutions around them are support-ive and encouraging to a greater extent than what is perceived by the low-growth group. It needs further investigation to check whether such perceptual differences are due to the differences in the objective reality itself or because of the fact that the high-growth group possesses greater degrees of political skills and so are able to mobilize better support for their enterprises. The latter seems to be the fact at least in the case of institutional support because, with a sample drawn from the same country, it is possible that both the groups of respondents were assessing the sup-port and encouragement received from the same/similar institutions.

Chi-square analysis of the cross-tabulation between religious affilia-tion and growth index has yielded a non-significant Chi-square value, indicating that religious affiliation of the entrepreneur is not a factor dis-tinguishing between high-growth and low-growth ventures. It is likely that the values of Protestantism have now become part of the general social fabric that irrespective of one's religious affiliation, the economic value system remains more or less the same. Alternatively, it should be presumed that the original proposition about the Protestant Ethic (Weber, 1930, originally published in German in 1905) was itself an untested proposition. An indication of this approach of Weber may also be found in his assertion that Indian religions are too 'other worldly' and therefore would not support 'worldly' activities like entrepreneurship (Weber, 1958), whereas in actual practice it can be seen that there are exception-ally good entrepreneurs (such as the Marwaris and the Jains) among the Indian religious groups. Apparently, Weber's analysis was based on the professed religious beliefs rather than the practiced ones and was not tested empirically. Another possible explanation for the relatively better entrepreneurial performance of the Protestant groups (as observed by Weber) is that the 'revolting' groups would be having greater desire for independence, which is associated with entrepreneurial behavior. The responsible factor, therefore, could be the psychological characteristic rather than the religious ideology.

The non-significant result obtained about religious affiliation is also supported by the relatively low scores of the respondents on the practice of their religion. This may be seen from B-4, on which both the groups have a mean score of around 2.2, with the difference in means at a very low level of -0.009 (vide Table 3.8), which indicates that whatever be the religious affiliation, the belief in and practice of religious principles are low among these entrepreneurs. In a similar manner, a few other variables, which were identified by some previous researchers as characteristic of successful entrepreneurs (such as the physical and psychological deprivations in childhood, and the refugee/outsider-status of the individual in the society), have received low scores in both the groups, although with relatively high values of non-significant differences in their means at −0.226 and +0.309 respectively. Such findings point to the need for a review of these theories, along with an analysis of the high-scored variables and low-scored variables in all the four variable groups, which will be taken up below.

Variables With High and Low Mean Scores

The comparative analysis presented above shows forth the variables that are significantly different for the high-growth and low-growth groups. These variables, however, need not be the ones which are the most or the least characteristic of entrepreneurs. These will be shown only by the absolute magnitude of the scores. This section, therefore, makes an analysis of the highest and lowest scoring variables in each category of variables, namely, policies, traits, motives, and the background. Even though these are presented separately for the high-growth and low-growth groups, there is no implication that these are contrasting characteristics of the two groups. In fact, it should be emphasized that, except for the variables identified as significant in the *t*-tests mentioned in the above section, there are no statistically significant differences between the two groups. Even on some of the significantly different variables, the levels of significance are not very high. Similarly, the absolute values of group means are also relatively low. It appears that there are more similarities than differences between the high-growth and low-growth groups. The tables that follow (Tables 3.9–3.16) should be understood with this perspective clearly in mind.

The process of selecting the variables was quite simple. Variables with group means above 5 on the 7-point scale were selected as the most favored policy or the most characteristic feature of the policy or the most characteristic feature of the venture/entrepreneur. On the other hand, variables with group means below 3 were selected as the least favored ones. In case of variable groups for which the scores were relatively low (for example, personal policies or traits), variables with group means up to 4.60 were selected as the most characteristic. Similarly, where the scores were relatively high (e.g., motives), the cut-off for the least favored/characteristic variables was raised up to 3.57. The choice of 5 and 3 was

Table 3.9.   Entrepreneurial policies: Most favored policies.

High-growth group	Low-growth group
1. P-6. Acquire knowledge of technology involved (6.27, 1.08)	1. P-6. Acquire knowledge of technology involved (6.36, 1.16)
2. P-5. Continuous search for new ideas (6.13, 0.90)	2. P-7. Assemble the best talents (6.29, 1.01)
3. P-7. Assemble the best talents (6.13, 1.042)	3. P-5. Continuous search for new ideas (6.21, 0.92)
4. P-14. Quality at any cost (6.00, 1.02)	4. P-19. Spreading of risks (5.57, 1.64)
5. P-11. Minimize borrowed funds (5.47, 1.20)	5. P-11. Minimize borrowed funds (5.36, 1.39)
6. P-13. Related diversification (5.37, 1.43)	6. P-14. Quality at any cost (5.36, 1.59)
7. P-2. Develop one's own new idea rather than borrow (5.33, 1.47)	7. P-2. Develop one's own new ideas rather than borrow (5.32, 1.39)
8. P-19. Spreading of risks (5.27, 1.66)	8. P-33. Organic growth with a relatively small start-up (5.29, 1.18)
9. P-33. Organic growth with a relatively small start-up (5.07, 1.76)	9. P-4. Deviate from goals for profitable opportunities (5.00, 1.54)
10. P-29. Judgmental rather than analytical decisions (5.03, 1.10)	
11. P-16. Use of professional systems, techniques and people (5.00, 1.62)	

Note: Figures in brackets are the means and standard deviations in that order.

determined by the fact that they represented agreement and disagreement, respectively, on the measurement scale. In the tables, the figures given in brackets below each variable are the group mean and the standard deviation, respectively, for that variable. Since it was already clarified that there is no intention of contrasting the variables for the two groups for want of statistical significance, the following analysis will present these policies and characteristics as generally applicable to successful entrepreneurs. As there is no control group of unsuccessful entrepreneurs or successful non-entrepreneurs, this analysis cannot be taken as a statistically rigorous one.

1. Policies
Among the most favored policies of entrepreneurs/enterprises (see Table 3.9), one finds that entrepreneurs are keen to familiarize themselves

with the technology involved in the business and supplement this with the recruitment of talented people. There is an emphasis on the development of one's own ideas and on continuous search for new ideas. The image of the company is built by strictly adhering to quality standards. These entrepreneurs believe in relatively small start-up with a minimum amount of borrowed funds and an emphasis on organic growth using mainly the funds generated internally. The growth strategy of the high-growth group is that of related diversification, which is based on the principle of spreading risks. Although the low-growth group also believes in spreading risks, the strategy of related diversification is not among the high-scoring variables in this group. Obviously, one cannot expect a high score for this 'growth strategy' for the low-growth group. In the high-growth group, there is a reference to their decision-making style. Though they use professional systems, techniques, and people, the final criterion for making decisions is their own judgment. In the low-growth group, there seems to be a greater emphasis on opportunities rather than on one's own goals as the guiding principle for business directions.

As for the least favored policies (see Table 3.10), competition on the basis of pricing is the most prominent. Partners are rarely chosen mainly

Table 3.10.   Entrepreneurial policies: Least favored policies.

High-growth group	Low-growth group
1. P-25. Low price-policy (2.13, 1.43)	1. P-25. Low-price policy (2.57, 1.75)
2. P-3. Waiting passively for new ideas to emerge (2.20, 1.42)	2. P-15. Building image primarily through advertisements and publicity (2.61, 1.34)
3. P-8. Choosing partners for capital contribution (2.53, 1.43)	3. P-3. Waiting passively for new ideas to emerge (2.71, 1.86)
4. P-9. Subcontracting as much as possible (2.87, 1.81)	4. P-24. Aggressive marketing (2.75, 2.07)
5. P-15. Building image primarily through advertisements and publicity (2.90, 1.61)	5. P-28. Sponsoring public interest activities (2.79, 1.40)
	6. P-17. Strict rules and procedures (2.89, 1.66)
	7. P-8. Choosing partners for capital contribution (2.93, 1.84)

Note: Figures in brackets are the means and standard deviations in that order.

for the money they can contribute. Similarly, advertisements and publicity are not seen as the primary means of building the company's image. In the high-growth group, there is a reluctance to subcontracting the work, which is compatible with the emphasis we have observed above on developing one's own capabilities. In the low-growth group, we find an 'aversion' to aggressive marketing, sponsoring of public interest activities, and to strict rules and procedures in the organization. The first two of these are required only if the venture has high growth ambitions. The last one (the absence of strict rules and procedures) is probably because the organization is not large enough to need rules and procedures or because it is run primarily by the members of the same family or relatives and friends of the principal promoter, who may not like to be bound by rules, as they see themselves as the owners of the venture.

2. Personality Traits

Among the most characteristic traits of the entrepreneur, the following seem to be prominent (see Table 3.11): (1) desire to excel in one's field, (2) love for challenging work, (3) confidence about managing one's enterprise well, and (4) dislike for authority. In addition to the above, the high-growth group seems to be affected by a sense of dissatisfaction with the status quo and a desire to change things. As for the desire to excel, it may be observed that both the groups are relatively high on this trait, even

Table 3.11.   Entrepreneurial traits: Most characteristic traits.

High-growth group	Low-growth group
1. T-22. Desire to be the best in one's field (6.20, 1.22)	1. T-22. Desire to be the best in one's field (5.36, 1.57)
2. T-18. Pleasure in doing difficult things (5.30, 1.37)	2. T-18. Pleasure in doing difficult things (5.07, 1.15)
3. T-6. Confidence in managing one's enterprise well (5.20, 0.85)	3. T-6. Confidence in managing one's enterprise well (4.93, 1.63)
4. T-15. Dislike for authority (4.83, 1.44)	4. T-15. Dislike for authority (4.86, 1.38)
5. T-21. Constant dissatisfaction and an itch for changing things (4.60, 1.43)	

Note: Figures in brackets are the means and standard deviations in that order; the cut-off score was lowered to 4.60 for this group of variables as the scores were generally low.

Table 3.12.   Entrepreneurial traits: Least characteristic traits.

High-growth group	Low-growth group
1. T-19. Complacency about one's knowledge of business (2.03, 1.38)	1. T-19. Complacency about one's knowledge of business (2.32, 0.983)
2. T-11. Breaking promises (2.13, 1.48)	2. T-7. External attribution of failures (2.71, 1.49)
3. T-16. Changing goals in the face of difficulties (2.37, 1.16)	3. T-1. Absence of scruples (2.79, 1.52)
4. T-4. Leaving business and getting back to employment (2.43, 1.72)	4. T-16. Changing goals in the face of difficulties (2.79, 1.34)
5. T-7. External attribution of failures (2.50, 1.08)	5. T-12. Aversion to hard work (2.82, 1.77)
6. T-14. Preference for exercising authority rather than using persuasive methods (2.53, 1.01)	6. T-4. Leaving business and getting back to employment (2.82, 2.11)
7. T-12. Aversion to hard work (2.57, 1.48)	7. T-11. Breaking promises (2.89, 1.75)
8. T-1. Absence of scruples (2.90, 1.81)	
9. T-25. Inability to mobilize support from others (2.93, 1.74)	

Note: Figures in brackets are the means and standard deviations in that order.

though in our earlier analysis we have noted that the differences in the scores are statistically significant. It, therefore, appears that the difference is in the intensity of the desire and not in the direction.

As for the personality traits that are the least characteristic of entrepreneurs (see Table 3.12), there are seven of them that are common to both low-growth and high-growth groups, which are as follows: complacency about one's knowledge of business; external attribution of failures; aversion to hard work; absence of scruples; breaking promises; changing goals in the face of difficulties; and leaving the business to take up employment. The high-growth group is low on two other traits, namely, preference to use authority than persuasion and inability to mobilize support from others. Analyzing the traits that emerged as the least characteristic of entrepreneurs, it could be stated that entrepreneurs are hardworking individuals with a desire to constantly improve the knowledge and understanding of their businesses. They are not generally deterred by setbacks in their business and would not want to leave it to take up employment, even if the latter would give them similar emoluments. They attribute their failures to themselves and try to learn from these as well. In this context, it should be recalled that in an earlier part of the analysis, the low-growth group was found to be willing to change goals for the sake of exploiting the emerging opportunities in the environment. What we have found here about their not changing the goals in the face of difficulties is different. What is implied here is that difficulties would not deter the low-growth group from their goals, but opportunities would.

The willingness to change goals in the pursuit of new opportunities, observed in the case of the low-growth group, may be interpreted as 'opportunistic' behavior, which is traditionally ascribed as a characteristic of high-growth entrepreneurs rather than the low-growth ones (Smith, 1967). The use of the word 'opportunistic' by Smith (1967) is to be understood as 'opportunity-based' and was used for distinguishing these entrepreneurs from the 'craftsman' entrepreneurs, who focus primarily on their own technical skills and build the business around that. The opportunistic entrepreneurs, on the other hand, have better education, social awareness, flexibility, and future orientation, which make them visualize the future needs of the society and lead the growth of their ventures accordingly. In other words, they tend to have growth orientation based on a longer-term vision of opportunities consistent with their own goals.

The kind of 'opportunism' observed in this study on the part of the low growth group, however, seems to be for deriving short-term benefits. This will become clearer when we examine this result along with the finding of the statistically significant difference between the two groups in the matter of breaking promises for short-term gains. It should be cautioned here that though the difference is statistically significant at $p \leq 0.10$, both the groups disagree with the practice. The difference is only in the strength of their disagreement. This is also borne out by the fact that both the groups have low scores on the belief that everything is fair in business as long as it produces results (ref: Variable T-1 in Section III of the Questionnaire). The relatively lower degree of 'opportunism' shown by the high-growth group may be in the interest of protecting the long-term image of the company, which obviously is essential for sustained growth.

3. Motives

The motives for undertaking entrepreneurial activity, according to this study, are somewhat different, at least in priority, from what have been identified by prior researchers (see Table 3.13). Achievement motive

Table 3.13.   Entrepreneurial motives: Most characteristic motives.

High-growth group	Low-growth group
1. M-9. Enjoyment of work (6.27, 0.91)	1. M-15. Desire for independence (5.64, 1.55)
2. M-11. Development and utilization of one's skills, knowledge, and capabilities (5.63, 1.03)	2. M-11. Development and utilization of one's skills, knowledge, and capabilities (5.18, 1.25)
3. M-15. Desire for independence (5.63, 1.07)	3. M-16. Need for involvement in decisions (5.11, 1.52)
4. M-16. Need for involvement in decisions (5.47, 1.38)	4. M-9. Enjoyment of work (5.07, 1.63)
5. M-12. Achievement of targets (5.33, 1.32)	

Note: Figures in brackets are the means and standard deviations in that order.

figures as relatively high only in the high-growth group. Even in this group, it appears as the lowest of the five motives. Power motive is not high in either group even though the difference between the two groups on this measure is statistically significant, which implies that although power is not the major impetus for entrepreneurial start-up, the growth-seekers are goaded by it to a greater extent than their low-growth counterparts.

The most important of the motives seems to be an intrinsic interest in the work, development and utilization of one's capabilities, and a desire for independence and involvement in directing one's own affairs. It should be noted that the order of importance varies between the high-growth and low-growth entrepreneurs. It may not be accidental (though not statistically substantiated) that the strongest motive of the low-growth group is the desire for independence, but the strongest for the high-growth group is the interest in the work. It appeals to logic that the former (low-growth group) is in business for reasons extrinsic to the 'business' of the business and so are not particularly interested in making it grow big. They are happy so long as they can have an 'independent' existence. In the exercise of such independence, it is natural that they would also choose an activity which they enjoy, except in cases where it is absolutely impossible, which is unlikely. This is why the motive of interest in work is also relatively high for the low-growth group (even though it is the last on the 'high' list) and not necessarily because it is their most important motive. This fact is also borne out by the statistically significant difference observed between the two groups on the motive of enjoyment of work. Apparently, the findings of Collins and Moore (1970) that the most dominant motive of entrepreneurs is a desire for independence is more or less supported by this study. The group mean is almost the same (5.63 and 5.64) for the two groups. The difference, however, is that the high-growth group is significantly higher than the low-growth group on their interest in the work and their need for power. It seems that the growth-seekers are stronger on intrinsic motives.

As was to be expected, deontic motive (doing things because it is one's duty) was among the weakest in both the groups of entrepreneurs (see Table 3.14). Similarly, they do not work because the external agencies controlling the resources are supportive, or even because they are in need of getting feedback or knowing the results of their actions. The last of these is somewhat surprising because it has been proposed in achievement motivation theory as a component of the need for achievement. In large organizations, where employees are nothing more than cogs in the machine, very few people are able to know and assess the impact of their performance. The *n-Ach* theory is that the entrepreneurial person is uncomfortable with such a situation, from which he/she tries to escape by starting up his own venture. He/she can now not only satisfy his/her need for achieving something but also have the information on what has been achieved at each stage and associate the results with his/her actions. It appears that the need for feedback and for the knowledge of results is relatively low among

Table 3.14.   Entrepreneurial motives: Least characteristic motives.

High-growth group	Low-growth group
1. M-10. Deontic motive (3.10, 1.58)	1. M-8. Need for social status (3.43, 1.35)
2. M-4. Need for support from those who control resources (3.20, 1.45)	2. M-10. Deontic motive (3.43, 1.99)
3. M-17. Need for feedback and knowledge of results (3.57, 1.07)	3. M-17. Need for feedback and knowledge of results (3.46, 1.29)
	4. M-4. Need for support from those who control resources (3.48, 1.33)
	5. M-20. Need to have clean and healthy surroundings (3.51, 1.24)

both the groups, even though the need for achievement is relatively high in the high-growth group. One of the implications of this finding is that probably there is a need to re-examine the concept of achievement motivation itself, with a view to finding out whether it is an independent motive in the first place, and if so, whether it is constituted by the four components identified by prior researchers, namely, the need to achieve results as per the standards set by oneself, the need to achieve better results than others, the preference for moderate and calculated risks, and the need to get regular and correct feedback and to know the results of one's actions.

In addition to the above three motives, there were two other motives which were found to be weak in the low-growth group. They are the need for social status, on which the difference between the two groups was statistically significant, and the need to have clean and healthy surroundings. It seems that the high-growth group sees enterprise growth as a means to attain better social status. Similarly, with the growth of the enterprise, one would be able to set up offices separate from the factory and enjoy cleaner and healthier surroundings. The latter motive having been classified as a hygiene factor was not expected to play any important influence on the decision to set up an entrepreneurial venture. But it sounds logical that it could be a potent influence (though not statistically significant at $p \leq 0.10$ level) on growth decisions.

4. Background and Early Experience

Looking at the 'high scorers' among the background variables, one gets the feeling that there is not much support for the theories proposed by McClelland (1961), Hagen (1962), and several other theories developed subsequently in these traditions (see Table 3.15). We do not find entrepreneurs to have suffered from parental neglect, local displacement, material deprivation, psychological deprivations, and the like. On the contrary, both the groups are high on happiness during their childhood days. They have also received good support and encouragement from their friends and relatives. For the high-growth group at least, it cannot be said that their entrepreneurial start-up was a result of their being unsuccessful in their previous occupation. They were successful and probably well-adjusted individuals, contrary to the observations of Kets de Vries (1977, 1985) about the 'dark side' of the entrepreneurial personality, and it was probably this taste of prior success that gave them the confidence to start on their own. The start-up does not seem to be a reaction to parental neglect, deprivations, unhappiness, failures, and frustrations.

Table 3.15. Background and early experience of entrepreneurs: Most characteristic background variables.

High-growth group	Low-growth group
1. B-20. Support from friends and relatives (5.70, 1.10)	1. B-11. Happy childhood (5.50, 1.21)
2. B-16. Deep interest in a variety of activities in different fields (5.41, 1.53)	2. B-16. Deep interest in a variety of activities in different fields (5.31, 1.32)
3. B-22. Entrepreneurship as a result of purposeful action (5.37, 1.39)	3. B-20. Support from friends and relatives (5.15, 1.29)
4. B-19. Success during the period immediately preceding start-up (5.22, 0.934)	4. B-22. Entrepreneurship as a result of purposeful action (5.12, 1.66)
5. B-11. Happy childhood (5.15, 1.61)	5. B-14. Feeling of having been cared for by elders during childhood (5.00, 1.63)

Note: Figures in brackets are the means and standard deviations in that order.

There are two other high-scoring variables to be taken note of. One of them suggests that the entrepreneurial individual is one who has had interest in a variety of activities in different fields during his/her childhood. This fact assumes importance against the theory that entrepreneurship involves some degree of innovativeness and the observation that one of the major routes to creativity and innovation is the cross-fertilization of apparently unrelated ideas, especially from different fields. The second 'high score' has implications for the paradigm of entrepreneurship research, which debates whether entrepreneurship is an outcome of the environmental influences or of the strategic choices of the individual. In one of the earlier studies by the author (Manimala, 1992b), the theory of environmental determinism was found to be unsupported at least in so far as it concerns the task environment. The findings of this study suggest that, if the task environment is not conducive and not able to provide the business-specific resources of money, trained labor, physical space, etc., the entrepreneurial individual would identify alternate ways of functioning and/or would develop such resources for themselves. Conversely, even if all these resources are provided to a non-entrepreneurial individual, he/she may not be able to create and manage a venture. The important issue, therefore, in the development of entrepreneurship is to focus on the general environment comprising the economic, social, cultural, educational, and legal-political environment that helps in the formation and development of entrepreneurial individuals in the society. Such individuals would then be able to develop the facilities of the task environment or to find alternatives for them, if they are not there, and/or utilize the available facilities for the benefit of their ventures. The perceptions of entrepreneurs reported in this study also seem to support the above finding. Entrepreneurs in both the groups have felt that their being entrepreneurs is largely the result of their own purposeful action and not of chance events created by environmental forces.

Since the findings of this study are based on self-report data (unlike those of the previous one), it may be argued that the perceptions of entrepreneurs would be colored by the 'actor-observer bias' (Jones & Nisbett, 1971; Bruno & Tyebjee, 1982). But according to this theory, it is the actors who should attribute things to external factors whereas observers (e.g., researchers on entrepreneurship) should hold the actors responsible. Since it is the reverse in the present case where the actors feel very strong about their own roles in shaping their destinies, it is unlikely to be colored by the actor-observer bias. It may especially be noted that even in the case of failures, where external attribution is more likely to happen (Rotter, 1966), our sample of respondents has accepted their own responsibility (see Table 3.12). These findings based on subjective measures are also supported, as noted above, by the findings of the author's earlier study which was based on objective measures derived from the analysis of real-life events. Hence, the strategic choice paradigm (proposing that entrepreneurship is primarily a function of the strategic choices of the entrepreneurial individual rather than that of the influences of the environmental factors), under which this study was conducted, can be considered to be an appropriate paradigm.

As mentioned above, there were many surprises among the low scores on background variables (see Table 3.16). Some of the dominant hypotheses proposed by prior researchers have not received any support from this study. Belief in and practice of one's religion are the least supported, with the lowest mean scores in both the groups. Similarly, local displacement and psychological deprivations have also been scored low in both the groups. Notwithstanding these, there seems to be some evidence to show that entrepreneurs still have to struggle their way to the top. This is indicated by the low levels of education they possess. It seems they are

Table 3.16. Background and early experiences of entrepreneurs: Least characteristic background variables.

High-growth group	Low-growth group
1. B-4. Belief in and practice of religion (2.22, 1.19)	1. B-4. Belief in and practice of religion (2.23, 0.99)
2. B-8. High levels of education (2.85, 1.99)	2. B-8. High levels of education (2.62, 1.33)
3. B-15. Local displacement of ancestral family (2.89, 1.99)	3. B-13. Psychological deprivations in childhood (2.65, 1.70)
4. B-13. Psychological deprivations in childhood (2.96, 2.03)	4. B-7. Self-employment by the members of one's ancestral family (2.85, 1.46)
	5. B-15. Local displacement of ancestral family (2.89, 2.03)
	6. B-6. High education levels of ancestral family (2.92, 0.80)

Note: Figures in brackets are the means and standard deviations in that order.

bright individuals who could not pursue their studies for one reason or another. An entrepreneurial career then is perhaps the only way for them to come up in life. The extent to which they would want to come up also seems to be determined by the education levels of their ancestral families. The latter is one of the few background variables on which there is a significant difference between the high-growth and low-growth groups. As individuals, entrepreneurs in high-growth groups are low on educational attainments. But the high-growth group belongs to relatively better-educated families. It is probably in relation to this benchmark that the high-growth groups have higher targets for enterprise growth.

Concluding Remarks

The lessons learned from the comparative analysis of the high-growth and low-growth ventures are enlightening. Further analysis would depend on what has emerged in the analysis above. There are, apparently, more similarities between the two groups than differences, as there are very few variables that differentiate the two groups with high levels of significance (that is, $p \leq 0.05$). Moreover, the absolute scores on the significantly different variables are not high in many cases. It is only in relative terms there is a difference, not because the particular variable is the highest scoring in one group and the lowest in the other. It therefore implies that the differences between the two groups in terms of the dominant features of entrepreneurial policies, traits, motives, and the background variables are not substantial. In the context of this finding, it would be legitimate for us to do a combined analysis of the data to arrive at the most significant dimensions of the differences. It may also be noted that some of the dominant hypotheses from prior research, especially about the background, traits, and motives of entrepreneurs, were found to be unsupported.

In the light of the above, further analysis of the data will be modified as follows:

- Mean scores of each variable for all entrepreneurs will be computed with a view to preparing a list of variables most and least characteristic of entrepreneurs in general. For want of a control group of non-entrepreneurs, these lists cannot be taken as distinguishing features of entrepreneurs, but they will surely indicate the directions for future research.
- The principal dimensions of entrepreneurial policies, motives, traits, etc. will be obtained through separate factor analyses of each group of variables. The relationships among these will be tested through a correlation analysis of the factors that emerge.
- The 16 variables that are significantly different for the high-growth and low-growth groups will be subjected to factor analysis, which would yield the principal orientations of growth-seeking entrepreneurs. These factors will be used in the subsequent regression analysis and discriminant analysis. The results will be compared, if appropriate, with the regression and discriminant analyses performed using the factors obtained from all the variables.
- As the significant differences between the two groups are few, it is proposed to use the industry growth measure also in the regression analysis to assess the relative contribution of the venture-specific or person-specific variables and the industry-specific (growth) variable to enterprise growth.

Chapter 4

General Entrepreneurial Concerns and Orientations

High- and Low-Scoring Variables for the Whole Sample

In the comparative analysis of high-growth and low-growth ventures presented in the previous chapter, it was found that there are more similarities than differences between the two groups. There is sufficient reason, therefore, to do a combined analysis of the data with a view to identifying the dominant concerns of entrepreneurs/new enterprises. One of the simplest of such analyses is to find out the most and least characteristic variables in the different sets of variables such as policies, traits, motives, and background variables. An appropriate cut-off for the most characteristic variables would be a mean score above 5.00, because 5.00 is the point of agreement on the scale. Similarly, we have used a mean score of 3.00 as a cut-off point for the least characteristic variables because that is the point of disagreement on our scale. These cut-off points were slightly adjusted by 0.50 points where the scores were generally high or low. Thus, in one case, the higher cut-off was 4.50, and, in another case, the lower cut-off was 3.50. These are explained at the bottom of the tables concerned (see Tables 4.1–4.4). The tables are self-explanatory. There is no need for discussing these at length, especially because similar trends were observed in the comparative analysis presented in the previous chapter. We shall therefore summarize the trends in each table within a paragraph each.

Table 4.1.   (a) Policies with mean scores above 5.00 for the entire sample ($N = 90$) and (b) Policies with mean score below 3.00 for the entire sample ($N = 90$).

Code no.	Description of variable	Mean	Standard deviation
(a) Policies with mean scores above 5.00 for the entire sample ($N = 90$)			
P-6	Acquire skills and knowledge in the technology of the business	6.30	1.15
P-7	Assemble the best talents	6.18	1.07
P-5	Constant search for new ideas	6.11	1.05
P-14	Quality at any cost	5.52	1.42
P-19	Spreading of risks	5.43	1.54
P-13	Related diversification	5.39	1.37
P-33	Relatively small start-up and organic growth using internal resources	5.31	1.47
P-2	Develop one's own new ideas rather than borrow	5.30	1.46
P-11	Minimize borrowed funds	5.23	1.47
(b) Policies with mean score below 3.00 for the entire sample ($N = 90$)			
P-3	Passively waiting for new ideas to emerge	2.29	1.52
P-25	Low price policy	2.42	1.56
P-8	Choosing partners for the capital contribution	2.56	1.49
P-15	Building image primarily through advertisement and publicity	2.81	1.47
P-24	Aggressive marketing	2.98	1.85
P-28	Sponsoring of public interest activities	2.98	1.38

As far as the policies are concerned (see Table 4.1), there is an emphasis on capability building, constant search for new ideas, maintenance of quality, risk management, and organic growth. Related diversification or staying within one's own experience and competence may be considered a sub-strategy of capability building or risk management. Organic growth orientation, as we have explained elsewhere, is a preference for a relatively small start-up and the subsequent growth, relying mainly on internally generated resources. By implication, therefore, there is a tendency to minimize borrowed funds.

Among the least characteristic policies are the low-price policy, high-pressure selling, choosing partners mainly for their contribution to capital, and involvement in public interest activities. It may be mentioned that even though entrepreneurs generally do not want to get involved in the larger social issues, we have earlier observed a significant difference in this regard between the high-growth and low-growth ventures. The high-growth ventures are more inclined to getting involved in public interest activities and would probably do so when the enterprise becomes 'cash-rich' and is at the threshold of growth. Another important point that comes to light is that there are very few entrepreneurs who believe that they can survive by a strategy of low pricing and/or high-pressure selling. Since there is no difference between the high-growth and low-growth ventures on this policy, one should presume that even for survival, an enterprise cannot depend on low-pricing or high-pressure selling. Developing a competitive advantage for oneself in some area or the other is a must; and in this sense, every entrepreneur has to be an innovator, as was proposed by Schumpeter almost a century ago (Schumpeter, 1934).

As the scores were generally low on personality traits, the cut-off point for the high-scoring variables was lowered to 4.50 (see Table 4.2). Of the four high-scoring variables, one had a mean score of less than 5.00. Prominent among the high-scoring variables are the desire to be the best in one's field, pleasure in doing difficult tasks, confidence about managing one's enterprise, and constant dissatisfaction with what is happening around. It then becomes evident that the entrepreneurial individual's desire to excel and itch for changing things have to be supported by a willingness to undertake difficult tasks and confidence in one's own abilities. This is also supported by the lowest-scoring variables, which were observed to be the following: low on complacency feelings; low on aversion to hard work; low on external attribution of failures; low on breaking promises or violating the moral and ethical norms; and low on treating business as a mere source of income. It can be inferred from these that entrepreneurial individuals are hard-working individuals, who love their business more than as a mere source of income, want to learn new things, and attribute failures to their own actions. Moreover, they do believe that business is also bound by certain norms of ethical behavior.

Unlike in the case of personality traits, the scores on motives were generally on the higher side (see Table 4.3). Hence the cut-off for the lowest scoring variables was raised to 3.50. There are several motives which were found to be high for entrepreneurial individuals, such as enjoyment of one's work, desire for independence, development and utilization of one's capabilities, and so on. It may be noted that the need for achieving

Table 4.2.   (a) Traits with mean scores above 4.50* for the entire sample (*N* = 90) and
(b) Traits with mean scores below 3.00 for the entire sample (*N* = 90).

Code no.	Description of variable	Mean	Standard deviation
(a) Traits with mean scores above 4.50* for the entire sample (*N* = 90)			
T-22	Desire to be the best in one's field	5.84	1.30
T-18	Pleasure in doing difficult tasks	5.20	1.24
T-6	Confidence in managing one's enterprise	5.10	1.27
T-21	Constant dissatisfaction and an itch to change things	4.53	1.44
(b) Traits with mean scores below 3.00 for the entire sample (*N* = 90)			
T-19	Complacency that one knows everything that is needed for the conduct of one's business	2.13	1.11
T-11	Breaking promises for gains	2.54	1.56
T-12	Aversion to hard work	2.58	1.48
T-4	Business as an income substitute	2.69	1.78
T-7	External attribution of failures	2.87	1.30
T-1	Absence of moral scruples	2.96	1.71

Note: *4.50, instead of 5.00, is chosen here as the high-score cut-off because the scores in this section were generally low.

targets and standards is at the bottom of the 'high-score' list, implying that achievement motive may not be the distinguishing motive of entrepreneurs. This hypothesis is also supported by the positioning of the "need for feedback and knowledge of results" in the 'low-score' category. This motive has traditionally been considered to be a component of the achievement motive. There are indications in this study for a need to redefine the concept of achievement motive, regarding which we hope to have deeper insights from the factor analysis to be discussed below. Two other low-scoring variables conform to the pattern of motives expected. Entrepreneurs are rarely motivated because of external support. Similarly, they are unlikely to be motivated by a sense of obligation.

The high scorers and low scorers among the background variables (see Table 4.4) seem to go against the accumulated wisdom of the researchers on the background and early experiences of entrepreneurs. Entrepreneurs in the present sample have had a relatively happy childhood and have enjoyed parental care and support during childhood.

Table 4.3. (a) Motives with mean score above 5.00 for the entire sample ($N = 90$) and (b) Motives with mean scores of 3.50* or below for the entire sample ($N = 90$).

Code no.	Description of variable	Mean	Standard deviation
(a) Motives with mean score above 5.00 for the entire sample ($N = 90$)			
M-9	Enjoyment of one's work	5.66	1.42
M-15	Desire for independence	5.62	1.26
M-11	Development and utilization of one's capabilities	5.34	1.21
M-16	Involvement in decisions affecting oneself	5.32	1.32
M-18	Variety in tasks so as to avoid boredom	5.11	1.40
M-5	Reputation and recognition within or outside	5.10	1.11
M-12	Achievement of targets and standards set by oneself or others	5.07	1.48
(b) Motives with mean scores of 3.50* or below for the entire sample ($N = 90$)			
M-4	Support from those who control resources	3.32	1.41
M-10	Deontic motive/working because of a sense of duty	3.40	1.77
M-17	Need for knowing the results of one's actions	3.53	1.22

Note: *3.50, instead of 3.00, is chosen here as the low score cut-off because the scores in this section were generally high.

Their belief in religion is weak and so too naturally its practice. They are low on psychological deprivations, and very few have had ancestral families that have experienced local displacements. There was no tradition of self-employment in these families either. Educational accomplishments of the entrepreneurial individual are relatively low. Prior experience of start-up, successful or unsuccessful, is limited, which would imply that the 'theory of the experienced entrepreneurs' is unsupported. According to this theory, entrepreneurs get 'stabilized' with a project only after having done a few 'project-hopping'. The learning and experience gathered from prior attempts would make the subsequent attempt more productive and successful. The prior attempt would also serve as a 'corridor' for seeing newer and better opportunities (Ronstadt, 1988). However, the present findings do not offer any support to this theory. Most of our respondents have stuck with their first ventures and have steered them successfully without the benefit of any prior experience of venture start-up. Alternatively, it is possible that they would have derived the relevant experience (and the 'corridor-view') from their prior employment.

Table 4.4.   (a) Background variables with mean scores above 5.00 for the entire sample
($N = 84$) and (b) Background variables with mean scores below 3.00 for the entire sample
($N = 84$).

Code no.	Description of variable	Mean	Standard deviation
(a) Background variables with mean scores above 5.00 for the entire sample ($N = 84$)			
B-20	Support from friends and relatives	5.43	1.25
B-22	Purposeful action towards entrepreneurship	5.39	1.50
B-16	Diversity of interests during childhood	5.35	1.42
B-11	Childhood happiness	5.29	1.46
B-19	Feeling of success prior to start-up	5.04	1.05
B-14	Parental care	5.01	1.75
(b) Background variables with mean scores below 3.00 for the entire sample ($N = 84$)			
B-3	Unsuccessful attempts before the present start-up	1.30	0.60
B-2	Successful attempts before the present start-up	1.68	0.98
B-4	Belief in and practice of one's religion	2.26	1.05
B-13	Psychological deprivation during childhood	2.71	1.83
B-8	Educational accomplishments	2.81	1.29
B-7	Self-employment in ancestral family	2.89	1.31
B-15	Local displacement of ancestral family	2.95	2.04

Note: The sample size for this analysis is 84, because six respondents did not furnish data on all
variables.

A few points on the positive side of the background need to be highlighted. Entrepreneurial individuals were interested in a variety of activities in several fields during their childhood. They have also received
support and encouragement from individuals as well as institutions for
their entrepreneurial ventures. Juxtaposing these with what has been identified and discussed in the previous paragraph, one may venture to pro-
pose a new hypothesis regarding the 'entrepreneurial background'. These
are bright individuals who had been well supported and cared for by
parents and elders during childhood but could not pursue high levels of
education probably because of their shifting interests in different fields.
They realize that only an entrepreneurial career is available to them if they
want to make it big in life, and they strive for it relying primarily on their
own actions, but with support and encouragement from other individuals
and institutions.

Major Concerns and Orientations

One way of identifying the major concerns of entrepreneurs is the identification of high- and low-scoring variables, as described above. While this method is simple, it leaves out a large number of variables which are neither very high nor very low, but may contribute to one or the other principal dimensions or orientations. In order to identify the principal dimensions of the variables or the orientations underlying them, each of the variable groups was subjected to factor analysis. As we have mentioned in the chapter on methodology, the number of respondents (90) was considered to be on the lower side at least for one factor analysis, namely, for the policy group, which has 33 variables. In order to supplement the sample size, data were obtained from another 64 Indian respondents, and the variables were subjected to two sets of factor analysis, one using the sample of 90 and the other using the sample of 154. Since there were no major differences in the grouping of variables, it was finally decided that the sample size of 90 would be retained for the factor analysis, so that this analysis (like the other ones) would be based on the British sample alone. The results of the three sets of hierarchical factor analysis (on policies, traits, and background variables) and of one single-stage factor analysis (on motives) are presented in Tables 4.5–4.11. The purpose of the factor analysis was to identify the major dimensions underlying the variables. They are discussed under the four headings as follows.

Policy Orientations

The first-stage factor analysis yielded fourteen factors (see Table 4.5). Factor scores were computed for these, which then became the variables for the second-stage factor analysis. The six final factors that emerged out of this analysis are given in Table 4.6. A brief explanation of each of these is given below.

P-I. Social Orientation: Factor 1 of the first-stage factor analysis was retained as Factor I in the second stage as well. There is some difficulty in interpreting this factor because the policy of having strict rules and procedures within the organization also has combined with the two policies of fostering linkages and associations outside. In spite of the apparent lack of compatibility among the variables, there is an indication that this factor refers to the external orientation of these entrepreneurs, which

Table 4.5.   Hierarchical factor analysis of policies, Stage I: Details of 14 factors (loadings ≥ 0.50).

Factor no.	Variable no.	Description	Factor loading	Factor name given
PF-1	P-17	Strict rules and procedures and no experimentation within	.704	Social orientation
	P-26	Industry and professional associations	.641	
	P-28	Sponsoring of public interest activities	.501	
PF-2	P-19	Spreading of risks	.536	Risk management
	P-21	Collecting systematic information	.809	
PF-3	P-16	Professionalization	−.552	Lack of professionalism
	P-30	Monetary gains exclusively for partners	.500	
	P-31	Minimum sharing of information	.708	
	P-32	Minimizing investments through improvisation, make-shift arrangements, etc.	.671	
PF-4	P-12	Competition avoidance through product differentiation	−.614	Conformism
	P-23	Rewarding employees more for loyalty than performance	.805	
PF-5	P-27	Seeking support primarily from friends and relatives	.794	Self-reliance
	P-29	Reliance on one's own judgment for decision-making	.689	
PF-6	P-4	Deviating from goals for profits	.671	Opportunity orientation
	P-18	Testing before venturing out	−.728	(Hit-and-miss attitude)
PF-7	P-13	Related diversification/staying within one's experience	.797	Maintaining quality
	P-14	Quality at any cost	.621	through experience
PF-8	P-15	Building image primarily through advertisement and publicity	.825	High-pressure selling
	P-24	Aggressive marketing	.735	

Table 4.5.   (*Continued*)

Factor no.	Variable no.	Description	Factor loading	Factor name given
PF-9	P-6	Acquire knowledge of the technology involved	.840	Acquisition of technology by oneself
PF-10	P-11	Minimizing borrowed funds	.888	Organic growth
	P-33	Relatively small start-up and organic growth using internal resources	.605	
PF-11	P-1	Preference for tried and tested products and services	.515	Beaten path orientation
	P-3	No active search for new ideas	.820	
PF-12	P-10	Borrowing technology	.867	Borrowing technology
PF-13	P-2	Developing one's own technology rather than borrowing	.768	Developing/ Subcontracting technology
	P-9	Sub-contract as much as possible	.606	
PF-14	P-7	Assemble the best talents	−.500	Choose partners and employees for their special capabilities
	P-8	Choose partners for their capital contribution	.769	

would imply that those who are 'outward looking' and so are not able to pay much attention to 'internal matters' would leave them largely to rules and procedures.

P-II. Risk Management: This factor is constituted by factors 2 and 3 of the first-stage factor analysis. The factors called 'risk management' and 'lack of professionalism' have combined with opposite signs for the loadings. The various components of the prior factors can be seen in Table 4.5. Since the sign of the second-factor loading is negative, it should be interpreted here as 'professionalism'. It sounds logical that the different ways of managing risk are combined to form one factor. Spreading risks on to different projects, collecting systematic information on new projects, and

Table 4.6.   Hierarchical factor analysis of policies, Stage II: Details of six final factors (loadings ≥ 0.50).

Factor no.	First-stage factor number and description		Factor loading	Factor name given
P-I	PF-1	Social orientation	.615	Social orientation
P-II	PF-2	Risk management	.516	Risk management through
	PF-3	Lack of professionalism	−.705	professionalism
P-III	PF-5	Self-reliance (one's own judgment and support from close circles)	.711	Self-reliance
P-IV	PF-9	Acquisition of technology by oneself	.628	Organic growth using
	PF-10	Organic growth	.562	one's own knowledge and resources
P-V	PF-7	Maintaining quality through experience in the field	.645	Image and sales through quality
	PF-8	High-pressure selling	−.544	
P-VI	PF-13	Sub-contract, rather than borrow technology, if one's own technology is not available	.599	Capability development
	PF-14	Choose partners and employees for their special capabilities	.577	

using professional systems and techniques are all methods of coping with uncertainty and risk. Hence, this factor can be called the risk management policy.

P-III. Self-reliance: There is only one factor of the previous stage in this final factor. The variables relate to the policy of relying primarily on one's own judgment for decision-making and of seeking support from closer circles of friends and relatives in times of crisis. The indication here seems to be that of an orientation opposite to that of Factor P-I. The picture is that of a 'one-man show' where the person relies more on his/her own judgment and would not so much be guided by professional analysis or rules and procedures. In case of a need for external help, this person would prefer to seek help from friends and relatives and so would not find it necessary to enlarge the network of one's influence through professional associations or public interest activities. The factor, therefore, seems to relate to a policy of self-reliant and self-contained operations.

P-IV. Organic Growth: Preliminary factors 9 and 10 have combined to form this final factor. There are three elements contributing to this factor. First of all, the entrepreneur or the entrepreneurial team feels that there should be some familiarity within the team with the technology of the business, which they would acquire. The second aspect is the minimization of borrowed funds, and the third is to start the enterprise on a relatively small scale and develop it using internally accumulated resources. Though this factor looks very similar to the one we described as 'self-reliance' above, there are some differences. Learning the technology oneself does not imply that the entrepreneur would want to do it all by himself/herself. He/she would not mind hiring professionals but only at a stage when he/she would be able to afford to pay them. Similarly, minimizing borrowed funds is not necessarily because of any aversion to such funds, but because of the apprehension that the business may not be able to service such funds, which was also clearly seen in the findings of the previous study by the present author. This is the reason why some entrepreneurs do have a preference for a relatively small start-up and organic growth using internally generated and accumulated resources. The reason for adopting such policies is a concern for the viability of the enterprise rather than a temperamental preference of the entrepreneur for self-reliance. Therefore, it is not difficult to understand why the factor analysis has identified two separate factors, 'self-reliance' and 'organic growth', which have apparently similar contents.

P-V. Image through Quality: This factor is mainly about the maintenance of quality. Looking at the contributing variables, it appears that the policy of maintaining consistent quality is adopted mainly for the long-term image of the company. This is probably the reason why preliminary factor no. 8, relating to aggressive marketing and building of company image through advertisements and publicity combined with this factor with a negative loading. Image can be built through the quality of products and services and/or through advertisements and publicity. Though there is nothing inherently incompatible with these two strategies being adopted at the same time, during the start-up period and early phase of growth, it appears that there may be a choice for the entrepreneur between the two, probably because of the paucity of resources during that period. When there is competition for limited resources, the priority will have to be for quality rather than for advertisements and publicity. It may be recalled that the statements in the questionnaire referred to the primary means of image-building. Obviously, both cannot be primary, and with most entrepreneurs, maintenance of quality seems to be more important than advertisements and publicity, for building the long-term image of the enterprise. The policy of related diversification, which has also got loaded on to this factor, seems to offer further support to this fact.

Although the policy of related diversification (as opposed to the policy of unrelated diversification) is advocated by many researchers as the major strategy for ensuring stable growth due to the possibility of achieving synergies by sharing or transferring resources (Weiss, 2016), the factor analysis conducted for this study does not reveal it to be an independent policy. Related diversification is apparently a way to ensure that the firm has competence in the new area it enters and that the quality of its products and services is not adversely affected due to the lack of experience in the new area. This would imply that if the firm is confident of maintaining quality standards in the new area, it does not have to worry about whether the new area is related or unrelated to its existing operations, thus providing a rationale for growth through unrelated diversification, which is not very unusual either. Alternatively, as Bowonder and Miyake (1992a,b) point out, the concept of relatedness itself may have to be redefined. Traditionally, related diversification is understood as getting into areas related by similar products or, at the most, processes. Bowonder and Miyake (1992a,b) have identified another kind of relatedness commonly adopted by Japanese companies, where the relating factor is the core competence of the firm. In this way, a cement company diversifying into electronics can be viewed as related diversification through their core competence in ceramics. Similarly, a steel manufacturer may 'relatedly' diversify into electronics through their core competence in process control. In the ultimate analysis, therefore, 'related diversification' does not emerge as an independent policy of an enterprise. It depends on some other policy factors such as sustaining one's long-term image through maintenance of quality, developing and expanding one's core competence into other areas, and so on. This may be the reason why in our analysis related diversification did not emerge as an independent factor but combined with the 'quality-image' factor.

P-VI. Capability Development: The last factor is a combination of preliminary factors 13 and 14 and is about capability building. Of the four variables in this factor, two are about the choice of people, and the other two are about technology. There are obviously two ways of managing technology, developing one's own technology, and subcontracting from others when such capabilities are not available internally. As far as the people are concerned, one should look for the best talents in the field. Even in the choice of partners and associates, the primary consideration should be their capabilities rather than the capital they can contribute.

Major Dimensions of Entrepreneurial Personality

The twenty-five variables under the personal policies of the principal promoter yielded nine factors in the first stage of factor analysis (see Table 4.7) and five factors in the second and final stage (see Table 4.8).

These factors would suggest the major dimensions of entrepreneurial personality and are briefly described below.

T-I. Internal Locus of Control: Factor I is a combination of preliminary factors 5 and 7. Considering the variables involved in this final factor, it was called the 'Internal locus of control' factor, as it contains both the variables on attribution. Successes are attributed to oneself, and failures are not attributed to external factors. In the preliminary factor 5, the desire to excel in one's field has combined with external attribution of failure, with opposite signs of loadings, indicating that the desire to excel should be supported by reliance on one's own effort. Preliminary factor 7 also has similar contents. Along with 'success through one's own action' and 'lack of external support' there is a negatively loaded variable on taking risks without proper assessment of them. The message is that the entrepreneur should calculate risks and proceed to success through one's own action without relying much on external support. The final factor, therefore, can be legitimately called the 'Internal locus of control' factor.

An obvious inference from the constitution of this factor is that risk-taking ability, which in the popular mind and according to early researchers (Cantillon, 1755; Knight, 1921; Mill, 1848) was the first and probably the most important of entrepreneurial traits, does not seem to be an independent trait at all. In other words, it is not because these individuals have a propensity to take risks that they initiate entrepreneurial ventures. On the contrary, it is because they are in love with a project and want to see it

Table 4.7. Hierarchical factor analysis of personality traits, Stage I: Details of 9 factors (loadings ≥ 0.50).

Factor no.	Variable no.	Description	Factor loading	Factor name given
TF-1	T-2	No experiments with one's style of management	.667	Conformism
	T-3	No need to generate alternatives in decision situations	.767	
	T-10	Would not like any social deviants in the enterprise	.664	
TF-2	T-15	Dislike for authority	.767	Revolt against the establishment
	T-21	Constant dissatisfaction and an itch for change	.760	
TF-3	T-23	Concern for others not understanding oneself	.780	Deviance
	T-24	Preference to work alone		
TF-4	T-6	Confidence about managing one's enterprise well	.655	Persistence even in difficult tasks
	T-16	Changing goals in the face of obstacles	−.544	
	T-18	Pleasure in doing difficult things	.722	
TF-5	T-7	External attribution of failures	.803	Desire to excel through one's own effort
	T-22	Desire to be the best in one's field	−.513	
TF-6	T-1	Absence of moral scruples	.797	Absence of moral scruples
	T-11	Breaking promises for gains	.775	
TF-7	T-8	Success through one's own action	.658	Reliance on one's own actions rather than on luck or external support
	T-13	Risk-taking rather than calculating its impact	−.621	
	T-25	Lack of external support	.593	
TF-8	T-9	No worry about future	.519	Future wellbeing through hard work
	T-12	Aversion to hard work	−.799	
TF-9	T-5	Discomfort with uncertainties	.827	Getting things done as a matter of routine
	T-20	Comfort with legitimate authority and discomfort with political action	−.505	

Table 4.8. Hierarchical factor analysis of personality traits, Stage II: Details of 5 factors (loadings ≥ 0.50).

Factor no.	Variable no.	Description	Factor loading	Factor name given
T-1	TF-5	Desire to excel through one's own effort	.671	Internal locus of control
	TF-7	Reliance on one's own actions rather than on luck or external support	.604	
T-2	TF-1	Conformism	.701	Conformism
	TF-3	Deviance	−.649	
T-3	TF-2	Revolt against the establishment	.635	Desire to improve things through hard work
	TF-8	Future wellbeing through hard work	.658	
T-4	TF-4	Persistence even in difficult tasks	.730	Comfort with political processes
	TF-9	Getting things done as a matter of routine	−.638	
T-5	TF-6	Absence of moral scruples	.833	Ethical dimension

implemented that they gear themselves up to face the risks involved in it. This is probably the difference between speculators and gamblers on the one hand, and entrepreneurs on the other. In fact, it could be stated that the latter have an aversion to taking risks, as was also found in the author's previous study (Manimala, 1988a, 1999). They try to avoid, reduce and/or manage risks through information management, step-by-step testing against reality, and spreading of risks. It is in this sense that some researchers have described entrepreneurs as risk avoiders and not really risk takers. They would surely avoid those risks that are perceived as pure games of chance (McClelland, 1961; Lipper, 1985; Bellu, 1988; Davidsson, 1988). It is therefore not difficult to understand why some researchers have found no significant difference between executives and entrepreneurs on objective risk-taking behavior (Brockhaus, 1980; Sexton & Bowman, 1983; Krasner & Ray, 1984). A similar finding of 'no difference' between entrepreneurs and non-entrepreneurs in their risk-taking behavior was reported by Palich and Bagby (1995), where they have also observed that the difference is that some situations, which are generally perceived as risky, are perceived as opportunities by the entrepreneurial individuals. In any case, it can be safely inferred that the propensity to take risks is not an independent trait. It may be considered to be a component of the 'locus-of-control' factor. As a hypothesis, it could be stated that individuals with internal locus of control would have their own goals and plans, for the attainment of which they would be able and willing to manage the risks involved. On the other hand, individuals with an external locus of control would not set any goal for themselves and would naturally let themselves be carried away to where fate or luck would take them. This is probably the reason why the desire to excel, the desire to achieve goals through one's own efforts, and the aversion to speculation and gambling got combined with the locus-of-control factor. Perhaps, it is also an indication that the concept of locus of control also needs to be reexamined and redefined, emphasizing the role of goals and risk management.

T-II. Conformism: The second factor deals with the conformism-deviance dimension. The preliminary factors on conformism (factor no. 1) and on deviance (factor no. 3) have combined with opposite loadings, indicating that this dimension is about the extent to which the individual conforms to existing systems and practices, or deviates from them. Prior factor 1 has variables such as sticking to one's style, dislike for social deviants, and the lack of eagerness for generating alternatives. The deviance factor has variables expressing concern for others not understanding oneself and preference for working alone.

T-III. Desire for Constant Improvement: This factor is a combination of preliminary factors 2 and 8. The former has two variables: one about constant dissatisfaction and an itch for changing things, and the other about dislike for authority. This is probably because those in authority are generally entrusted with the task of protecting the existing structures, systems, procedures, etc. The second prior factor in this group also has two variables: one relating to optimistic feelings about the future of the enterprise and the other relating to willingness to work hard. This dimension, therefore, is about an optimism about the future based on one's dissatisfaction with what is happening around and a desire to change things through hard work.

T-IV. Comfort with Unstructured Situations: This dimension seems to be a natural sequel to the previous one. Changing things is difficult to accomplish if one relies only on the given structures, systems, rules, and procedures. One should have considerable skills and ease for persuading people to accept the new directions and act upon them. This is probably why comfort with the unstructured situations has emerged as a separate dimension. The constituent variables of this dimension are a propensity to undertake difficult tasks, confidence about managing these well, persistence in goals against obstacles, tolerance of ambiguities, and comfort with political processes. In short, it is about the individual's ability to accomplish things in unstructured situations. Such individuals take up difficult tasks and pursue their goals with confidence and persistence because they have high tolerance for uncertainties and are comfortable with the political processes, which implies an ability to give a structure to an unstructured situation.

T-V. Ethical Orientation: The last dimension is about ethical orientation. There are two variables loaded on to this factor: one on the attitude that anything is fair in business and the other on breaking promises for monetary gains. A low score on this dimension, therefore, is indicative of high levels of ethical orientation and vice-versa.

Major work motives

The 20 statements on motives initially chosen on the basis of prior research on human motives were factor-analyzed to identify the major work motives of an individual. As the factors were relatively well defined at the first stage itself, there was no need for a second-stage factor analysis. The six factors that were identified in the factor analysis, along with the details of the variables and their loadings, are given in Table 4.9 and are briefly explained as follows:

M-I. Self-actualization: This dimension combines many variables which were traditionally considered to be separate motives. Prominent among these are self-actualization, self-development, accomplishing new things, and achievement of targets and standards. The factor seems to refer to achieving something through self-actualization. However, the kind of achievement that is implied here is somewhat different from the concept proposed by McClelland (1961). Achievement of targets and standards is just one component of the factor defined above, whereas for the concept defined by McClelland (1961), this was the major component, with a bifurcation of this into a desire to achieve one's own targets and a desire to excel in comparison with others. Two supporting components of

Table 4.9. Factor analysis* of work motives: Details of variables and loadings.

Factor no.	Variable no.	Description	Factor loading	Factor name given
M-1	M-1	Money motive	−.607	Self-actualization
	M-11	Capability development and utilization	.779	
	M-12	Achievement of targets and standards	.628	
	M-13	Desire to do something new and path-breaking	.595	
	M-14	Desire to express oneself through work	.638	
M-2	M-9	Enjoyable/interesting work	.714	Enjoyable work
	M-18	Avoidance of boredom	.671	(Nature of work)
	M-19	Contribution to society	.677	
	M-20	Clean and healthy surroundings	.782	
M-3	M-7	Desire for influencing others	.619	Desire for autonomy
	M-15	Desire for independence	.641	and power
	M-16	Desire to be involved in decisions affecting oneself	.758	
	M-17	Desire to know the results of one's actions	.647	
M-4	M-5	Desire for reputation and recognition	.606	Status motive
	M-6	Desire for top position	.853	
	M-8	Desire for social status	.655	
M-5	M-2	Family obligations	.586	Affiliation motive
	M-3	Desire to belong to a group	.616	
	M-4	Support from those who control resources	.828	
M-6	M-10	Working because it is one's duty	.894	Deontic motive

Note: *There was no need for a hierarchical factor analysis for this set of variables, as the variables got grouped neatly into six dimensions in the first stage itself.

McClelland's *n-Ach* are the propensity to take calculated risks and the need to get regular and correct feedback. In our analysis, this last variable has combined, as we shall see later, with the power motive. As for the achievement/self-actualization motive as defined by the present data, there are four positively loaded components in it and one negatively loaded component. The positively loaded variables, in the order of the magnitude of their loadings, are as follows: (i) capability development and utilization; (ii) desire to express oneself through work; (iii) achievement of targets and standards; and (iv) desire to do something new and path-breaking. The negatively loaded variable is the money motive. The way this was stated in the questionnaire indicates a need for present and future financial security. The factor, therefore, suggests that too much concern for financial security may be antithetical to self-development/ achievement. It is unlikely to imply that high achievers are not interested in money. What it probably implies is that if a person is worried primarily about financial security, he/she may not take a path of achievement. It is also suggestive of the ability and willingness of the individual to take calculated risks as proposed by McClelland (1961). The concept of achievement/self-actualization motive that has emerged in this study has the following five components: (a) expressing oneself through work, (b) creating something new, (c) achieving targets and standards, (d) developing one's capabilities for these, and (e) the ability and willingness to forego some amount of financial security.

The enlargement/modification of McClelland's concept of achievement motive, combining it with the features of a few other motives, is implied in the findings of this study, as noted above. Two of the components added to this concept deserve to be commented upon. One of them is the desire to express oneself through work, which is very similar to the concept of self-actualization enunciated by Maslow (1954). The second is the desire to create something new, which Khandwalla (1985) has identified as a separate motive, distinguishing it from the desire to achieve high standards on routine and humdrum tasks. This study, however, finds that it is part of the self-actualization or achievement motive. Taking a second look at the constituents of this factor, it appears that this factor should be described in terms of self-actualization rather than achievement. This is probably why the highest loading is for the variable relating to the development and utilization of one's capabilities, and the second highest is for the variable relating to the expression of oneself through work. Since each person is unique, the drive for actualizing oneself through specialized work using one's own unique capabilities is likely to lead to something new. In the process of such movement toward the goals of self-actualization through work, it is but natural that one sets targets and standards, which also need to be achieved. In this sense, achievement motive, as defined by prior researchers, is only a means to self-actualization. The next factor on the nature of work would support this contention, in the sense that achievers would like to work on the tasks they would enjoy, and not on any tasks that may get assigned to them. It appears, therefore, that not all individuals with a high need for achievement or self-actualization motive are likely to become entrepreneurs, unlike what was originally proposed by the theory of achievement motivation. If such individuals get enjoyable work in existing organizations, enabling them to 'actualize' themselves and to achieve their goals, there should be no reason why they would take to entrepreneurship. This hypothesis has logical appeal but has to be tested using further data.

M-II. Nature of Work: The second dimension among the motivators is the nature of work. The variables which are loaded on to this factor are interesting work, task variety, contribution to society, and clean and healthy surroundings. All of these obviously relate to the nature of work. There are various ways in which work can be interesting. The intrinsic interest of the person in the work is perhaps the most important component of this factor. The variety in the tasks involved is a component which would reduce monotony and boredom. Clean and healthy surroundings would add to the 'enjoyability' of the work in an extrinsic manner. It was somewhat puzzling to have the variable 'contribution to society' loaded on to this factor. On closer scrutiny, it would appear that this variable also relates to the nature of the job. The question is whether the individual's work is contributing to the interests of the society at large. As far as the entrepreneur is concerned, the perceived contribution he/she makes to the society can become his super-ordinate goal (Sherif, 1958; Blake & Mouton, 1992) and enhance the meaningfulness of his/her work. The four variables, therefore, describe different aspects of the nature of work.

M-III. Power Motive: What was described in Maslow's (1954) hierarchy of needs as 'ego needs' got split into two factors in the present analysis. One of them can be called the power motive and the other the status motive. (The former, namely, the power motive, will be the next dimension to be discussed.) The dimension we have described here as power motive has four variables in it, which represent two aspects of power, namely, the power to decide one's own affairs and the power to influence others. There are two variables indicating the former, which are the desire for independence and the desire to have involvement in decisions affecting oneself, which incidentally has the highest loading. The second aspect of power is what is commonly understood about power, namely, the power to influence others. A variable that is slightly odd in this group is the desire to know the results of one's actions. This was proposed by prior researchers as a component of achievement motive (McClelland, 1961). It is likely that since the components of achievement motive (as they got defined in this study) were mostly things under the individual's control, knowledge of results on these may not be a psychological necessity. On the other hand, since power motive pertains to matters affecting oneself and to the efforts to influence others, the knowledge of results may be felt to be essential. Anxiety about the decisions affecting oneself and the non-predictability about others could be the underlying reasons why the desire to know the results has become a component of the power motive rather than of the self-actualization/achievement motive.

M-IV. Status Motive: The second part of what Maslow (1954) called 'ego needs' is the status motive. According to the present analysis, there are three components to this factor, namely, the desire for top position, the desire for social status, and the desire for reputation and recognition. It appears that power and status need not always go with each other, as was conceptualized by Maslow in combining the two under the 'ego needs'. For example, the reputation, recognition, and status attained by high achievers in various fields (such as artists, poets, writers, musicians, and similar others) need not be accompanied by increases in personal or positional powers. Even a top position need not always have powers with it. Ceremonial positions with high status but with very little power are examples of such situations, and there may be people who would love to have such status without the powers and responsibilities, so that they could avoid the botherations associated with these. Conversely, there may be power-wielding persons (e.g., goons), who have no status in the society. It is therefore logical that the power and status motives have emerged as two independent factors in the present analysis.

M-V. Affiliation Motive: There are three components for the affiliation motive, as it got defined in the present analysis. They are the need to belong to a family, the need to work with a peer group, and the need to get support and encouragement from those who control resources. Belongingness, therefore, seems to operate at two levels, namely, that of personal life and of work life. The latter, in turn, has two components:

one indicating the individual's relationship with peers and the other with superiors. It may be noted that the concept of belongingness, as defined here, is somewhat different from the traditionally defined 'social needs', a part of which (namely, the need to be in high-status groups) got associated with the 'status motive'. Therefore, the factor discussed here refers only to the belongingness or affiliation motive required for one's regular life and work.

M-VI. Deontic Motive: The sixth factor is constituted by a single variable. This is the motivation arising from a sense of duty, a feeling of obligation. It may be noted that this kind of motive has rarely been mentioned in the existing body of literature on motivation. The inclusion of this motive in the questionnaire was prompted largely by the observed inability of the other motives to explain the motivation for certain types of jobs. It was never implied that entrepreneurs would be motivated primarily by a sense of duty. In fact, it is the other way; entrepreneurs hardly perceive their work as a means to fulfill their obligations to someone, as we have seen in the previous chapter in the section on high-scoring and low-scoring variables. Of course, it is possible that social entrepreneurs are different in this regard, as they may be motivated by a sense of obligation to the larger society. The reasons, therefore, for including this variable in this study were two-fold. First of all, it gave us an opportunity to test if this motive (working because of a sense of duty) is an independent motive or a part of any other motive. The factor analysis has shown that it is an independent motive because it has emerged as a separate factor, all by itself. Second, when this study is later expanded to entrepreneurs of different types, or belonging to different cultures and/or to non-entrepreneurs, it is likely that this motive is high in some groups such as social entrepreneurs, non-entrepreneurs, or low-growth entrepreneurs in some cultures. One of the salutary outcomes of this study is that it has provided some empirical evidence in support of the hypothesis that deontic motive is an independent work motive for individuals. In other words, this study has led to the 'empirical identification' of a new motive, which does not find any place in the mainstream research literature on motivation, although there are plenty of discussions on it in the religious and spiritual literature.

At the conceptual level, some researchers have talked about the need for defining a new motive which would capture the inner urge of an individual to fulfill one's obligations through work. Schwartz (1983), for example, questioned McGregor's (1960) assertion that work is as natural as play. Had it been the case, there would not have been any need for people to be paid for work. There is no denying that there are a few individuals who enjoy their work and would do it even if there is no pay. But that is the exception rather than the rule. A large majority of activities which are classified as work will have an element of unpleasantness associated with them. Few people would enjoy tasks like cleaning the toilets or reading the proof of a telephone directory. Besides, there are very few jobs that can be really enriched even with the addition of autonomy, skill-variety, task-significance, feedback, and task-identity, as is assumed by the job-enrichment schemes. This is probably why the job enrichment movement has failed to produce any spectacular results. In fact, there are many cases where trade unions have demanded extra remuneration for doing enriched jobs! Enrichment, therefore, does not seem to make the job more enjoyable. Similarly, matching jobs with persons also seems to be an unrealistic proposition, viewed especially in the context of many nations finding it difficult to provide any jobs, matching or non-matching, to a large number of people. Another intriguing fact about work is that even those who dislike their work would not like to stop working in spite of their being financially well off. All these may point to the existence of some internal compulsions for the individual to work, which may be called the 'Deontic Motivation'.

The major difference between the deontic motive and the other motives is that for the latter, rewards follow work or are concurrent with work, but for the former, rewards precede work (Manimala, 1987). For example, the wages are paid after the work is completed or after a stipulated period of work. Some other rewards, such as enjoyment from work, are derived simultaneously as the work is done. In the case of deontic motive, however, the rewards are received in advance and as a consequence, the individual develops a sense of obligation. The natural process of the development of deontic motive may be seen in the bringing up of a child. When a child is born into a family, it is unconditionally accepted as a member of the family and is given everything it needs, irrespective of its future potential for work. The grown-up individual, therefore, develops a sense of obligation towards his/her parents, elders, the society and the country, and discharges this obligation by working for the latter's benefit. This is probably why the ancient Indian scriptural text, the *Bhagavad Gita*, advocates the individual to do one's duty without thinking of the reward. The exhortation apparently is to do the duty *because* the reward has already been received. Be that as it may, the question arises whether such a motive could be made to operate in the modern workplace. It seems the Japanese practice of lifetime employment works on the basis of this principle. At the time of joining an organization, the employee, so to say, gets an unconditional acceptance as its member, which creates a sense of obligation in the employee who then works for the organization with high levels of commitment.

In this context, it was interesting to watch in a Japanese film called "Oshin" how a wealthy family persuades a reluctant seven-year-old girl from a poor family to work for the former as a babysitter. They send a bagful of rice to the poor girl's house as advance pay for one year. The child then has no way but to work. Later on, this child is allowed by the employer to go to school, indicating that there is an acceptance for her into the employer's family. In other cultures, employers would generally refrain from making advance payment of wages for fear that the potential employee may exploit the situation by not joining or by not working properly even if he/she joins (as the wages are already received). The assumption is that once the wages are given away there is nothing at the employer's disposal to control the employee and that the latter would have no stakes in the situation and so would not work. Similarly in most cultures, employers would not take up the responsibility of developing the employees in areas which do not have direct and immediate relevance to the work to be performed. Even in the matter of work-related skills, employers would be happier to recruit people who are already trained in the required skills. The underlying philosophy is that the employer is responsible to compensate the employee only to the extent of the work done. Development of his/her skills/potential or anticipating his/her personal needs is not considered to be the responsibility of the employer. Hence the loyalty and feeling of obligation would be toward those who help him/her on these rather than toward the employer or the work. For creating deontic motivation in employees, the employer has to offer a compensation package comprising the work-related rewards, the overall development of the employee, and the anticipatory care of his/her needs as a person. In short, the difference is very simple. It is the difference between accepting the employee as a member of the family, on the one hand, or treating him/her as an outsider, on the other.

As noted above, the deontic motive would perhaps be the most powerful motive for making people work for others, especially when performing unpleasant tasks of the lower order. The motivational patterns observed among the Japanese workers may be better explained by deontic motive than by the other well-researched motives. It should, however, be noted that while this motive may offer some explanation to certain types of employee motivation, it would be largely irrelevant to entrepreneurial motivation. However, we have discussed this motive in some detail because the concept itself is relatively new and unresearched and because we expect to find some differences in this motive between the 'experimental' and 'control' groups when the present research design is subsequently used for further investigation on other categories of entrepreneurs and/or non-entrepreneurs. As far as this study is concerned, our contribution is limited to the 'empirical' identification of deontic motive as an independent motive.

Dimensions of the Background

The background variables (Section V of the Questionnaire) yielded eight factors in the first stage (see Table 4.10) and four factors in the second stage (see Table 4.11) of factor analysis. The contents of these four factors are briefly discussed as follows.

B-I. Personal Interests and Choices: This factor is constituted by the combination (with opposite loadings) of prior factors on personal interests and choices and on prior entrepreneurial experience. It appears that as the entrepreneurial experience for the individual increases, the scope of exercising one's interests and choices narrows down. In other words, the person with entrepreneurial experience is likely to be constrained by the requirements of his existing business and would not be absolutely free to pursue one's own interests. Hence, the opposite loadings. It also sounds logical in the light of the findings by researchers (discussed in Chapter 1) that entrepreneurs may restrict the growth of their enterprises because growth may entail the performance of some activities which may not suit the interests and capabilities of the entrepreneur. The first factor, therefore, relates to the purposeful actions, choices, and interests of the individual.

B-II. Support and Encouragement: This is the factor with the largest number of variables loaded onto it. There are eight of them, which constitute two of the prior factors. One of these with six variables relates to the childhood welfare and happiness of the entrepreneurial individual. Three of these variables are with positive loadings and three with negative, indicating that the meanings of one group of three will have to be reversed for

Table 4.10.   Hierarchical factor analysis of background variables, Stage I: details of eight factors (loadings ≥ 0.50).

Factor no.	Variable no.	Description	Factor loading	Factor name given
BF – 1	B-11	Childhood happiness	−.803	Childhood welfare and happiness*
	B-13	Psychological deprivation	.687	
	B-14	Parental care	−.540	
	B-15	Local displacements	.615	
	B-17	Disappointments	.595	
	B-18	Satisfaction	−.540	
BF – 2	B-8	Level of education	.592	Accomplishments before start-up
	B-19	Pre-start-up success	.781	
BF – 3	B-6	Ancestral family's level of education	.819	Family status
	B-12	Affluence in the family	.769	
BF – 4	B-1	Age at the time of start-up	.789	Age and experience
	B-9	Prior work experience	.777	
BF – 5	B-4	Belief in and practice of religion		Personal interests and choices
	B-22	Purposeful action towards one's goals	.753	
	B-16	Diversity of interests	.500	
BF – 6	B-20	Support from friends and relatives	.663	Support and encouragement
	B-21	Support from institutions	.881	
BF – 7	B-2	Number of prior successful ventures	.586	Entrepreneurial experience
	B-3	Number of prior unsuccessful ventures	.810	
BF – 8	B-10	Nature of previous employment	.805	Nature of previous employment

Note: *In computing the factor scores, we have reversed the positively loaded variables in the first factor (BF – 1), so that the dimension could be described as "Childhood welfare and happiness".

arriving at a coherent group of variables in the factor. The components of this factor, therefore, are childhood happiness, absence of psychological deprivations, absence of local displacements, absence of disappointments, and a feeling of satisfaction about one's life until the start-up of the venture. The second factor has two variables, which are about support and

Table 4.11.   Hierarchical factor analysis of background variables, Stage II: Details of four final factors (loadings ≥ 0.50).

Factor no.	Variable no.	Description	Factor loading	Factor name given
B – I	BF-5	Personal interests and choices	.726	Personal interests and choices
	BF-7	Entrepreneurial experience	−.677	
B – II	BF-1	Childhood welfare and happiness	.668	Support and encouragement
	BF-6	Support and encouragement	.577	
B – III	BF-3	Family status	.680	Prior work experience
	BF-8	Nature of previous employment	.533	
B – IV	BF-2	Accomplishments before start-up	.839	Accomplishments before start-up

encouragement from individuals and institutions. The overall burden of the final factor, therefore, seems to be the support and encouragement received by the individual both during childhood as well as during the start-up of his/her venture.

B-III. Prior Work Experience: The combination of prior factors on family status and nature of previous employment to form this final factor was somewhat puzzling. Family status had two variables, namely, ancestral family's level of education and affluence during childhood in one's own family. Nature of previous employment refers to the kind of organizations the individual has worked with, indicating progressively higher scores for jobs in industry, especially the ones related to the current business. Examining these two sets of variables, it may be argued that family status can be a surrogate variable for the person's childhood experiences at work. The status of the family will no doubt be a major determinant of the kind of chores and odd jobs one gets to perform during childhood. If the ancestral family had high levels of education and/or if one's own family was financially well off, the chances are that a member of this family engages himself/herself in jobs and chores of higher status than if otherwise. Hence the overall content of this factor can be interpreted as the nature of prior work experience.

B-IV. Accomplishments before Start-up: This final factor is constituted by two variables, namely, the person's educational accomplishments and his/her success in other activities during the period immediately before the start-up. This factor is therefore on the individual's accomplishments before starting the venture. The high or low scores on this will indicate whether it is the individual who is otherwise successful or unsuccessful who takes up entrepreneurship.

Factors of the Distinguishing Variables

The *t*-tests on variables discussed in Chapter 3 have revealed that there are just 14 variables for which the difference between the high-growth and low-growth groups is statistically significant. Since a large number of variables are not significantly different, the factors derived from them may not be of much help in distinguishing between the high-growth and low-growth groups. The differences between the two groups in terms of these factors are unlikely to be statistically significant. Hence, it was necessary to find another way to focus attention on the distinguishing variables and to make parsimonious use of them in explaining the difference between the high-growth and the low-growth groups. It was therefore decided to identify the major dimensions of the distinguishing variables by subjecting these variables together to a factor analysis, disregarding the conceptual categories of policies, traits, motives, etc. Since the policy group had only three significant variables but had two other similar ones which were close to 90% confidence level, we have included the latter also in the factor analysis, making a total of 16 variables for this analysis. Six factors emerged from this, which can be considered to be the factors distinguishing growth ventures from others. These factors, along with the variables and their loadings, are given in Table 4.12. A brief description on each follows:

D-I. Power and Status: The first factor is constituted predominantly by the motive variables. Three out of four motives got loaded on to this factor. They are the desire for social status, the desire to influence people, and the desire for top position. Along with these, there is a negatively loaded trait variable (T-14), with a loading slightly lower than 0.50. This variable is on the individual's preference for exercising legitimate authority than persuasive power. Since the loading is negative, we should include the opposite meaning of the variable to constitute the factor. Thus, the growth-seeker seems to be a person interested in the positional as well as personal power with a preference to operate the latter. This sounds

Table 4.12. Factor analysis of variables significantly different for the high-growth and low-growth groups.

Factor no.	Variable no.	Description	Factor loading	Factor name given
D – I	M-6	Desire for top position	.641	Desire for position, power, and status (power motive)
	M-7	Power motive/desire to influence	.758	
	M-8	Desire for social status	.826	
	T-14	Exercising the authority rather than persuasion	−.462	
D – II	P-14	Quality at any cost	.526	Pursuit of excellence
	P-28	Sponsoring of public interest activities	.569	
	M-9	Interest in and enjoyment of one's work	.599	
	T-22	Desire to be the best in the field	.707	
D – III	B-20	Support from friends and relatives	.769	Support and encouragement
	B-21	Support from institutions	.815	
D – IV	T-3	Complacency about one's knowledge	−.762	Learning motive
	B-6	Ancestral family's level of education	.745	
D – V	P-18	Testing before venturing out	.748	Reality Orientation
	P-21	Collecting systematic information	.690	
	T-11	Breaking promises for gains	−.490	
D – VI	P-20	Decentralized set-up and autonomy to the lower levels	.877	Decentralization and delegation

sensible because the positional power of the entrepreneur can be effective only within his enterprise, whereas a growing enterprise will have a lot of things to be organized in collaboration with external agencies, for which persuasive skills and powers are the most appropriate.

D-II. Pursuit of Excellence: There are four variables — two policy variables, one motive variable, and one trait variable — loaded on to this factor. All of them refer to excellence of some kind. The trait variable (T-22) is about the desire to be the best in one's field. The motive variable (M-9) is about the motivation provided by an enjoyable job. It appears that the best performances occur when the task in itself is enjoyable for the individual. The two policy variables are on ensuring the quality of products and services and on sponsoring public interest activities. These are two methods by which the enterprise can draw customer/public support for his/her pursuit of excellence. This is especially true of quality, which works as a 'double-edged sword'. It is an outcome of the enterprise's pursuit of excellence and a means of ensuring public support for such pursuits. The overall burden of this factor, therefore, is the pursuit of excellence, which is essential for growth.

D-III. Support and Encouragement: This factor is constituted exclusively by the background variables. Two of the three significant background variables have been combined to form this factor. These are about the support from friends and relatives and from institutions. It may be that the growth-seekers were fortunate to have received better support and encouragement from other individuals and institutions. Alternatively, these individuals may have persuaded other individuals and institutions, and elicited support and encouragement from them. The latter looks like a more plausible hypothesis especially in view of the finding that the growth-seekers are also power-seekers and are comfortable with the exercise of persuasive power (see Factor D-I above). Besides, as we have noted elsewhere in this book, both the samples having been drawn from the same country, their assessment of institutional support would be with reference to the same/similar institutions. The differences, therefore, should be attributed largely to the respondents' capability to elicit support from such institutions, rather than the supportiveness or otherwise of the institutions.

D-IV. Learning Motive: Here is a motive constituted by 'non-motive' variables. There are a trait variable and a background variable combining with opposite loadings to form this factor. Complacency about one's grasp of every situation has a negative loading, whereas ancestral family's level of education has a positive one. Combination of these two variables is obviously difficult to explain. For the time being, we would designate it as the willingness to learn from new situations.

D-V. Reality Orientation: There are three variables constituting this factor, namely, two positively loaded policy variables and one negatively loaded trait variable. The policy variables relate to collecting systematic information and testing before venturing out. Both of these are about reality testing. The trait variable is about breaking promises for gains. Since the loading is negative for this variable, it should be reversed for the purpose of constructing the factor. It appears that the long-term realities of any situation would not permit the breaking of one's promises. The overall content of the factor, therefore, is a reality orientation on the part of the entrepreneurial individual.

D-VI. Decentralization and Delegation: The last factor has only one variable, which refers to decentralization and delegation. It is natural that, as the organization grows large, it becomes increasingly difficult for one individual to manage it directly. In other words, the growth-seeker should be prepared to trust people and delegate some of his powers to them. The association between enterprise growth and delegation/decentralization is fairly well acknowledged. What is not very clear is whether growth causes delegation/decentralization or whether a willingness on the part of the entrepreneur to forego absolute control over the enterprise causes growth.

Factor Mean Scores: High and Low

This chapter began with the identification of high-scoring and low-scoring variables with a view to finding out some characteristic features of entrepreneurs in general. The next step was to identify the major concerns and orientations of entrepreneurs through factor analysis of the variables in separate groups, which generated 21 factors in four categories, in addition to the six factors obtained from the 16 distinguishing variables. This section, which is the last of this chapter, examines the high- and low-scoring factors so as to understand the characteristic concerns and orientations of entrepreneurs. The means and standard deviations of the 21 factors in the four categories of variables are given in Table 4.13. The high scorers are marked with '*' and the low scorers are marked with '@' in the table. The norm for deciding the high and low scores is similar to that adopted for the variables, with a small difference. The principle remains the same, which is that a high score is one that is around or above 5, and a low score is one that is around or below 3. Since the factor scores are aggregations of variable scores, it should be expected that the scores

Table 4.13.   Means and standard deviations of 21 factors generated from four variable groups ($N = 84$).

Factor no.	Description	Mean	Standard deviation
P – I	Social orientation	3.317@	1.045
P – II	Managing risks through professionalization	4.544*	0.888
P – III	Self-reliance	3.988	1.232
P – IV	Organic growth using one's own knowledge and resources	5.589*	0.929
P – V	Image and sales through quality	5.256*	0.893
P – VI	Capability development	4.932*	0.819
T – I	Internal locus of control	4.274	0.942
T – II	Conformism	3.914	0.743
T – III	Desire to improve through hard work	4.530*	0.843
T – IV	Ease of dealing with difficult and unstructured situations	4.836*	0.730
T – V	Absence of moral scruples	2.798@	1.333
M – I	Self-actualization	4.714*	1.031
M – II	Enjoyable/interesting work	4.756*	1.053
M – III	Desire for autonomy and power	4.667*	0.861
M – IV	Status motive	4.489	1.065
M – V	Affiliation motive	3.395@	1.060
M – VI	Deontic motive	3.393@	1.715
B – I	Personal interests and choices	4.857*	0.624
B – II	Support and encouragement	4.429	0.935
B – III	Previous work experience	3.500@	0.814
B – IV	Accomplishments prior to start-up	3.500@	0.974

Note: *are high-scoring factors; @ are low-scoring factors.

would move a little toward the center of the scale due to averaging. Hence the higher scores would get slightly depressed and the lower scores slightly elevated. It was, therefore, decided to classify the means above 4.50 as high scores and the means below 3.50 as low scores. The high scorers and low scorers thus identified are presented in Table 4.14.

According to the above criterion, there are four high-scorers and one low-scorer among the policy orientations. The high-scorers are

Table 4.14. High- and low-scoring factors in the four categories.

High scorers		Low scorers	
I. Policies			
P-IV	Organic growth (5.59, 0.93)	P-I	Social orientation (3.32,1.05)
P-V	Image and sales through quality (5.26, 0.89)		
P-VI	Capability development (4.93, 0.82)		
P-II	Managing risks through professionalization (4.54, 0.89)		
II. Traits			
T-IV	Ease of dealing with difficult and unstructured situations (4.84, 0.73)	T-V	Absence of moral scruples (2.80, 1.33)
T-III	Desire to change things for the better through hard work (4.53, 0.84)		
III. Motives			
M-II	Enjoyable work (4.76, 1.05)	M-VI	Deontic motive (3.39, 1.72)
M-I	Self-actualization (4.714 , 1.031)	M-V	Affiliation motive (3.40, 1.06)
M-III	Desire for autonomy and power (4.67, 0.86)		
IV. Background			
B-I	Personal interests and choices (4.857, 0.624)	B-III	Prior work experience (3.50, 0.81)
		B-IV	Accomplishments prior to start-up (3.50, 0.97)

Note: Figures in brackets are means and standard deviations in that order.

(1) organic growth, (2) image and sales through quality, (3) capability development, and (4) managing risks through professionalization. These are, therefore, policies that all entrepreneurs follow to ensure the survival of their enterprises. The only low-scoring factor in this group is social orientation, which implies that this is not a policy followed by all entrepreneurs. It may be noted that the variance on this factor is slightly higher, indicating that enterprises differ more on this factor than on others. Moreover, the *t*-tests discussed in Chapter 3 also showed that on the

dimension of social orientation the difference between the high-growth and low-growth ventures was statistically significant.

The high- and low-scorers among the 'trait' factors indicate that the entrepreneurial individual has a desire to change things for the better, toward which he/she would take up difficult and challenging tasks and accomplish them through hard work, especially using persuasive skills. In this process, he/she would try to avoid unethical practices. Internal locus of control was theoretically expected to be high but was marginally low. Similarly, conformism was expected to be low but was around 4.00, meaning neither high nor low.

Among the motives, the highest score was for enjoyable work, followed closely by self-actualization, and desire for autonomy and power. Self-actualization, as defined here, contains parts of achievement motive (McClelland, 1961) and Pioneering-Innovative (PI) motive (Khandwalla, 1985). Additionally, it has 'capability development' and 'expressing oneself through work' as two major components. Hence, it is more appropriate to call it self-actualization rather than achievement or PI. In fact, both these variables can be interpreted in terms of their contribution to the individual developing and actualizing himself/herself. Thus, the driving force for an entrepreneur seems to be the desire to actualize oneself through enjoyable work, for which he/she needs power over oneself (which is the autonomy component of power motive) and over others (which is the influence component). As expected, the deontic motive and the affiliation motive were the lowest for entrepreneurs. The status motive with a mean of 4.49 can be classified as a high scorer. With a slightly higher standard deviation, this motive may be a distinguishing motive of the growth-seeker, as we have observed in the previous chapter. Finally, prior theory about affiliation motive being low for entrepreneurs has found support in this study as well.

As for the background variables, two factors stand out: one as a high scorer and the other as a low scorer. Personal interests and choices for the individual seem to be the most dominant one among background factors. Though the second factor, namely, the one on childhood happiness, support, and encouragement, is technically in the 'indifference zone', its mean score of 4.43 is relatively high. This observation is of special importance against the predictions by prior researchers that the entrepreneurial individual has had an unhappy childhood devoid of care, welfare, support, and encouragement. The trends emerging from this study are contrary to the assertions of prior research in this regard. Similarly, the low-scoring factor seems to contradict the hypotheses on the nature of previous work experience. On this factor, a high score indicates experience in related jobs, which also does not seem to be important.

Mean Scores of Distinguishing Factors

The factors discussed in this section are the ones generated from the variables that were significantly different for the high-growth and low-growth groups. These are already included under the 'general factors' discussed in the previous section. The reason for pulling these variables out and identifying the underlying factors is to test whether these factors would better explain the growth phenomenon. These tests, mainly correlation and regression, will be discussed in the next chapter. In this section, we shall just introduce these factors, along with their means and standard deviations (see Table 4.15). The constitution of the factors has already been discussed elsewhere in this chapter. It was observed there that the scores on the distinguishing variables were not necessarily high or low scores in absolute terms and that the differences were to be understood in relative terms. Factor analysis of these variables has yielded six dimensions, on which the present sample of entrepreneurs has relatively high scores. It may be seen from Table 4.15 that four out of the six factors have mean scores higher than 4.50. Besides, from the fact that the standard deviations of these factors are higher than for the general entrepreneurial orientations discussed above, it appears that these will provide better explanations for the difference between high-growth and low-growth ventures.

Table 4.15. Factors of distinguishing variables (along with their means and standard deviations).

Factor no.	Description	Mean	Standard deviation
D-I	Power motive	4.43	0.95
D-II	Pursuit of excellence	4.96	0.88
D-III	Support and encouragement	4.73	1.18
D-IV	Learning motive	4.66	1.34
D-V	Reality orientation	4.60	1.07
D-VI	Decentralization and delegation	4.19	1.62

Concluding Remarks

This chapter was devoted to the identification of the most and least characteristic features of enterprises/entrepreneurs in terms of their policies, traits, motives, and background. The variables were also factor analyzed in their respective groups for identifying the major concerns and orientations underlying these variables. There were 21 such factors, six of policies, five of traits, six of motives, and four of the background. The high scorers and low scorers among these were identified. In addition, factors were generated from the 'distinguishing variables', identified in the previous chapter. These two sets of factors will be separately examined in the next chapter to determine their discriminatory and explanatory powers. The reason for the separate analysis is obvious. From the nature of the scores and the *t*-tests conducted earlier, it appears that a large number of variables are unable to distinguish between high-growth and low-growth ventures. Therefore, it was felt that the factors obtained from the distinguishing variables would do the job better. Since the latter are fewer in number, the explanation would be more parsimonious as well. The next chapter, therefore, will look for explanations for growth behavior separately among the two sets of factors.

Chapter 5

Inter-linkages among Factors and their Association with Enterprise Growth

Chapter 4 was devoted primarily to the identification of the major concerns and orientations of entrepreneurial individuals through factor analyses of the different variable groups. This chapter investigates the inter-relationships among these factors, with a view, hopefully, to providing partial explanations to the phenomenon of enterprise growth. Since the t-tests discussed in Chapter 3 showed that there are but a few variables that are significantly different for the high-growth and low-growth ventures and that, even for these, the confidence level is not very high, we do not expect that the general entrepreneurial orientations can provide any explanation to the phenomenon of enterprise growth. Hence, we extracted another set of factors from the variables that are significantly different for the two groups. This chapter will begin with an analysis of inter-correlations among these two sets of factors separately. Performance variables such as profitability and enterprise growth will be added to these two sets with a view to finding out how these are correlated with the other variables. Since there is no theoretical reason to expect correlations between industry growth and the person-specific or enterprise-specific variables, the former is not included in the correlation analysis.

Inter-correlations among the 21 General Entrepreneurial Factors and the 2 Performance Variables

Of the 253 possible correlations among the 23 variables mentioned above, there are 49 significant ones (at $p \leq 0.05$). This is 19.37% of the total possible number of correlations. The details of the significant correlations can be seen in Table 5.1.

The most striking feature of the correlation matrix is that profitability is correlated neither with any of the general entrepreneurial orientations nor with enterprise growth. Similarly, enterprise growth is also not significantly correlated with any of the variables, except for a negative correlation with variable T-V which is the absence of moral scruples. Though this correlation is statistically significant, it is obviously small. However, one may venture a hypothesis that enterprise growth would partly depend on the long-term image of the enterprise, which in turn, is a function of the entrepreneur's integrity as well. It was rather surprising that growth or profitability was not related to any other features of the entrepreneur, not even the policies. Perhaps, as Eisenhardt and Schoonhoven (1990) have found, enterprise growth is a function of industry growth and nothing else. In that case, a question may be asked why even in a growing industry, only some firms grow and others do not. There is, therefore, some reason to believe that growth is also influenced by some factors which are specific to the enterprise or the entrepreneur. Though we may not identify these factors in this study, it would still be unwise to rule out their existence based on the present findings. In the next section of this chapter, we shall make one more attempt to determine the correlates of enterprise growth using the factors derived from the distinguishing variables.

Before this second exercise in correlation analysis is taken up, we should take a look at the significant correlations among other variables in the first matrix (Table 5.1). Most of these variables are significantly correlated with about four to five other variables. There is thus a case for reducing the factors further by combining a few of these highly correlated factors through another factor analysis of the 21 factors. This will be taken up later.

Table 5.1. Inter-correlation matrix for the 21 factors belonging to four categories, namely, policies, traits, motives, and background and two performance variables, namely, profitability and enterprise growth ($N = 70$).

Factors	Variables	P-I	P-II	P-III	P-IV	P-V	P-VI	T-I	T-II	T-III	T-IV	T-V	M-I	M-II	M-III	M-IV	M-V	M-VI	B-I	B-II	B-III	B-IV	PRF	E.GR
P-I	Social orientation	1.00	–	–	–	–	–	–	.25	–	–	–	–	.35	.25	–	–	–	.23	–	–.25	–	–	–
P-II	Managing risk through professionalism		1.00	–.36***	–.29**	–	–	–	–	–	–.23*	–.34**	–	–	–	–	–	–	–	–	–	–	–	–
P-III	Self-reliance			1.00	.26	–	–	–	–	–	–	–	.22*	–	–	–	–	–	–	–	–	–	–	–
P-IV	Organic growth using one's own knowledge and resources				1.00	–	–	.29**	.20*	–	.22*	–	–	–	–	–	–	–	.20*	–	–	–	–	–
P-V	Image and sales through quality					1.00	–	–.20*	–	–	.24*	–	–	.21*	–	–	.25*	–	–	–.24*	–	–.20*	–	–
P-VI	Capability development						1.00	–	–	–	–	–	–	–	–	–	–	–	–	–	–	–	–	–
T-I	Internet locus of control							1.00	–	–	–	–	–	–	–	–	–	–	.32	–	–	.37	–	–
T-II	Conformism								1.00	–	–	–	–	–	–	–	–	–	–	.24	–	–	–	–
T-III	Desire to improve things through hard work									1.00	–.38***	.32***	–.26*	.23*	–	–	.34***	–	–	–	–	–	–	–
T-IV	Ease with difficult and unstructured situations										1.00	–	–.21*	–	–	–	–	–	–	–	–	–	–	–
T-V	Absence of moral scruples											1.00	–.24*	–	–	–	–	–	–	–	–	–	–	–.21
M-I	Self-actualization												1.00	.38***	.45***	.31**	–	–	–	–	–	–	–	–
M-II	Enjoyable/interesting work													1.00	.25*	.38***	–	–	–	.24*	–	.32***	–	–
M-III	Desire for autonomy and power														1.00	.45***	.28*	–	–	–	–	–	–	–
M-IV	Status motive															1.00	.28*	–	–	.24*	–	.29**	–	–
M-V	Affiliation motive																1.00	–	–	.55***	–	–	–	–
M-VI	Deontic motive																	1.00	–	–	–	–	–	–
B-I	Personal interests and choices																		1.00	–	.33***	–	–	–
B-II	Support and encouragement																			1.00	.33***	–	–	–
B-III	Previous work experience																				1.00	–	–	–
B-IV	Accomplishments prior to start-up																					1.00	–	–
PRF	Profitability																						1.00	–
E.GR	Enterprise growth																							1.00

Notes: '–' indicates a correlation not significant at $p \leq 0.05$; '*' indicates a correlation significant at $p \leq 0.05$; '**' indicates a correlation significant at $p \leq 0.01$; '***' indicates a correlation significant at $p \leq 0.005$.

Inter-correlations among the 6 Distinguishing Factors and the 2 Performance Variables

Among these eight variables, there are 28 possible correlations. Seven out of twenty-eight, which is 25%, have turned out to be significant at $p \leq 0.05$ (see Table 5.2). Profitability is associated with the desire for power and status, with a low but significant correlation. The correlation between power and profits is rather low, possibly because there are various other ways by which an individual can acquire power and status.

Enterprise growth is significantly correlated with two factors. They are 'reality contact' and 'decentralization and delegation'. It may be noted that both these are policy variables, indicating that there may be some substance in the author's hypothesis that entrepreneurial performance would be a function more of the enterprise policies than of the entrepreneur's traits, motives, and background. It was the same hypothesis that prompted the previous study as well (Manimala, 1988a, 1999). However, there are some differences between the two studies. For example, the performance variables chosen for investigation were different for the two studies. For this study, it is the growth of the enterprise, whereas for the previous one, it was innovativeness. Similarly, the previous study did not investigate the role of traits, motives, and background of entrepreneurs in determining the innovativeness of their enterprises, whereas in this study,

Table 5.2.   Inter-correlation matrix for the six 'distinguishing factors' and two performance variables, namely, profitability and enterprise growth ($N = 75$).

Factors/variables	D-I	D-II	D-III	D-IV	D-V	D-VI	PRF	E.GR
D-I Desire for power and status	1.00	.21*	–	–	–	–	–	–
D-II Pursuit of excellence		1.00	.26*	–	.20*	–	–	–
D-III Support and encouragement			1.00	–	–	–	–	–
D-IV Desire to learn from, and deal with new situations				1.00	–	–	–	.13
D-V Reality contact					1.00	.21*	–	.20*
D-VI Decentralization and delegation						1.00	–	.21*
Profitability (PRF)							1.00	
Enterprise growth (E.GR)								1.00

Notes: '–' indicates a correlation not significant at $p \leq 0.05$; '*' indicates a correlation significant at $p \leq 0.05$.

we have data on these aspects as well. So, the previous study could not say anything about the relationship between enterprise innovativeness and the traits, motives, and the background of the entrepreneur, even though it found that some policies of the enterprise were associated with its innovativeness. The study on enterprise growth was a little more ambitious in the sense that we wanted also to examine the role of traits, motives, and background of the entrepreneur in promoting enterprise growth. However, as we have seen in Chapter 3, very few of these variables turned out to be significant in the *t*-test.

Moreover, when these trait-motive-background variables, along with the significant policy variables, were subjected to factor analysis to yield six factors, it is only two of the factors, both of which are policy factors, that turned out to be significantly associated with enterprise growth. The correlations are not high enough to indicate that our initial hypothesis is strongly supported. A variation of this hypothesis, which, however, is not a direct inference from this or the previous study by the author, could be that the background, traits, and motives may have an influence on the start-up of the venture, but after that it is the policies of the enterprise that would determine the venture's success, innovativeness, or growth. Though this study may not be capable of examining the validity or otherwise of the above hypothesis, it is possible that some of these variables may have undergone changes during the period from the start-up period to later periods. As we have collected data with reference to the two time periods, it should be possible for us to compare these through *t*-tests. This will be discussed in a subsequent section of this chapter.

A word about the two significant correlations with enterprise growth is in order. One is with 'decentralization and delegation' and the other with what we called 'reality contact'. These two refer to the way the entrepreneur/enterprise goes about doing the business and does not seem to have much to do with the background, traits, and motives of the entrepreneur. Growth, apparently, is the result of systematically collecting information, testing the market stage-by-stage, and initiating responsive actions. Once the enterprise grows, there is an increasing need for decentralization and delegation, as it is impossible for a single individual to monitor and manage the large number of activities involved in a growing organization. While this seems to be a plausible causal hypothesis, influences in the opposite directions cannot be ruled out — that growth has caused a change in the policies (rather than policies causing growth). After all, a correlation signifies only an association, without saying anything about the direction of such association. There is, however, a provision in the design of this study for determining the causal direction, if any. Enterprise growth can be regressed on the start-up policies with respect to decentralization, delegation, information gathering, and test marketing. If this regression analysis shows significant associations, it would imply that the policies have caused enterprise growth, since the policies have temporally preceded growth. Before taking up such an analysis, it is advisable to check whether there are significant differences between start-up characteristics and later characteristics of the enterprise/entrepreneur. These two aspects will be discussed later in this chapter.

The four other significant correlations are between: (a) power motive and the pursuit of excellence, (b) support and encouragement and the pursuit of excellence, (c) reality contact and the pursuit of excellence, and (d) reality contact and decentralization/delegation. Barring the last one, all the others involve the factor relating to the pursuit of excellence. It seems that the pursuit of excellence is caused by a desire for power and status, support and encouragement received by the entrepreneur during childhood and during the start-up, and the policies of collecting information and pre-testing one's actions. While this causal relationship is also a hypothesis, the causal role of one of these variables can be affirmed with greater confidence. It is that of 'support and encouragement'. This group of variables have been measured with reference to earlier time periods, namely, those of childhood and of the start-up period. So, it is legitimate for us to presume that this group of variables would exert a causal influence on the pursuit of excellence.

The Combined Entrepreneurial Factors (CEF)

The correlation analysis of the 21 factors derived from the four groups of variables showed that the inter-correlations among these were fairly high. Hence it was proposed that a further factor analysis of these may be useful. The attempt here was to break the conceptual segregations made in terms of background, trait, motive, and policy variables. It is hoped that, in this way, we may arrive at what may be called the 'combined entrepreneurial factors' (CEF). Eight such factors emerged in the factor analysis, which are presented in Table 5.3. A brief description on each of these factors follows:

Table 5.3. Combined entrepreneurial factors (CEF) derived using factor analysis of the 21 dimensions identified from the four variable groups ($N = 84$).

CEF no	Variable no	Description	Loading	CEF name given
CEF-I	T-III	Desire to improve things through hard work	0.50	Autonomous and interesting work for improvements
	M-I	Self-actualization	0.66	
	M-II	Enjoyable work	0.69	
	M-III	Desire for autonomy and power	0.70	
	M-IV	Status motive	0.67	
	B-IV	Accomplishments before start-up	0.46	
CEF-II	T-II	Conformism	0.63	Affiliation motive
	T-IV	Ease of dealing with difficult and unstructured situations	−0.52	
	M-V	Affiliation motive	0.74	
	B-II	Support and encouragement	0.75	
CEF-III	P-II	Managing risks through professionalization	−0.57	Self-reliance
	P-III	Self-reliance	0.77	
	P-IV	Organic growth using one's own knowledge and resources	0.56	
	P-VI	Capability development	0.56	
CEF-IV	P-I	Social orientation	−0.77	Self-orientation
	B-III	Previous work (job and family) experience	0.75	
CEF-V	T-I	Internal locus of control	0.64	Internal locus of control
	B-I	Personal interests and choices	0.78	
CEF-VI	T-V	Absence of moral scruples	−0.83	Ethical orientation
CEF-VII	P-V	Image and sales through quality	0.84	Quality orientation
CEF-VIII	M-VI	Deontic motive	0.89	Deontic motive

CEF-I: Autonomous and Interesting Work: The first combined factor is constituted by six prior factors, of which four are motive factors and one each from the trait and background factors. The trait factor is the desire to improve things through hard work, which may have been supported by the background of prior accomplishments (before start-up); and the motive factors are those of self-actualization, enjoyable work, desire for autonomy and power, and the status motive. The overall content of this factor may be designated as 'Autonomous and Interesting Work' for bringing about continuous improvements.

CEF-II: Affiliation Motive: The second combined factor is clearly the need for affiliation. There are three positively loaded factors and one negatively loaded factor in this combined factor. The starting point of the affiliation motive can be inferred as the love, care, support, and encouragement received by the individual especially during the childhood. This is probably why the factor of support and encouragement got included here with a relatively high loading of 0.75, which is a slightly higher loading than the 0.74 of the old factor of Affiliation Motive. The factor of conformism indicates that people with a high need for affiliation would conform to the norms of the society so that they would be accepted by the society and thus can belong to it. One of the benefits of affiliation to a group is that the group would structure many situations for the individual and would assist the individual in the performance of difficult tasks. It, therefore, implies that those who are comfortable with difficult tasks and unstructured situations may feel a lower need for affiliation. It may be for this reason that this factor has a negative loading on this combined factor. CEF-II, comprising four old factors — namely, Affiliation Motive, Support and encouragement from others, and Conformism with positive loadings, and Ease of dealing with difficult tasks and unstructured situations, with a negative loading — can be designated as Affiliation Motive.

CEF-III: Self-reliance: This combined factor relates mainly to the self-reliance for the management of one's enterprise. This is why seeking professional help has got a negative loading on it. There are three other factors on it, all of which have positive loadings. These are self-reliance with respect to ideas, technology and know-how, organic growth using one's own knowledge and resources, and the development of one's own skills and capabilities. This combined factor seems to represent a craftsman's attitude of generating one's own business ideas based on one's own expertise, and using one's own resources and with very limited professional help from outside. Most start-ups are likely to be in a craftsman style because that would give the entrepreneur the much-needed confidence in his/her venture. Besides, the scarcity of resources and the lack of reputation during the initial stages would make it difficult for the entrepreneur to attract outside talents and resources. It is only at a later stage, when the organization grows, that professional help and outside financial resources, namely, borrowed funds and investment partnerships, are sought for and accepted. One of the reasons for the 'growth unwillingness' of entrepreneurs (discussed in Chapter 1), which is also shown by the statistics that more than 90% of new ventures remain small long after their start-up, may be this inclination for self-reliance and the consequent refusal to accept external resources.

CEF-IV: Self-orientation: The high negative loading (−0.77) of social orientation on this combined factor suggests that this factor may be on self-orientation. However, the second prior factor, which has high positive loading (+0.75) on this combined factor, is not very clear in this regard. This prior factor had the variables of ancestral family's affluence and the nature of one's prior employment. One may have to probably strain an interpretation that those who are affluent or those who take up employment are generally more concerned with their own welfare than that of others.

CEF-V: Internal Locus of Control: The bearing of this factor is clearly that of internal locus of control. The two prior factors that have got loaded on to this (Internal locus of control, and Personal interests and choices) are on the aspects of self-direction and of assuming responsibility for one's own actions and choices.

CEF-VI: Ethical Orientation: This as well as the subsequent two combined factors have only one prior factor each loaded on to them. The present one had two variables in its prior factor, both relating to unethical practices: one on breaking promises and the other on ends justifying the means. A low score, therefore, on the combined factor would indicate high levels of ethical orientation. This prior factor (Absence of scruples) is loaded here with a very high negative loading of −0.83, and hence the new factor may be called 'Ethical Orientation'.

CEF-VII: Quality Orientation: Like CEF-VI, this factor ("Image and sales through quality", with a positive loading of +0.84) also had two variables on its prior factor: one relating to the building of image through quality and the other, a negatively loaded variable on aggressive marketing, implying that there is no need of aggressive marketing if one is careful about maintaining the quality of one's products and services. The overall burden of this factor, therefore, is that quality is probably a 'double-edged sword'. It helps the enterprise in improving its sales as well as image, most probably with a reversal of the sequence; the strict adherence to quality would enhance the image of the company's products and services, which in turn would increase the sales.

CEF-VIII: Deontic Motive: This is a single-variable factor whose content and relevance have been explained in the previous chapter. Entrepreneurs are low on this motive, for obvious reasons. It may, however, be useful in studies comparing entrepreneurs and non-entrepreneurs, or in studies comparing different types of entrepreneurs in different cultures. The relevance of this motive for the philanthropic work of the British entrepreneur, Dame Stephanie Shirley, is clearly seen in her statement: "I do it because of my personal history; I need to justify the fact that my life was saved" (see Appendix-1).

Changes in Traits, Motives, and Policies

An important issue that we proposed to examine was whether the traits and motives of the entrepreneur and/or the policies of the enterprise changed over time. One prevalent hypothesis is that traits and motives are relatively stable but policies would change depending on the exigencies of the business. Though our analysis has shown that this hypothesis is largely true, it has also shown that there are a few traits and motives which change with entrepreneurial activity. The changes are identified through *t*-tests and are presented in Tables 5.4 to 5.6. A brief analysis of these changes is presented as follows.

(a) Changes in Traits

As may be seen from Table 5.4, there are ten variables that have changed over time. Of these, the changes in seven variables are significant at $p \leq 0.05$. The remaining three are significant at $p \leq 0.10$. All the changes,

Table 5.4.   Changes in personality traits over time: *t*-values of traits that are significantly different over two time periods (D.F. = 89).

Trait no.	Description	Start-up mean	Later mean	*t*	P	Remarks
T-2	Confidence about one's management style and aversion to experimentation	3.88	3.39	−3.45	0.001	Decreases
T-3	Sticking to a few tried and tested solutions and not wasting time on generating new ideas.	3.62	3.31	−1.89	0.062	Decreases
T-7	External attribution of failures	3.03	2.87	−2.24	0.028	Decreases
T-12	Feeling that the workload is a little too much	2.39	2.58	1.71	0.091	Increases
T-13	Gambling instinct	4.48	1.09	−3.24	0.002	Decreases
T-14	Preference to use authority than persuasion	3.32	3.02	−3.28	0.001	Decreases
T-15	Aversion to taking instructions	4.88	4.76	−1.74	0.086	Decreases
T-17	Avoidance of failure situations	3.71	3.90	1.94	0.055	Increases
T-19	Complacency about one's knowledge	2.32	2.13	−1.94	0.055	Decreases
T-25	Doing it oneself and not taking help and support from others	3.36	3.08	−2.78	0.007	Decreases

except two, are decreases from the previous (start-up) level. The two variables that showed increases from the previous level are the tendency to avoid failure situations and the feeling that the workload is a little too much. This is supported by the substantial decreases in the gambling instinct and in the external attribution of failures. Another set of variables that apparently go together with the reduction in the gambling instinct and the external attribution of failures is a reduction in complacency about one's knowledge and skills. In addition to the statement specifically referring to this aspect, there are two other statements which show the same direction. One of them is on the confidence about one's management style and the consequent aversion to experimentation, and the other is on the preference to exercise authority rather than persuasion. Both are decreasing. Finally, there is a decrease in the tendency to do everything oneself. All these changes are consistent with the theory that entrepreneurs are generally more optimistic at the time of start-up (Baron & Shane, 2005), which gradually changes into a more realistic attitude later. Almost all the changes in entrepreneurial traits observed above are indicative of this movement from 'over-optimism' to realism.

The effect of entrepreneurial experience on personality traits as observed in this study, whether in a growing company or otherwise, is mainly about three areas: namely, the areas of risk-taking behavior, attitude toward learning, and the involvement of others in the business. The change in the risk-taking behavior is to be expected. It is but natural that there is a greater need for taking risks during the start-up than later when the firm is well established. The ambivalent results on the risk-taking behavior of entrepreneurs in prior studies could be partly explained by this finding. Since most of the studies on entrepreneurial characteristics have the existing entrepreneurs as subjects, the findings may not be a true representation of their behavior during the start-up period. Hence in this study, we added a section for rating the variables as experienced during the start-up period, which has brought out the possibilities of change in entrepreneurial traits, motives, and policies.

Complacency or over-confidence about one's knowledge and style is another trait that changes with entrepreneurial experience. It appears that the self-confidence and optimism of entrepreneurs are higher during start-up than later. As they grapple with the complexities and uncertainties of entrepreneurial life, their confidence is shaken a little bit and they realize the inadequacies of their own knowledge, skills, and styles. While this explanation sounds logical, a common-sense line of argument is that experience would increase the confidence and optimism. Research studies, however, have failed to support this line of argument. For example, a large-sample study of 2,994 entrepreneurs by Cooper *et al.* (1986) showed that there is substantial decline in the entrepreneur's confidence and optimism in comparison to the start-up period. Similar findings were reported by Baron and Shane (2005), cited above. One of the consequences of this would be the increasing tendency to seek help and support from others rather than follow the do-it-oneself policy.

(b) Changes in Motives

Motives are apparently more stable than traits and policies. Though there are six out of twenty motives showing changes that are significant at $p \leq 0.10$, only three of them are significantly different at $p \leq 0.05$ (see Table 5.5). Of the latter three, the money motive is the only one to have decreased. Established entrepreneurs, whether growing or otherwise, can

Table 5.5. Changes in motives over time: *t*-values of traits that are significantly different over two time periods (D.F. = 89).

Motive no.	Description	Start-up mean	Later mean	*t*	P	Remarks
M-1	Money motive	4.69	4.37	−2.41	0.018	Decreases
M-6	Desire for top position	4.87	4.71	−1.74	0.085	Decreases
M-15	Desire for independence	5.27	5.62	3.42	0.001	Increases
M-16	Desire for involvement in decisions affecting oneself and one's enterprise	4.99	5.32	3.18	0.002	Increases
M-18	Desire for variety in tasks	4.93	5.11	1.79	0.077	Increases
M-19	Desire to contribute to the society	4.76	4.93	1.89	0.063	Increases

be presumed to be making enough profits to satisfy their financial needs. Hence, getting more money may not be a motivator for them. This is in accordance with Maslow's theory. However, the two motives whose strength has increased merit special attention. These two motives are related to each other, one of them being the desire for independence, and the other the desire to be in control of oneself by being a party to the decisions affecting oneself or one's enterprise.

The peculiarity of these motives seems to be that they are not satiable in the sense that the money motive is. The more you exercise your independence, the more you want to remain so. Similarly, a person who has been in control of his/her own destiny would not like to abdicate his autonomy. These are, therefore, motives that cannot be 'satisfied' in the strict sense and may not be covered by the general dictum that a satisfied need will not be a motivator. The three other motives mentioned in Table 5.5, which are significant at $p \leq 0.10$, also illustrate this point. Desire for variety in tasks is increasing, probably because of the boredom of having to perform repetitive tasks while carrying out the regular business. So too, there is an increase in the desire to contribute to the society, which would also sound logical, as entrepreneurs at the start-up stage may not have the time or resources to spend on societal concerns. On the other hand, the desire for a top position is decreasing. It may be because the entrepreneur has been at the top of his/her organization for few years, and hence the desire to be on top is no longer a motivator. Apparently, this is a motive that gets satiated, unlike the former two. One important point that emerges from the findings under this section on changes in motives over time is that there may be a need for classifying human motives into satiable and non-satiable, similar to the well-known classification of motives by Herzberg *et al.* (1959) into motivators and hygiene factors. It appears that among the human motives, some are satiable and others are not. One plausible hypothesis is that what used to be classified as primary motives are satiable but may recur periodically, whereas the secondary motives would become stronger with the efforts to satisfy them.

There is also a likelihood that the importance, relevance, and strength of secondary motives can vary with individuals, groups, and professions. For independence and the control over one's own affairs, which have emerged as non-satiable motives in this study, there may be different outcomes for other groups. These hypotheses are worth investigating, especially because the most appropriate motivator for any individual would be the one that grows in greater strength with the efforts to satisfy it. The reason why financial and other such incentives fail on repeated administration is not far to seek. Against such a context, it is heartening to note that there might be some motives which would not become irrelevant and weak in the process of satisfying them.

(c) Changes in Policies

As expected, it was in policies that we found the largest number of changes (see Table 5.6). Twenty out of the 33 policies have changed. Traits and motives are apparently more stable than policies. The mere continuance in business itself seems to warrant some changes in policies, implying that a few policies that were appropriate during the start-up would not be found useful later. Such changes in policies are more necessary for high-growth ventures, as the growing organization would change its features and therefore require new policies to support the new features.

Among the policy variables that have undergone changes, one can identify two major groups: one is a reduction in the 'low-cost/low-price orientation' and the other is an increase in professionalism. A strategy of low price $(P - 25)$ may be useful initially for gaining entry into the market, but will not be sustainable in the long run without compromising on profits or quality. In a similar way, there is very little scope for enterprises to continue to work on improvised facilities or sub-contract arrangements for their infrastructure, even though these are very useful strategies for minimizing investments especially when the projects are at the testing stage. For the same reason, the strategy of organic growth will be more

Table 5.6.   Start-up and later policies of enterprises: *t*-values and other details of policies significantly different at $p \le .10$ (D.F. = 89).

Policy no.	Description	Start-up mean	Later mean	*t*	P	Remarks
P – 2	Preference to develop own ideas rather than to borrow them from others	5.04	5.30	1.72	0.090	Increases
P – 3	Lack of special efforts for developing new ideas	2.71	2.29	–2.77	0.007	Decreases
P – 5	Continuous search for ideas	5.73	6.11	3.00	0.004	Increases
P – 7	Recruiting talented people	5.91	6.18	3.32	0.001	Increases
P – 10	Technical collaboration with others	3.24	3.48	1.79	0.077	Increases
P – 16	Use of professional systems & procedures	4.03	4.58	4.86	0.000	Increases
P – 18	Test-marketing	3.74	4.11	2.78	0.007	Increases
P – 19	Spreading of risks	4.89	5.43	3.57	0.001	Increases
P – 20	Decentralization & delegation	3.84	4.20	2.61	0.011	Increases
P – 21	Collecting systematic information	4.16	4.41	2.40	0.019	Increases
P – 23	Rewarding employees for loyalty than for performance	3.48	3.27	–2.47	0.018	Decreases
P – 25	Low-price strategy	2.64	2.42	–1.99	0.049	Decreases
P – 26	Industry and professional associations	3.68	4.16	3.26	0.002	Increases
P – 27	Seeking support primarily from friends and relatives	3.34	3.04	–2.13	0.036	Decreases
P – 28	Sponsoring public interest activities	2.79	2.98	2.00	0.049	Increases
P – 29	Reliance on one's judgment rather than on professional analysis for decision-making	5.13	4.88	–1.94	0.056	Decreases
P – 30	Restricted sharing of monetary gains	4.01	3.56	–3.81	0.000	Decreases
P – 31	Restricted sharing of information	3.91	3.31	–3.94	0.000	Decreases
P – 32	Minimizing investments through sub-contracting, improvisation, etc.	4.04	3.66	–2.71	0.008	Decreases
P – 33	Start small and grow big organically using internal resources	5.68	5.31	–2.69	0.009	Decreases

useful during the start-up phase than later. Once the organization has built up its capabilities for supporting and servicing external resources, the policy of relying entirely on internal resources may not help the enterprise to realize its full potential at a pace fast enough to compete and survive in the field. Hence there is an increasing tendency for seeking and securing external resources, which may take the form of financial as well as technical collaborations.

The second group of policy variables that have changed over time indicates a movement toward greater degrees of professionalism. This is but a logical consequence of the changes of the other kind discussed above. When the enterprise decides to get out of the mode of 'self-contained' and rather sub-optimal operations based on the principle of minimizing resources, there is hardly any alternative to the professionalization of management. Search for ideas and collection of information for decision-making will be more and more systematized, and talented professionals will be recruited for managing these and other related operations. There will be a greater emphasis on performance rather than loyalty in matters relating to employee rewards and remuneration. Similarly, there will be a change in the decision-making style itself, in the sense that the reliance on hunches and gut feelings will be reduced in favor of greater use of inputs, resources, data, and analysis from people other than the entrepreneur himself/herself. Extending this logic, therefore, the entrepreneur has also to share information and business gains with these constituencies. Naturally, there is a decrease in the restrictiveness shown by entrepreneurs vis-à-vis sharing of information and gains.

Two other changes in policies are also worth mentioning. One is the increasing tendency toward spreading risks. Apparently, the adage, "Don't put all your eggs in one basket", is more applicable to the later stages of enterprise growth rather than the start-up period. In this context, a distinction made by an entrepreneur sounds interesting. He said that the proverb quoted above was a merchant's rule of thumb, whereas an entrepreneur at the time of start-up should follow the opposite policy, which is similar to what is being followed by a hen. The hen will not put her eggs in different baskets but will put them all in one basket and concentrate her energy on them so that they all would hatch. It, therefore, makes sense that at the start-up stage, the entrepreneur should be concerned with risk management rather than risk-spreading. The latter strategy is more appropriate at a later stage when the enterprise is more or less on its own and so the entrepreneur could afford to turn his/her attention to other matters as well. Similar is the case of entrepreneurs getting involved in public interest activities. This policy has shown an increase in strength indicating that image-building exercises such as this would be more appropriate only after the enterprise has established itself.

A word about the policies that have not changed over time is also in order. Some of these are as follows: the preference for innovative products; choosing the course of action based on goals rather than opportunities; acquiring and developing the knowledge relevant to one's business; choosing partners for their special capabilities rather than for the money; sub-contracting of work; minimizing borrowed funds; avoiding competition by the appropriate choice of product-market mix; launching units in areas related to one's previous experience; attitude toward product quality, advertisement, and publicity; attitude toward experimentation, innovation, supervision, and control; preference for aggressive marketing; and so on. These may be considered the more stable kinds of policies, which may be determined more by the preferences of the entrepreneur than by the stages in the enterprise's developments over time.

Explanatory and Discriminatory Powers

One of the most important uses of the analysis of inter-relationships among variables is to see whether the phenomenon under observation can be explained and/or predicted by any other variables. The literature on enterprise growth had suggested that the entrepreneur's characteristics and/or certain policies followed by the enterprise may determine enterprise growth. Accordingly, we have performed a regression analysis of enterprise growth on the distinguishing factors and on industry growth and enterprise profitability. There was no reason for high expectations on the output of the regression analysis, because of the low correlations among the factors, as we have observed in the early part of this chapter. In fact, among the 21 general entrepreneurial factors, there was only one factor which had a significant correlation with enterprise growth. This was a negative correlation with the absence of moral scruples. In any case, as the correlations in this group of variables were low and non-significant, there was no need to do regression on these.

The next option was to regress enterprise growth on the distinguishing factors, with which the correlations were better but not high enough for expecting any significant output from the regression. Needless to say, the results were non-significant, and the percentage explained was negligible. In this regression, we had used the 'later-period scores' for the distinguishing factors. Though the R-square was 0.105, the adjusted R-square was negative (−.003) and negligible. F-statistic also was very low (.97) and was not significant. The present combination of variables, therefore, provided hardly any explanation to enterprise growth. It was rather surprising that even industry growth which was found in some studies as a major determinant of enterprise growth did not provide much explanation. Its beta-value was 0.16, for which the *t*-value (1.24) was significant only at $p \leq 0.22$. One reason for this low power of explanation even for industry growth could be that industry growth may be a necessary condition but not a sufficient condition for enterprise growth. It may be true that sustained growth of enterprises can be achieved only in a growing industry, but all enterprises in a growing industry need not be growing as well. Apparently, the other components of this 'package of determinants' are yet to be identified.

Since we have found in an earlier analysis that venture characteristics, especially policies, do change over a period of time, it was interesting to check whether the start-up period scores would make a difference in the variables' power of explaining enterprise growth. This analysis has also got a methodological justification, as we have explained in Chapter 2. The time gap between these variables and the growth variable would enable us to make causal hypotheses, if the regression was to be found significant. It was with this possibility in view that we performed a second regression analysis using the start-up period scores. The result, however, was not significant. The significance levels were even lower than in the analysis using the 'later-period scores'. Thus, the present data are shown to be insufficient for identifying the causes of enterprise growth. All that we have identified in the previous chapters is the association of certain policies of the venture or characteristics of entrepreneurs, with high-growth ventures.

We have also made an attempt to see if the relationships in the reverse direction are stronger, by regressing the distinguishing factors on enterprise growth. The results were somewhat better with adjusted R-square improving up to 7%. This highest value was obtained for the regression of 'pursuit of excellence'. R-square was 0.17 and adjusted R-square was 0.07 with an F-statistic of 1.26 significant at $p \leq 0.13$. The better values of this regression are not due to the variable of industry growth, whose beta-value is low (0.03) and non-significant. The two beta-values that are significant at $p \leq 0.05$ are those of factor 3 (support and encouragement) and factor 1 (desire for position, status, and power), implying that pursuit of excellence is significantly associated with support and encouragement during childhood and start-up and with the need for power. Since support and encouragement relate to an earlier period, they can be inferred as a cause of the pursuit of excellence. The reverse analysis, however, has not been able to settle the issue of enterprise growth causing the other characteristics.

Concluding Remarks

Given the kinds of correlations among the relevant variables, it was not surprising that the regressions were non-significant. However, in the light of prior research and theory, there has to be some explanation for the growth phenomenon using the variables we had studied. The reasons for the low correlations could probably be due to the kind of measurement of the variables. For example, growth was measured by us using a combined index. Though this is perfectly logical and is capable of being a better measure in certain cases, the combination can produce an 'averaging effect' and may affect the correlations. Distortions may also have crept in because we have used subjective measures for profitability and industry growth. In the proposed cross-cultural analysis using part of the present data, it is possible to segregate the different indices of growth and do separate analysis for each. Similarly, in future analyses, it is not difficult to get/ compute objective data on industry growth and/or profitability. These options will have to be looked into in subsequent analyses/studies.

An implication for further analysis in this study has also to be noted. Since the correlations were generally low, and the regressions not significant, we have dropped a few other regressions which were mentioned in the Methodology chapter as other possible ways of analyzing the data. Similarly, it is evident that discriminant analysis also will not produce any significant results. Besides, as we have observed above, the sample had more of similarities than differences among its constituents, and so the relevance of cluster analysis is also doubtful. For these reasons, we have decided not to proceed with further analysis of the present data. The next chapter therefore will be the concluding chapter, which would provide an overview of the findings, and an assessment of the contributions of the present research along with its implications and limitations, and would indicate the directions for further research in this area.

Chapter 6

Conclusion

The findings of this study on growth venture policies and their relationships with the characteristics of the founders of these ventures can be classified into two categories, namely, those pertaining to entrepreneurs in general and those pertaining to growth ventures in particular. Though the primary objective of the study was to look at growth ventures in terms of their policies and founder characteristics, an incidental outcome was a few insights on the policies and characteristics of entrepreneurs in general. Since the latter was 'incidental', these results have not been contrasted with the characteristics of non-entrepreneurs, and to that extent, such findings will have to be taken as tentative and are more useful as hypotheses for further research than as proven conclusions. This final chapter, therefore, will discuss the findings of this study, assess its contributions to entrepreneurship theory and practice, discuss its limitations, and indicate directions for future research.

Summary of Findings

As we have noted above, the findings of this study can be grouped into two main categories: one relating to growth ventures and the other to entrepreneurship in general. These two are briefly summarized as follows.

Growth Venture Characteristics

A major part of this study was devoted to the comparative analysis of the characteristics of high-growth and low-growth entrepreneurs.

Moreover, we have also explored the linkages between enterprise growth and other firm-level and industry-level variables such as the firm profitability and the industry growth. The findings of these analyses are summarized as follows.

Profitability, industry growth, and enterprise growth

In order to test the hypothesis that growth does not necessarily follow from profitability, the correlation coefficient was computed between profitability and enterprise growth, which was found to be low (0.058) and non-significant. Thus, it may not be unlikely to have highly profitable but stagnating enterprises. This finding may be treated as providing partial support to the hypothesis of 'growth unwillingness' on the part of some entrepreneurs. A second hypothesis which we wanted to test was that enterprise growth is largely a function of industry growth. The correlation (0.221, significant at $p < 0.03$) is not high enough to suggest that industry growth is the only or even the major determinant of enterprise growth. However, since the correlation is statistically significant, it should be inferred that there is a definite relationship between industry growth and enterprise growth. A plausible hypothesis would be that enterprises would find it difficult to sustain their growth unless the concerned industry is also growing. However, even in a growing industry, it is not necessary that all enterprises would be experiencing growth.

Growth venture policies

There were only three policies that were significantly different (at $p \leq 0.10$) for the low-growth and high-growth ventures. They were (a) involvement in public interest activities, (b) quality orientation, and (c) decentralization and delegation. The three anchors of growth seem to be in the product, the organization, and the society. On these vital orientations, the growth-seeker is significantly stronger than the ordinary entrepreneur.

Distinguishing personality traits

Among the personality traits, there were four, which were significantly different (at $p \leq 0.10$) for the two groups. They were (a) a desire to be the best in one's field, (b) a preference for using persuasive power rather than authority, (c) continuous search for new ideas and alternatives, and (d) adherence to one's promises. This is indicative of an orientation to excel, supported by the search for new ideas, political skills, and ethical orientation. The growth-seeker is one who would pursue excellence in an ethical manner, through novel ideas and persuasive skills.

Distinguishing motives

The four motive variables which were shown to be different for the high- and low-growth entrepreneurs can be grouped under two categories. One of them relates to the nature of work. The growth-seeker is more particular that he/she should be doing tasks which are interesting and enjoyable. The second motive is the desire for power, which includes the desire to have position, status, and power. Apparently, the growth-seeker tries to secure position, power, and status through the performance of interesting and enjoyable tasks involved in his/her venture.

Distinguishing features of the background

Very few of the background variables were significantly different for high-growth and low-growth ventures. Growth-seekers come from better edu-cated ancestral families and receive better support and encouragement from friends, relatives, and institutions. Apparently, the latter (better support and encouragement) can be better explained by the higher levels of the growth-seeker's political skills rather than by the objective realities of the situation. This is especially true of the institutions, as both the groups are drawn from the same region and so would be rating the same/similar institutions.

The distinguishing factors

The variables which were found to be significantly different for the two groups were subjected to factor analysis with a view to finding out the fac-tors that might distinguish between the high-growth and low-growth groups. There were six factors that emerged from this analysis, which were:

- desire for position, status, and power,
- pursuit of excellence,
- support and encouragement from others,

- desire to learn,
- reality contract, and
- decentralization and delegation.

Enterprise growth is apparently a means to secure status, power, and position through a pursuit of excellence nourished by a constant desire to learn based on the collection of real-life data and information, with the support of people/institutions within and outside the enterprise.

Explanatory and discriminatory powers

Though the above factors emerged from the variables that had significantly different *t*-values for the two groups, their power to explain the growth behavior and discriminate between the high-growth and low-growth ventures was relatively low. F-statistic of the regression was not significant at 95% confidence level. The *t*-values of the beta-coefficients were also not significant. The percentage explained (R-square) was just 8%. Adjusted R-square was negative and negligible. It seems that the explanation for enterprise growth will have to be sought in some other factors as well. Presumably, the factors identified in this study will support enterprise growth only in combination with a few other factors, which were not investigated by this study. The latter may relate to the socio-economic conditions, product-market choices, and the growth stage of the industry. Since the correlations of these variables with enterprise growth were low and the regressions were not significant, other analyses such as discriminant analysis and path analysis were not performed.

General Entrepreneurial Characteristics

An analysis of the mean scores of variables has revealed the characteristics of entrepreneurs in general. These were, however, based on high and low scores alone, and not on a comparison with a control group consisting of respondents from non-entrepreneurial professions. The characteristics identified using high and low scores are briefly described as follows.

Characteristic policies

Among the high-scoring policies are the acquisition of knowledge and skills relevant to one's business, being in an area related to one's previous experience, continuous search for and development of new ideas, minimizing borrowed funds, quality orientation, and organic growth relying primarily on internal resources. The low scorers are the low-price policy, choice of partners primarily for capital contribution, image-building primarily through advertisements and publicity, aggressive marketing, and sponsoring of public interest activities. Though the last one was found to be significantly high for the growth-seekers, it seems that entrepreneurs in general do not like to get involved in public interest activities. This may be a function primarily of affordability and the need for creating a public image and so would be more appropriate at the growth stage.

Characteristic traits

Entrepreneurs have a desire to be the best in their fields. They are stimulated by a constant dissatisfaction about the existing state of affairs and the love for accomplishing difficult tasks. They also have a high degree of confidence in their ability to manage their enterprises. In fact, their confidence is substantially higher during the start-up than later, as was revealed in the analysis of changes in policies, traits, and motives. Entrepreneurs are hard-working individuals with relatively high ethical orientation and willingness to take responsibility for their own actions.

Characteristic motives

Entrepreneurs would like to be doing such activities as they can enjoy and in which they can develop and utilize their skills and capabilities. Desire for variety in tasks, achievement of targets and standards, and desire for reputation and recognition, which are also high, may be associated with the desire for doing interesting work. Another strong motive for the entrepreneur, which increases in strength over time, is the desire to be independent and to be involved in decisions affecting oneself. While they would surely appreciate and make use of the support and encouragement from others, this may not be the reason for their being entrepreneurs. It is also unlikely that they would be motivated by a sense of obligation, which is a low-scoring motive for this combined sample.

Characteristic features of the background

Unlike what has been observed by prior researchers, entrepreneurs in the present sample have had happy childhoods characterized by parental care and support from friends and relatives. Very few of them have experienced local displacements or psychological deprivations. Their educational accomplishments are also relatively low, and they are not very particular about religious beliefs and practices. Prior experience of entrepreneurship, either in the family or for themselves, is also rare. Before the start-up of their first ventures, they were successful individuals with deep interests in a variety of activities and have become entrepreneurs through purposeful action rather than being swayed into this career by environmental pressures and/or opportunities. Thus, this study has not found any support for some of the dominant sociological theories about the entrepreneurial background, which attribute entrepreneurship to displacements and deprivations (physical and/or psychological).

Major dimensions of entrepreneurial characteristics

Factor analysis of the four variable groups have shown the major dimensions of these variables, which were discussed in detail in Chapters 4 and 5. The factors are listed as follows in four groups.

1. Dimensions of Policies
   Six factors emerged from the two-stage factor analysis. They were named as follows:
   (i)   Social orientation
   (ii) Risk management through professionalization
   (iii) Self-reliance
   (iv) Organic growth
   (v)   Image and sales through quality, and
   (vi) Capability development
2. Dimensions of Traits
   Trait variables yielded five factors in the two-stage factor analysis. They were named as follows:
   (i)   Internal locus of control
   (ii) Conformism
   (iii) Desire to improve things through hard work
   (iv) Comfort with political processes, and
   (v)   Ethical orientation
3. Dimensions of Motives
   Motive variables got grouped into six fairly well-defined factors in the first stage itself. The contents and the constitution of these factors,

as explained in the text, have suggested the following names for them:
- (i) Self-actualization motive
- (ii) Desire for enjoyable/meaningful work
- (iii) Desire for autonomy and power
- (iv) Status motive
- (v) Affiliation motive, and
- (vi) Deontic motive

4. Dimensions of the Background

Background variables got grouped into four factors in the two-stage factor analysis. These factors were named as follows, as explained in the text:
- (i) Personal interest and choices
- (ii) Childhood welfare and happiness
- (iii) Experience in the family and on the prior jobs, and
- (iv) Accomplishments before start-up

Changes in policies, traits, and motives over time

It was hypothesized that policies are more likely to change than traits and motives. The latter two are considered to be relatively stable attributes of human beings. This hypothesis has been partially supported, as there were statistically significant changes in about 20 out of the 33 policy variables, compared to only ten among the 25 trait variables and six among the 20 motive variables. Another hypothesis that has received support from these findings is that there have to be changes in enterprise policies over time to accommodate the changing needs of the different phases of the new venture. This study has looked at only two time periods, the start-up period and the later period, and the results are summarized as follows:

1. Changes in Policies: Changes in policies were significant at $p \leq 0.10$ with reference to about 20 items. These may be grouped into the following five categories as follows: (a) reduction in the use of low-price strategies, (b) reduction in the use of organic growth strategies, (c) increasing professionalization, (d) increasing tendency toward spreading risks, and (e) increasing involvement in public interest activities. On the other hand, policies relating to quality, innovation, supervision, controls, partnership, etc. are relatively stable.

2. Changes in Personality Traits: Changes in personality traits were far fewer than those in policies. The directions of change can be indicated as follows: (a) greater tendencies to avoid failure situations, (b) reduction in gambling/risk-taking instinct, (c) reduction in complacency and over-confidence, (d) increasing use of persuasion than authority, and (e) increasing willingness for experimentation. The changes, therefore, pertain mainly to the risk-taking behavior, attitude towards learning, and the involvement of others in one's business.

3. Changes in Motives: Motives are perhaps the most stable among the three sets of variables. Changes in only three of them were significant at $p \leq 0.05$. Money motive has decreased, but the need for independence and the desire to be involved in decisions affecting oneself have become stronger. If the confidence level is lowered to 90%, changes in three other motives emerge as significant. Desire for a top position has decreased, but the need for variety in tasks and the desire to contribute to society have become stronger. These changes point to the need for a new classification of motives into *Satiable* and *Non-satiable* ones.

Combined entrepreneurial factors (CEF)

Since the inter-correlations among the factors generated from the four sets of variables were fairly high, the 21 dimensions derived from the four groups of variables were factor analyzed further. This analysis yielded eight final factors, which were designated as combined entrepreneurial factors. They are listed as follows: (i) autonomous and interesting work, (ii) affiliation motive, (iii) self-reliance, (iv) self-orientation, (v) internal locus of control, (vi) ethical orientation, (vii) quality orientation, and (viii) deontic motive.

Inter-relationships among variable groups

Inter-correlation matrix and the combined factor analysis revealed a few relationships among the 21 dimensions. It was observed that most of the high correlations were within the particular variable group, indicating that the conceptual boundaries between policies, traits, and motives are rather sturdy. Some of the most important 'cross-border' relationships are listed below. Those involving background variables are obviously more relevant because of their precedence in time and the possibility of causal linkages.

(a) Opportunities during childhood for pursuing one's own interests and for making autonomous choices are likely to develop internal locus of control in the individual (correlation coefficient, $r = 0.32$, significant at $p \leq 0.005$). (b) Parental care, support, encouragement, and happiness during childhood are related to pre-start-up accomplishments ($r = 0.33$, significant at $p \leq 0.005$) and to affiliation motive ($r = 0.55$, significant at $p \leq 0.001$). (c) Individuals with internal locus of control have had better accomplishments in life ($r = 0.37$, $p \leq 0.005$). (d) Conformism is associated with ethical orientation ($r = 0.38$, $p \leq 0.005$) and with affiliation motive ($r = 0.34$, $p \leq 0.005$). Most other high correlations are within each variable group. Notable among these are the inter-relationships among four motives, namely, self-actualization, enjoyable work, need for autonomy, and power and status motive.

Contributions of this Study and their Implications

Though this study was designed and executed with the primary objective of identifying the distinctive features of growth ventures and growth-seeking entrepreneurs, it has incidentally thrown some fresh light on a few traditionally well-researched issues in entrepreneurship. Hence the contributions of this research can be grouped under two major headings, namely, (a) contributions to the emerging area of growth-venture research and (b) contributions toward greater understanding of entrepreneurship in general, especially in terms of the review and re-examination of existing concepts and theories. A few points relating to these two aspects are highlighted below. Considering the limitations of this study, especially in terms of the relatively small sample size of 90, any generalization made here should be understood as hypotheses with some empirical support but needing further confirmation by research in different contexts.

Growth Venture Profile

The fourteen variables identified as significantly different for high-growth and low-growth ventures can and do throw some light on our understanding of growth ventures. A tentative profile may be drawn up based on the six factors derived from the distinguishing variables. It should be clarified that the difference between the two groups on the dimensions that follow is one of degree. The description of a growth venture profile in terms of these dimensions does not imply that these are totally absent among low-growth ventures. It is just a matter of higher intensity or greater emphasis in the high-growth group on the following dimensions:

- Desire for positional and personal power.
- Pursuit of excellence in the field of one's interest.
- Support and encouragement from people and institutions around (*Stated differently, it may be indicative of political skills and capabilities for ensuring support from others*).
- Divergent thinking and a desire for continuous learning.
- Reality contact and testing.
- Decentralization and delegation.

The emerging picture is that of someone who is motivated by the intrinsic interest in the work and is able to maintain high quality and excellence vis-à-vis the demands of the various stakeholders in collaboration with and mobilizing support from the external environment as well as internal constituents.

A major limitation of this profile arises from the fact that regression of enterprise growth on these dimensions was not significant. It would imply that growth may not be caused by any of these factors. Perhaps, it is the other way. When enterprises grow, these factors also may have to change. As far as can be inferred from the present findings, the determinants of growth are yet to be identified. It was rather surprising that even the factor of industry growth, which was significantly correlated with enterprise growth and was identified by some researchers as a major determinant of enterprise growth, was found to be non-significant in the regression analysis. It appears that industry growth may be a necessary condition for the sustained growth of an enterprise but may not be the sufficient cause.

Growth Unwillingness and Growth Facilitation

The growth unwillingness hypothesis has found some support from this study in an indirect manner. The low and non-significant correlation between profitability and enterprise growth would suggest that even highly profitable firms may also refuse to grow. Similarly, the significant correlation between industry growth and enterprise growth may suggest that external factors could also hinder or facilitate enterprise growth.

Background of the Entrepreneur and the Growth-Venture Model

Existing theories about the background of the entrepreneurial individual are largely unsupported by the findings of this study. Very few of the present respondents have reported parental neglect, material deprivation, local displacement, psychological traumas, etc. A large majority of them have had happy childhoods, and were cared for and supported by parents and elders. They also have had successful careers prior to the start-up of their first ventures, but not much entrepreneurial experience. As far as their religious affiliations are concerned, there is no indication that they adhere to the values of Protestant Ethics. In fact, a large majority of them are low on the belief in and practice of religion.

The findings on the background of entrepreneurs cannot probably be generalized, because the sample may not have been truly representative. However, since the bulk of the sample does not conform to the traditional models, one should also look for alternative explanations. One of them could be that people's attitude toward an entrepreneurial career has changed. Unlike in the last century and at the beginning of this one, entrepreneurship is a respectable career now, and therefore it is no more a career reserved for the socially marginalized and hapless individuals. Similarly, low levels of religious beliefs and practice do not necessarily imply that the values of Protestantism are totally rejected. It could be that these values have become part of the social values so that, irrespective of the individual's religious beliefs and practices, he/she may be sharing these values.

There are three other findings about the background of entrepreneurs from the analysis of the responses of this sample, which deserve special mention. One of them is the relatively low levels of education in the group, implying that there is indeed some kind of marginalization suffered by these individuals. They are educationally marginalized, if not socially. A new hypothesis, therefore, about the emergence of entrepreneurial individuals is that these persons, who are particular about doing enjoyable and interesting work using their special skills and capabilities, would try for such jobs. However, as they could not, for some reason or the other, get high levels of formal education, the chances of their getting enjoyable jobs were low. Therefore, an entrepreneurship career was perhaps the only way available to them for making it big in life and, of course, for doing an interesting job. Thus, it appears that it is the need for doing an interesting job, which has been blocked by certain entry barriers like low levels of education, that channelizes the person into entrepreneurship. The need for achievement, status, power, etc. can also be satisfied through entrepreneurship. Incidentally, one can be an achiever or wield power in many other careers as well. For example, a political career would give much more power to an individual compared to an entrepreneurial career. Similarly, if the person gets sufficient opportunities for doing an interesting job as a paid employee, he/she may not turn to entrepreneurship, as illustrated by the cases of large numbers of committed employees who enjoy their work and produce great results in existing organizations.

In this context, one should also make a distinction between 'start-up motives' and 'later motives'. If the start-up motive is the need to do enjoyable work utilizing one's special skills and capabilities, for which there are no opportunities in the existing organizations, one becomes an entrepreneur and creates a growth-oriented business. On the other hand, if the start-up motive was something else, like the desire for independence, need to earn a living, need to deal with unemployment, attraction of the special incentives offered by public institutions, etc., there is every chance of that person remaining a self-employed 'small business owner' and not becoming a growth-oriented entrepreneur. Furthermore, for venture growth to happen, the founder should be having a few other traits and motives such as the need for position, power and status, social orientation, political skills, reality-testing orientation, and the ability to involve people and manage through them. In other words, while enjoyable/interesting work is the starting point of growth-oriented entrepreneurship, there may not be any movement toward growth without the support of the other traits and motives mentioned above. For example, artisans and craftsmen can be on their own and do an enjoyable job, but their enterprises may not grow, for want of support from the other traits, motives, and skills. Thus, it is possible that the start-up motives are the same for different kinds of entrepreneurs. It is the combination of these with the other motives, traits, policies, and external environmental factors that would change the course. The model can be presented as shown in Fig. 6.1. It should, however, be clarified that in view of the non-significant regressions, this model will have to be treated as a partially supported hypothesis than as a proven theory. The partial support obviously comes from the comparative analysis made by us in Chapters 3 and 4.

The other two factors that have emerged from the analysis of the entrepreneur's background are that (i) during the childhood and adolescence these individuals have had deep interest in a variety of fields and (ii) they have worked their way to entrepreneurship through purposeful

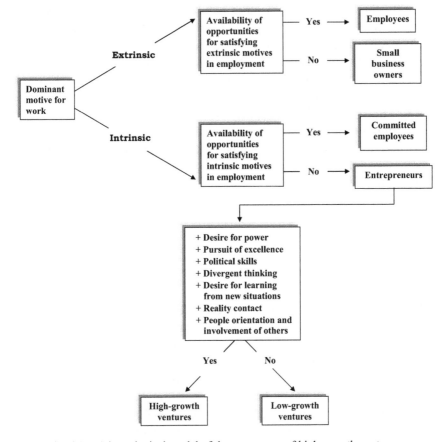

Fig. 6.1.   A hypothetical model of the emergence of high-growth ventures.

actions rather than being swept into it by circumstances. The relevance of these two aspects in understanding entrepreneurial behavior and the support they provide to two existing theories about entrepreneurship have been discussed in detail in the text. Diversity of interests may have prevented 'specialization' by these individuals and may have contributed to their 'educational marginalization' discussed above.

More importantly, diversity of interests is likely to lead to innovativeness, as innovations very often occur because of the unusual/unexpected combination of ideas from different fields. This may be the most common route to entrepreneurial innovation. The fact that the majority in our sample were individuals with deep interests in a variety of fields may indicate the possibility of a large number of them being innovative in some way or the other. There is thus indirect and partial support for the Schumpeterian theory that every entrepreneur is an innovator.

The other observation that is to be taken note of is that most of the respondents in the sample stated that their being entrepreneurs is the result of their own purposeful action and not of chance factors in the environment. This is a significant observation in view of the controversies on the paradigm of entrepreneurial action as well as research. There is some support here for the strategic choice paradigm as opposed to the population ecology paradigm. This is also in line with the findings of the author's earlier study, the details of which were discussed elsewhere in this book. In view of the findings of this study, we may also suggest modifications to a few other theories prevalent about entrepreneurship, which are discussed below.

Achievement Motive

This study has thrown some light on a few well-established concepts (traits and motives) and their role in explaining the entrepreneurship phenomenon. Achievement motive (McClelland, 1961) is one such concept which had a dominant role in guiding entrepreneurship research for more than two decades. This study, however, has brought out a few limitations of achievement motivation, both as a concept and as a critical factor for entrepreneurship. In the conceptual analysis performed with the help of factor analysis, achievement motive failed to emerge as an independent motive. It is, in fact, a part of man's need for expressing oneself through work, which was called 'self-actualization' by Maslow (1954). The other components of this motive are the desire to develop one's capabilities, and the desire to do something new. It is but natural that when an individual wants to express himself/herself through work, there is no way to do it except through the development of one's skills and capabilities. Since each individual is unique, there will be some uniqueness in his/her capabilities, which would lead to the accomplishment of something new and different. It is in the implementation of one's desire to express oneself through work or of one's desire to do something new and path-breaking that setting and achieving goals, targets, and standards become important. Therefore, it does not seem to be an independent motive by its own right. If, however, it is argued that the original concept of *n-Ach* was broader than the mere achievement of targets and standards, it is necessary to take a closer look at the concept of *n-Ach* as defined by McClelland (1961), which had four main components, namely, the desire to achieve targets and standards, the desire to do it better than others, the orientation to take moderate risks, and the desire to get feedback on one's actions. While it is true that the comparative performance dimension (doing things better than others) is not a part of the concept of 'Self-Actualization', the latter concept (as it got defined in this study) has a few more important dimensions under it, such as developing one's skills and capabilities, doing something new and path-breaking, and even achieving targets and standards (subject to the limits of one's self-concept and competencies). Comparing the two concepts, it could legitimately be hypothesized that *n-Ach* may not be a separate concept but can be subsumed into the concept of Self-Actualization (as it got defined in this study).

The second point about achievement motive, assuming that it is an independent motive, is its relevance for entrepreneurship. Our analysis has shown that the need to achieve targets and standards is relevant for performance in any career and is not something special for entrepreneurship. What emerged in our analysis as critical is the differences among individuals in terms of their intrinsic interest in work and/or their using work as a means for achieving their extrinsic objectives. It should be remembered that both these motives can be satisfied in employment, in which case the individual may not turn to entrepreneurship. However, if the opportunities for satisfying these are not available in employment, entrepreneurship becomes a major option, and it is the ones who have intrinsic love for the project on hand who would become growth-oriented entrepreneurs. The others would end up as small business owners. These and related aspects were explained in the model above. What is pointed out here is that the need for achieving targets and standards is not a sufficient motive for someone to become an entrepreneur. In fact, achievement-oriented people are found in any profession or any walk of life and are not confined to the field of entrepreneurship.

Power Motive

Unlike achievement motive, power motive and affiliation motive were found to be independent motives by this study. The concept of power motive, as it has emerged in this study, however, was slightly different from what was proposed in the conventional psychological theory. Power and status were considered to be two aspects of the human need called 'ego needs' by Maslow (1954). In our study, however, these two emerged as separate factors, independent of each other. It appears that there can be power without status and status without power, as we have discussed earlier. A more important finding of this study is on the components of power motive. The two major components are power over oneself and power over others. The former is represented by the desire for autonomy, independence, and involvement in decisions affecting oneself. The latter is the need for influencing others. It is apparently for this aspect that the desire to get feedback on the results of one's actions is important. The latter variable which was traditionally considered to be a part of achievement motive has combined with power motive in our analysis. The logic of this combination may be that it is the actions/responses of others that are more unpredictable than those of oneself. In addition to clarifying the concept of power motive, this study has also shown that this motive could be a determinant of growth performance, even though it may not be critical for start-up. The importance of the power motive for entrepreneurship has been recognized by earlier researchers (e.g., McClelland & Burnham, 1976). The contribution of this study is in identifying the stage at which it would turn critical. In other words, it is a characteristic more of the growth-oriented entrepreneurs than of the ordinary ones. The findings of a recent study by Ramsay *et al.* (2016) offer support to the observations made by us on the power motive and the achievement motive. In their study among university students, it was found that entrepreneurial intention was significantly associated with power orientation, but not with achievement orientation.

Affiliation Motive

As was observed in many prior studies (e.g., McClelland, 1961; McClelland & Burnham, 1976; Nandy, 1973), affiliation motive was found to be low for entrepreneurs in this study as well. In addition to the lack of association of affiliation motive with the entrepreneurial entry, Nandy (1973) has found that it is not associated with entrepreneurial competence either. Another issue that needs to be clarified is the different levels at which affiliation motive becomes operational. Obviously, it can include people of different contexts and levels of intimacy. For example, it operates at the family, social circles, and workplace. At the workplace, it operates at the peer level and also at the superior-subordinate level. This may be why the support and encouragement expected from superiors are shown as part of the affiliation motive. For entrepreneurs, the 'superiors' may be those people managing the regulatory and support institutions outside. Against this background, the low levels of affiliation motive on the part of entrepreneurs should be understood in a different sense — that they enjoy interacting with others but are not emotionally dependent on them (Decker *et al.*, 2012). However, the political skills and people-orientation identified by the present study as characteristics of growth-oriented entrepreneurs suggest that affiliation motive would also have a role to play in entrepreneurial success.

Deontic Motive

The concept and relevance of deontic motive have been discussed in detail in Chapter 4. It was observed there that deontic motive was expectedly low for entrepreneurs, but was included in the present investigation because of its potential for explaining the work behavior of some other groups (including non-entrepreneurs social entrepreneurs, etc.), which may serve as control groups when this study is extended to other cultures or other categories of entrepreneurs. As far as this study is concerned, its contribution with respect to this motive is its empirical identification as a separate motive.

Risk-Taking Ability

Risk-taking ability is one of the earliest traits to be identified as critical for entrepreneurs. As we have pointed out elsewhere, several recent studies have shown that risk-taking ability is not necessarily stronger among entrepreneurs than among other groups. In fact, in some studies, entrepreneurs were found to be risk-avoiders rather than risk-takers. In an earlier study by the present author (Manimala, 1988a, 1999), the more innovative entrepreneurs were found to be effective risk managers and not risk-takers in the strict sense. The innovative entrepreneur places himself/herself in a risky situation not necessarily because of his/her love of risks but because of his/her love for the project, which being new is inherently riskier, and warrants the management and reduction of these risks. This study has confirmed this hypothesis about entrepreneurs in general. There is something more to it than the moderate risk-taking proposed by McClelland (1961). Even moderate or calculated risks are not loved for their own sake. On the other hand, risks are perceived to be the 'necessary evils' that have to be encountered if one were to implement one's innovative pet projects. This is why in our analysis risk-taking behavior did not emerge as an independent trait. It combined with what may be called 'internal locus of control', or more appropriately the desire for self-direction. The components of this trait are a desire to excel, achieving goals through one's own efforts, aversion to gambling, willingness to work hard, and taking responsibility for one's actions and their outcomes. Two points, therefore, emerge from the above findings of this study. One is that entrepreneurs are motivated not by any love for risks, but by a love for their projects. The second is that the concept of locus of control may involve something more than the mere attribution of responsibility to oneself or others. The internal locus of control is apparently a consequence of one's desire to excel and willingness to work hard toward the achievement of excellence, even though the work involved would be inherently risky. Another issue that is relevant in this context is the differences in risk-perception. What is perceived as risky by an external observer may not be so risky for the doer, as the latter would be judging it based on his/her prior experience, training, and the insider knowledge of the situation.

Related Diversification

It was noted above that the risk-taking ability did not emerge as an independent trait. In the same manner, related diversification, though widely acclaimed as a major growth-strategy, failed to emerge as an independent strategy. It is shown as a means to ensuring quality through the synergies available in 'related' operations. This point will be clearer when this factor grouping is contrasted with another one involving the low-price strategy. The latter variable emerged as a factor all by itself, indicating that it is an independent strategy. Similarly, maintaining consistent quality and reliability of products and services is an independent strategy. However, related diversification has not emerged as an independent strategy but has combined with the factor of quality orientation. It seems that related diversification is a means for maintaining quality, which would imply that if quality can be ensured even in apparently unrelated areas, there is no harm in an enterprise following a growth path of unrelated diversification. This is why, in spite of the repeated assertions by academics that sustainable growth can be achieved only through related diversification, there are many examples of firms growing through unrelated diversification. There are a few studies (e.g., Michel & Shaked, 1984) that have shown that unrelated diversification would lead to better financial performance than related ones. This may be because the different sectors of business get affected differently by the changes in the environment, so that in unrelated diversification, all the units may not be affected in the same way by environmental adversities. In this context, it is interesting to note the findings of a study conducted in a developing country (Ramaswamy *et al.*, 2017) that unrelated diversification resulted in poorer performance (compared to related diversification) when the institutional environment improved due to pro-market reforms. Another finding about related/unrelated diversification in the context of firm growth is that the fast-growing small firms are focused on a single product/market, whereas the fast-growing large firms are diversified (Siegel *et al.*, 1993).

Yet another issue that emerges as important in this context is the need for developing a broader definition of the concept of 'relatedness'. Relationships through products and processes are readily recognized. However, it is often forgotten that other factors such as markets, distribution channels, raw materials, locations, tools/techniques, and core competencies can also cause synergistic relationships. As we have explained elsewhere, cement and electronics or steel and software may not be considered related according to the norms of conventional wisdom. But the former may be related through a company's core competence in ceramics and the latter through a core competence in process control. Both these diversifications, though apparently into unrelated products, are compatible with the strategy of maintaining consistent quality through relatedness, and therefore may be undertaken by firms. The point to be noted here is that it may be unwise to uncritically adhere to the traditional concept of related diversification. Diversification into any area would be acceptable so long as the enterprise feels confident about maintaining the quality and reliability of its products and services and minimizing its costs through synergistic operations. The main point that has been highlighted by this study is the need for redefining the concept of relatedness itself. By broadening the definition as explained above, most of the activities undertaken by entrepreneurs are likely to be perceived as related.

Changes in Policies, Traits, and Motives

Changes in policies, traits, and motives have been discussed in detail in Chapter 5. There is no need to repeat the contents of these changes here. It is sufficient here to highlight some implications of these findings as follows: (a) Traits and motives have been observed to be more stable than policies. (b) It may be possible for us to classify enterprise policies into those determined by the nature of the entrepreneur and those determined by the nature of the enterprise, the former being more stable. (c) Changes in policies are dictated mainly by the increasing complexities of the enterprise. (d) An important finding of this study is the discovery of two different kinds of motives, *Satiable* and *Non-satiable*, the former getting weaker and the latter getting stronger in the effort to satisfy them. Focus on the non-satiable needs may lead to the development of effective incentives and motivational techniques. (e) A part of the theoretical model proposed in Fig. 1.2 (indicated by the dotted lines in that figure) has found some empirical support from the above findings, as it is observed that the performance of the enterprise seems to have a long-term impact on the traits and motives of the entrepreneur as well as the policies of the enterprise.

Limitations of this Study

Limitations of this study arise primarily from the limitations of the method of mailed survey. These as well as the precautions taken by us to reduce their impact have been discussed in Chapter 2. We shall, therefore, mention a few other limitations below. These additional issues, along with those discussed in Chapter 2, will have to be taken into consideration while assessing the sturdiness of the present findings.

- Since the respondents for the control group were chosen from a database on the basis of their most recent sales performance, it is likely that they had been growing companies earlier and have suffered a temporary setback. Though we have later computed the growth index based on the data provided by the respondents, and not based on the figures taken from the database, there is a possibility of some high-growth enterprises having been classified as low-growth ones because of the temporary setback suffered by them during the relevant period.

- An opposite effect of including low-growth ventures among high-growth ones cannot be ruled out. This is because it was not possible for us to remove from the sample those enterprises that have had their start-ups in recent years. Hence, it is likely that the recently started ventures had a higher growth rate because of their smaller initial base.
- Since we could not control the start-up year, it was decided that there should be a control over the size of the enterprises. The initial decision was to include only those enterprises having a turnover between 5 and 10 million UK Pounds. It was then found that many of the fast-growing enterprises got excluded. So, the limit was raised to UKP 20 million. The gap between 5 and 20 million is also considerable and may have distorted the growth indices.
- In computing growth rates, a combined index based on four performance indicators was considered more realistic because it would eliminate the distortions that may be caused by the use of a single factor. However, as pointed out earlier, it could also lead to an 'averaging effect', thereby concealing the real differences.
- The severe recession that had been suffocating the British industries during the time when this survey was conducted had an adverse effect on the response rate, and therefore, we could not get data from a larger sample as per our original design and had to manage the analysis with 90 responses. The good news, however, is that the addition of a sizeable number of responses from a different context did not make any difference in the outcomes of number-sensitive analyses like the factor analysis.
- In the design of this study, it would have been better to have a few more control groups in addition to the 'low-growth' group, with which we compared the growth-venture characteristics. One such control group could have been from among the group of entrepreneurs who are generally referred to as 'small business owners' or 'craftsmen entrepreneurs'. This group would have brought out the differences between 'small business owners' and 'entrepreneurs' more sharply. It is, after all, from among 'entrepreneurs' that high-growth ventures arise, as we have seen from the model discussed above in this chapter. Such a comparison would have clarified if the differences are more due to their external circumstances than due to their own characteristics. Another control group could have been from among 'non-entrepreneurs', which would have brought out the differences, if any, between entrepreneurs and non-entrepreneurs.

In spite of the above limitations, the importance of some of our findings cannot be underestimated. The more prominent among them are as follows: the identification of the growth venture/entrepreneur characteristics; identification of the general entrepreneurial characteristics; redefinition of certain concepts traditionally being associated with entrepreneurship and an assessment of their roles in promoting entrepreneurship; critical examination of a few theories about entrepreneurship; and the proposal of alternative hypotheses. The new propositions arising from this study are called hypotheses (rather than theories) because of the nature of social science research findings, which often needs to get further confirmation from other studies. The new questions thrown up by this study and the directions for further research, therefore, are indicated in the next section.

Directions for Further Research

Enterprise growth is a *sine qua non* for economic growth, as the benefits to the economy from entrepreneurship (such as the creation of wealth and employment and thereby contributing to the welfare of the society) are derived mostly from the growing firms rather than the stagnating ones. For this reason, growth venture research has to go on, especially because the critical factors supporting growth may be different for different types of entrepreneurs, as was shown by the findings of Siegel *et al.* (1993), who made a comparative analysis of the characteristics of growth ventures among small and large businesses. Growth ventures among the small business group were characterized by focus on a single product/market, leaner management, and effective utilization of technology, whereas those in the large business group were diversified, had balanced and professional management, and maintained close customer contacts. The only factor that was commonly found in both the groups of growth-seekers is that the management had prior industry experience. While the present study could identify seven factors that are characteristics of growth ventures (namely, Desire for power, Pursuit of excellence, Political skills, Divergent thinking, Desire for learning from new situations, Reality contact, People orientation and involvement of others), it has also provided insights into the other possibilities of designing and conducting such studies. Considering the fact that growth venture research has not produced uniform outcomes, one of the important tasks of the present researcher at this stage is to generate alternate themes/hypotheses that may be of interest to future researchers. A few such themes for further research identified in this study are listed as follows.

- For computing the growth index, this study has used an average of means computed on the basis of four different criteria. While this is useful for removing the inadequacies of any single criterion, it may create an 'averaging effect', which precludes the assessment of the characteristics associated with different types of growths. In case a separate analysis is desired, it is possible to compute separate growth indices based on each of these performance indicators with a view to comparing high- and low-growth ventures identified on the basis of each criterion.
- In order to test the model proposed by us in this chapter on the emergence of small business owners, entrepreneurs, and growth entrepreneurs, three samples may be selected from these three groups and a comparative study of their policies, strategies, and other characteristics could be undertaken. Ideally, the samples should be selected from among enterprises that have had the start-up in the same year. In India, such a study can be undertaken in collaboration with any one of the large financial institutions whose clients are large enough and on whose performance the institutions have reliable data, which would help the initial classification. An example of the use of such a method is available in the study cited above (Siegel *et al.*, 1993), which analyzed the characteristics of growth ventures using two groups: one a sample of SMEs chosen from the Reynolds Database and the other a sample of large companies chosen from among the clients of PriceWaterhouse.
- Changes in entrepreneurial policies, traits, motives, etc. need to be studied in greater depth. The method of asking respondents to recall their past policies, traits, motives, etc. (as used in this study) has helped in revealing the directions of such changes. The ideal method, however, is a longitudinal study conducted at the start-up and later period, in which the lapse of time between the two studies can also be controlled for the respondents. It may be clarified that in this study the time period between the start-up and the data collection stage was obviously not equal for all the respondents.
- An observation that came out of the study of changes in entrepreneurial characteristics over time seems to have some potential for developing appropriate 'motivation theories' for different occupations. Studies for various groups could be designed and conducted with a view to

identifying the *satiable* and *non-satiable* motives of these groups. Incentives or motivational strategies designed around the non-satiable motives, which would become stronger in the attempt to satisfy them, have an obviously greater chance of success.

- Since the characteristics of entrepreneurs undergo changes by virtue of their being in an entrepreneurial career, the practice of studying existing entrepreneurs with a view to identifying their characteristics during the start-up time does not seem to be legitimate. Start-up characteristics could be identified using longitudinal studies, recall method, and/or the method of content analysis of undisguised published materials about them. The last of the three will be particularly useful for studies of entrepreneurial background.

- The results of this study have suggested the modifications and re-definitions of some concepts used in entrepreneurship research, such as achievement motive, power motive, risk-taking ability, locus of control, and related diversification. A new concept of deontic motive also has been empirically identified. The sturdiness of these concepts and/or their modifications will have to be tested using larger samples, and their relevance for entrepreneurship examined.

- While identifying and analyzing the 'general entrepreneurial' characteristics, this study did not have a control group to compare these with, which is a limitation of the study. Future studies of this kind could be conducted with control groups of non-entrepreneurs.

- Finally, cross-cultural studies using the present design or the ones suggested above could be undertaken to validate the new concepts and findings in other countries/cultures.

References

Advisory Council on Science and Technology, UK. (1990). *The Enterprise Challenge: Overcoming Barriers to Growth in Small Firms*. London: H M Stationery Office. July, 1990.

Aghion, P. and Howitt, P. (1992). A model of growth through creative destruction. *Econometrica*, **60**: 323–351.

Aghion, P. and Howitt, P. (1998). *Endogenous Growth Theory*. Cambridge, MA: MIT Press.

Alange, S. and Scheinberg, S. (1988). Swedish entrepreneurship in a cross-cultural perspective. In Kirchhoff, B. A., *et al.* (Eds.), *Frontiers of Entrepreneurship Research* (pp. 1–15). Wellesley, MA: Babson College.

Alpar, P. and Spitzer, D. M. Jr. (1989). Response behaviour of entrepreneurs in a mail survey. *Entrepreneurship Theory and Practice*, **14**(2): 31–44. Winter.

Anyadike-Danes, M., Hart, M. and Du, J. (2015). Firm dynamics and job creation in the UK: 1998–2013. *International Small Business Journal*, **33**(1): 12–27. January. doi.org/10.1177/0266242614552334.

Argyris, C. and Schon, D. A. (1974). *Theory in Practice: Increasing Professional Effectiveness*. San Francisco, CA: Jossey-Bass.

Audretsch, D., Klomp, L., Santarelli, E. and Thurik, A. R. (2004). Gibrat's law: Are the services different? *Review of Industrial Organization*, **24**: 301–324. https://doi.org/10.1023/B:REIO.0000038273.50622.ec.

Azoulay, P., Jones, B. F., Kim, J. D. and Miranda, J. (2020). Age and high-growth entrepreneurship. *American Economic Review: Insights*, **2**(1): 65–82. March. DOI: 10.1257/aeri.20180582.

Baggonkar, S. (2019). The Leela story: How the Nair family lost keys to its hospitality treasure. *Money Control*. https://www.moneycontrol.com/news/business/companies/the-leela-story-how-the-nair-family-lost-keys-to-its-hospitality-treasure-3665591.html. Accessed 18 Feb 2021.

Banerjee, P. (2019). Apple's latest feature is aggressive pricing strategy to take on rivals. *Livemint.* 12 September 2019. https://www.livemint.com/companies/news/apple-s-latest-feature-is-aggressive-pricing-strategy-to-take-on-rivals-1568226377458.html. Accessed 18 Feb 2021.

Barney, J. B. (1991). Firm resources and sustained competitive advantage. *Journal of Management,* **17**: 99–120. March. https://doi.org/10.1177/01492 0639101700108.

Baron, R. and Shane, S. (2005). *Entrepreneurship: A Process Perspective* (1st ed., p. 60). Mason, Ohio: South-Western Publishing.

Baum, J. R. and Locke, E. A. (2004). The relationship of entrepreneurial traits, skill, and motivation to subsequent venture growth. *Journal of Applied Psychology,* **89**(4): 587–598. https://doi.org/10.1037/0021-9010.89.4.587.

BBC News. (2019). Mukesh Ambani: India's richest man helps his brother avoid jail. https://www.bbc.com/news/business-47620861. Accessed 3 Jun 2020.

Begley, T. M. and Boyd, D. P. (1987). Psychological characteristics associated with performance in entrepreneurial firms and smaller business. *Journal of Business Venturing,* **2**(1): 79–93.

Bellu, R. R. (1988). Entrepreneurs and managers: Are they different? In Kirchhoff, B., Long, W., McMullan, W., Vesper, K. and Wetzel, W. (Eds.), *Frontiers of Entrepreneurship Research* (pp. 16–30). Wellesley, MA: Babson College.

Biography.com. (2014). Steve Jobs (1955–2011). *Biography Newsletter.* https://www.biography.com/business-figure/steve-jobs.

Belenzon, S., Shamshur, A. and Zarutskie, R. (2019). CEO's age and the performance of closely held firms. *Strategic Management Journal,* **40**(6): 917–944. https://doi.org/10.1002/smj.3003.

Beresford, R. and Saunders, M. (2005). Professionalization of the startup process. *Strategic Change,* **14**(6): 337–347.

Bertodo, R. G. (1990). The strategic alliance: Automotive paradigm for the 1990s. *International Journal of Technology Management,* **5**(4): 375–385.

Birch, D. (1987). *Job Creation in America: How Our Smallest Companies Put the Most People to Work.* New York: The Free Press.

Birch, D. and McCracken, S. (1982). *The Small Business Share of Job Creation: Lessons Learned from the Use of Longitudinal Data.* Washington, D.C: US Small Business Administration.

Birley, S. J. (1985). The role of networks in the entrepreneurial process. *Journal of Business Venturing,* **1**(1): 107–117.

Birley, S. J. and Westhead, P. (1990). Growth and performance contrasts between 'types' of small firms. *Strategic Management Journal,* **11**(7): 535–550.

Birley, S. J. and Westhead, P. (1994). A taxonomy of business start-up reasons and their impact on firm growth and size. *Journal of Business Venturing,* **9**(1), January: 7–31.

Blake R. R. and Mouton J. S. (1992). A model for identifying and developing commitment to superordinate goals. In Granberg, D. and Sarup, G. (Eds.), *Social Judgment and Intergroup Relations*. New York: Springer. https://doi.org/10.1007/978-1-4612-2860-8_10.

Block, Z. and MacMillan, I. C. (1985). Milestones for successful venture planning. *Harvard Business Review*, **63**(5): 184–196.

Boag, D. A. (1988). Growth strategies and performance in electronic companies. *Industrial Marketing Management*, **17**(4), November: 329–336.

Bowonder, B. and Miyake, T. (1992a). Innovation and strategic management: Diversification into emerging areas by Hitachi Ltd. ASCI Working paper. Hyderabad: Administrative Staff College of India.

Bowonder, B. and Miyake, T. (1992b). Management of corporate innovation: A case study from the Nippon Steel Corporation. *Creativity and Innovation Management*, **1**(2), June: 75–86.

Boyatzis, R. E. (1982). *The Competent Manager: A Model for Effective Performance*. New York: Wiley Interscience.

Bracker, J. S., Keats, B. W. and Pearson, J. N. (1988). Planning and financial performance among small firms in a growth industry. *Strategic Management Journal*, **9**: 591–603.

Brandstätter, H. (1997). Becoming an entrepreneur — A question of personality structure? *Journal of Economic Psychology*, **18**(2–3), April: 157–177.

Britannica. (1998). Honda Soichiro — Japanese Businessman. *Encyclopaedia Britannica*. https://www.britannica.com/biography/Honda-Soichiro.

Britannica. (2020). McDonald's: American Corporation. *Encyclopedia Britannica*. https://www.britannica.com/topic/McDonalds. Accessed 27 May 2020.

Britannica. (2021). Harland Sanders: American businessman. *Encyclopedia Britannica*. https://www.britannica.com/biography/Harland-Sanders. Accessed 2 Mar 2021.

Brockhaus, R. H. (1980). Risk-taking propensity of entrepreneurs. *Academy of Management Journal*, **23**(3): 509–520.

Brown, T. E., Davidsson, P. and Wiklund, J. (2001). An operationalization of Stevenson's conceptualization of entrepreneurship as opportunity-based firm behavior. *Strategic Management Journal*, **22**(10): 953–968.

Bruno, A. V. and Tyebjee, T. T. (1982). The environment for entrepreneurship. In Kent, C. A., Sexton, D. and Vesper, K. (Eds.), *Encyclopedia of Entrepreneurship* (pp. 289–307). New Jersey: Prentice-Hall.

Bryant, S. (2020). How many startups fail and why? *Investopedia*. https://www.investopedia.com/articles/personal-finance/040915/how-many-startups-fail-and-why.asp. Accessed 12 Feb 2021.

Busenitz, L. W., Plummer, L. A., Klotz, A. C., Shahzad, A. and Rhoads, K. (2014). Entrepreneurship research (1985–2009) and the emergence of opportunities. *Entrepreneurship Theory and Practice*, **38**: 1–20. July. DOI: 10.1111/etap.12120.

Calori, R. and Bonany, H. (1989). Growth companies in Europe: A case study. In S. Birley (Ed.), *European Entrepreneurship: Emerging Growth Companies* (pp. 27–48). Cranfield: EFER.

Cantillon, R. (1755/1931). *Essai sur la nature du commerce en general*. London: Macmillan 1931 (First published by the Marquis de Mirabeau in 1755).

Carland, J. W., Hoy, F., Boulton, W. and Cartland, J. (1984). Differentiating entrepreneurs from small business owners: A conceptualization. *Academy of Management Review*, 9(2): 354–359.

Chaganti, R., Chaganti, R. and Mahajan, V. (1989). Profitable small business strategies under different types of competition. *Entrepreneurship Theory and Practice*, 13(3), Spring: 21–35.

Chandler, A. D. (1962). *Strategy and Structure: Chapters from the History of the Industrial Enterprise*. Cambridge: MIT Press.

Christensen, C. R. and Scott, B. R. (1964). *Review of Course Activities*. Lausanne: IMEDE. (quoted in Churchill and Lewis, 1983, q.v.)

Churchill, N. C. and Lewis, V. L. (1983). The five stages of small business growth. *Harvard Business Review*, 61(3): 30–50.

Coad, A. (2007). *Firm Growth: A Survey*. CES Working Paper, HAL Archives-Ouvertes, Universite Paris, 14 May 2007. https://halshs.archives-ouvertes.fr/halshs-00155762. Accessed 18 Feb 2021.

Collins, O. F. and Moore, D. G. (1970). *The Organization Makers: A Behavioral Study of Independent Entrepreneurs*. New York: Appleton-Century-Crofts.

Colombelli, A., Haned, N. and Le Bas, C. (2013). On firm growth and innovation: Some new empirical perspectives using French CIS (1992–2004). *Structural Change and Economic Dynamics*, 26, September: 14–26.

Cooper, A. C., Dunkelberg, W. C. and Woo, C. Y. (1986). Optimists and pessimists: 2994 entrepreneurs and their perceived chances for success. In Ronstadt, R., Hornaday, J. A., Peterson, R., and Vesper, K. (Eds.), *Frontiers of Entrepreneurship Research* (pp. 563–577). Wellesley, MA: Babson College.

Cragg, P. and King, M. (1988). Organizational characteristics and small firms' performance revisited. *Entrepreneurship Theory and Practice*, 13(2): 49–64.

Craig, C. S. and McCann, J. M. (1978). Item non-response in mail surveys: Extent and correlates. *Journal of Marketing Research*, 15(2): 285–289. https://doi.org/10.2307/3151264.

Cyert, R. M. and March, J. G. (1992). *A Behavioral Theory of the Firm* (2nd ed.). Hoboken: Wiley-Blackwell. (First published in 1963).

Davidsson, P. (1988). On the psychology of continued entrepreneurship in small firms. Paper Presented at the 2nd International Conference on Recent Research in Entrepreneurship, December 5–6, 1988. Vienna: The University of Economics.

Davidsson, P. (1989). Entrepreneurship — And after? A study of growth willingness in small firms. *Journal of Business Venturing*, **4**: 211–226.

Davis, W. (1987). *The Innovators*. London: Ebury Press.

Deccan Herald. (2020). Anil Ambani's tale of riches to rags. https://www.deccanherald.com/business/business-news/anil-ambanis-tale-of-riches-to-rags-724063.html. Accessed 27 May 2020.

Decker, W. H., Calo, T. J. and Weer, C. H. (2012). Affiliation motivation and interest in entrepreneurial careers. *Journal of Managerial Psychology*, **27**(3): 302–320. https://doi.org/10.1108/02683941211205835.

Demirel, P. and Mazzucato, M. (2012). Innovation and firm growth: Is R&D worth it? *Industry and Innovation*, **19**(1): 45–62. DOI: 10.1080/13662716.2012.649057.

Denscombe, M. (2009). Item non-response rates: A comparison of online and paper questionnaires. *International Journal of Social Research Methodology*, **12**(4): 281–291. DOI: 10.1080/13645570802054706.

Dess, C. G. and Davis, P. S. (1984). Porter's (1980) generic strategies as determinants of strategic group membership and organizational performance. *Academy of Management Journal*, **27**: 467–488.

Dess, C. G. and Robinson, R. M. (1984). Measuring performance in the absence of objective measures. *Strategic Management Journal*, **5**: 265–274.

Dickerson, A. P., Gibson, H. D. and Tsakalotos, E. (1997). The impact of acquisitions on company performance: Evidence from a large panel of UK firms, *Oxford Economic Papers*, **49**(3): 344–361. July. https://doi.org/10.1093/oxfordjournals.oep.a028613.

Drucker, P. F. (1985). *Innovation and Entrepreneurship: Practice and Principles*. London: Heineman.

Dubini, P. (1988). The influence of motivations and environment on business startups: Some hints for public policies. *Journal of Business Venturing*, **4**: 11–26.

Duchesneau, D. A. and Gartner, W. B. (1990). A profile of new venture success and failure in an emerging industry. *Journal of Business Venturing*, **5**(5): 297–312.

Dunkelberg, W.G. and Cooper, A.C. (1982), Patterns of Small Business Growth, *Academy of Management Proceedings*, 409–413.

Dwyer, B. and Kotey, B. (2016). Identifying high growth firms: Where are we? *Journal of Management & Organization*, **22**(4): 457–475. DOI: 10.1017/jmo.2015.51.

Eisenhardt, K. M. and Schoonhoven, C. B. (1990). Organizational growth: Linking founding team, strategy, environment, and growth among US semiconductor ventures, 1976–88. *Administrative Science Quarterly*, **35**: 504–530. September.

ET Now Digital. (2020). Throwback: When Anil Ambani left behind elder brother Mukesh Ambani in net worth. https://www.timesnownews.com/business-economy/companies/article/throwback-when-anil-ambani-left-behind-elder-brother-mukesh-ambani-on-net-worth/559556. Accessed 3 Jun 2020.

Erdogan, B. Z. and Baker, M. J. (2002). Increasing mail survey response rates from an industrial population: A cost-effectiveness analysis of four follow-up techniques. *Industrial Marketing Management*, **31**(1): 65–73. https://doi.org/10.1016/S0019-8501(00)00117-6.

Feeser, H. R. and Willard, G. E. (1989). Incubators and performance: A comparison of high-growth and low-growth high-tech firms. *Journal of Business Venturing*, **4**: 429–442.

Ferber, R. (1966). Item non-response in a consumer survey. *Public Opinion Quarterly*, **30**: 399–415.

Fombrun, C. J. and Wally, S. (1989). Structuring small firms for rapid growth. *Journal of Business Venturing*, **4**: 107–122.

Foss, D. C. (1985). Venture capital network: The first six months of experiment. In Hornaday, J. A., Vesper, K. H., Timmons, J. A. and Shils, E. (Eds.), *Frontiers of Entrepreneurship Research* (pp. 314–324). Wellesley, MA: Babson College.

Galbraith, J. R. (1982). Stages of growth. *Journal of Business Strategy*, **3**(1), Fall: 120–126.

Gherhes, C., Williams, N., Vorley, T. and Vasconcelos, A. (2016). Distinguishing micro-businesses from SMEs: A systematic review of growth constraints. *Journal of Small Business and Enterprise Development*, **23**(4): 939–963. https://doi.org/10.1108/JSBED-05-2016-0075.

Gibb, A. and Dyson, J. (1984). Stimulating the growth of owner-managed firms. In Lewis, J., Stanworth, J. and Gibb, A. (Eds.), *Success and Failure in Small Business* (pp. 249–275). Aldershot, Hampshire: Gower.

Gibrat, R. (1931). *Les Inegalites Economiques*. Paris: Librairie du Recueil Sirey.

Gilmore, T. N. and Kazanjian, R. K. (1989). Clarifying decision making in high growth ventures: The use of responsibility charting. *Journal of Business Venturing*, **4**: 69–83.

Ginn, C. W. and Sexton, D. L. (1990). A comparison of the personality type dimensions of the 1987 Inc. 500 company founders/CEOs with those of slower growth firms. *Journal of Business Venturing*, **5**(5): 313–326.

Giunta, A., Nifo, A. and Scalera, D. (2012). Subcontracting in Italian industry: Labour division, firm growth and the North–South divide. *Regional Studies*, **46**(8): 1067–1083. DOI: 10.1080/00343404.2011.552492.

Granovetter, M. S. (1973). The strength of weak ties. *American Journal of Sociology*, **78**(6), May: 1360–1380.

Greiner, L. (1972). Evolution and revolution as organizations grow. *Harvard Business Review*, **50**(4): 37–46.

Growth Companies Register. (1988). *Vol. I: 1,000 Fastest Growing Private Companies & Vol. II: The Second 1,000 Fastest Growing Private Companies*. London: Financial Publishing Co. Ltd.

Hagen, E. E. (1962). *On the Theory of Social Change: How Economic Growth Begins*. Homewood, Illinois: Dorsey Press.

Hall, W. K. (1980). Survival strategies in a hostile environment. *Harvard Business Review*, 58, September/October: 75–80.

Hamel, G., Doz, Y. and Prahalad, C. K. (1986). Strategic partnerships: Success or surrender. Paper Presented at the Rutgers/Wharton Colloquium on Co-operative Strategies in International Business, New Brunswick, New Jersey, October 1986.

Hamel, G. and Prahalad, C. K. (1990). The core competence of the corporation. *Harvard Business Review*, **68**(3): 79–93.

Hamm, J. (2002). Why entrepreneurs don't scale. *Harvard Business Review*, **80**(12), December: 110–115.

Hanks, S. H., Watson, C. J., Jansen, E. and Chandler, G. N. (1993). Tightening the life-cycle construct: A taxonomic study of growth stage configurations in high-technology organizations. *Entrepreneurship Theory and Practice*, **18**(2): 5–30.

Harrigan, K. R. (1989). Strategic alliances: Their new role in understanding global competition. *The Columbia Journal of World Business*, **22**(2): 67–70.

Havnes, P. A. and Senneseth, K. A. (2001). Panel Study of firm growth among SMEs in networks. *Small Business Economics*, **16**: 293–302. June 2001. https://doi.org/10.1023/A:1011100510643.

Herzberg, F., Mausner, B. and Snyderman, B. (1959). *The Motivation to Work*. New York: Wiley.

HLV Ltd. (2021). Mumbai's only resort style business hotel: The Leela Mumbai. https://www.hlvltd.com/. Accessed 3 Jun 2020.

Honjo, Y. (2004). Growth of new start-up firms: Evidence from the Japanese manufacturing industry. *Applied Economics*, **36**(4): 343–355. DOI: 10.1080/00036840410001674277.

Hyde, R. L. (2019). How Walmart Model Wins with "Everyday Low Prices". *Investopedia*. 25 June 2019. https://www.investopedia.com/articles/personal-finance/011815/how-walmart-model-wins-everyday-low-prices.asp. Accessed 8 Feb 2021.

Jagannathan, R. (2014). Goodbye, Vimal: Why Mukesh Ambani is selling his father's first major business. *FirstPost*. December 2014. https://www.firstpost.com/business/corporate-business/goodbye-vimal-why-mukesh-ambani-is-selling-his-fathers-first-major-business-1999363.html. Accessed 23 Nov 2021.

Jarillo, J. C. (1988). On strategic networks. *Strategic Management Journal*, **9**: 31–41.

Jarillo, J. C. (1989). Entrepreneurship and growth: The strategic use of external resources. *Journal of Business Venturing*, **4**: 133–147.

Jensen, M. C. and Meckling, W. H. (1976). Theory of the firm: Managerial behaviour, agency costs and ownership structure. *Journal of Financial Economics*, **3**: 305–360.

Jo, H. and Lee, J. (1996). The relationship between an entrepreneur's background and performance in a new venture. *Technovation*, **16**(4): 161–171. https://doi.org/10.1016/0166-4972(96)89124-3.

Johns, W. H. and Linda, G. (1978). Multiple criteria effects in a mail survey experiment. *Journal of Marketing Research*, **15**: 280–284.

Jones, E. E. and Nisbett, R. E. (1971). *The Actor and the Observer: Divergent Perceptions of the Causes of Behavior*. Morristown, N.J.: General Learning Press.

Kamei, K. and Dana, L.-P. (2012). Examining the impact of new policy facilitating SME succession in Japan: From a viewpoint of risk management in family business. *International Journal of Entrepreneurship and Small Business*, **16**(1): 60–70.

Kane, T. (2010). The importance of start-ups in job creation and job destruction. *SSRN Electronic Journal*. Research Gate. July. DOI: 10.2139/ssrn.1646934.

Kang, T., Baek, C. and Lee, J.-D. (2020). Dynamic relationship between technological knowledge and products: Diversification strategy for firm growth. *Technology Analysis & Strategic Management*. DOI: 10.1080/09537325.2020.1834082. (Published online on 19 Oct 2020).

Kapur, D. (1985). Thermax: Hard sell and innovative design. *Business India*, 116–124. March 11–24.

Kazanjian, R. K. (1988). Relation of dominant problems to stage of growth in technology-based new ventures. *Academy of Management Journal*, **31**(2): 257–279.

Kets de Vries, M. F. R. (1977). The entrepreneurial personality: A person at the cross roads. *The Journal of Management Studies*, **14**, February: 34–57.

Kets de Vries, M. F. R. (1985). The dark side of entrepreneurship. *Harvard Business Review*, (November–December), 160–168.

Khandwalla, P. N. (1985). The PI Motive: A Base for Development. Working Paper No. 558, October. Ahmedabad: Indian Institute of Management.

Kim, J., Lee, C-Y. and Choc, Y. (2016). Technological diversification, core-technology competence, and firm growth. *Research Policy*, **45**(1), February: 113–124.

King, K. A., Pealer, L. N. and Bernard, A. L. (2001). Increasing response rates to mail questionnaires: A review of inducement strategies. *American Journal of Health Education*, **32**(1): 4–15. DOI: 10.1080/19325037.2001.10609392.

Kirchhoff, B. A. and Phillips, B. D. (1988). The effect of firm formation and growth on job creation in the United States. *Journal of Business Venturing*, **3**: 261–272.

Knight, F. (1921). *Risk, Uncertainty and Profit*. Boston: Houghton-Mifflin.

Kotter, J. and Sathe, V. (1978). Problems of human resource management in rapidly growing companies. *California Management Review*, **21**(2): 29–36.

Kourilsky, M. (1980). Predictors of entrepreneurship in a simulated economy. *Journal of Creative Behavior*, **14**(3): 175–199.

Krasner, O. J. and Ray, D. (1984). Entrepreneurs in robotics and biotechnology: Perceptions of problems and risks. Paper Presented at Babson Research Conference on Entrepreneurship, April 1984. Georgia Institute of Technology.

Krentzman, H. C. and Samaras, J. N. (1960). Can small business use consultants? *Harvard Business Review*, **38**(3): 126–136.

Kumar, M. S. (1984). Growth, Acquisition and Investment. Occasional Paper 56, Department of Applied Economics, University of Cambridge.

Kumar, R. S. and Balasubrahmanya, M. H. (2010). Influence of subcontracting on innovation and economic performance of SMEs in Indian automobile industry. *Technovation*, **30**(11–12), November–December: 558–569.

Laguir, I. and Besten, M. D. (2016). The influence of entrepreneur's personal characteristics on MSEs' growth through innovation. *Applied Economics*, **48**(44): 4183–4200. DOI: 10.1080/00036846.2016.1153792.

Lechner, C. and Dowling, M. (2003). Firm networks: External relationships as sources for the growth and competitiveness of entrepreneurial firms. *Entrepreneurship & Regional Development*, **15**(1): 1–26. DOI: 10.1080/08985620210159220.

Lee, N. (2014). What holds back high-growth firms? Evidence from UK SMEs. *Small Business Economics*, **43**(1): 183–195. DOI: 10.1007/s11187-013-9525-5.

Lewis, J. D. (1990). *Partnerships for Profit: Structuring and Managing Strategic Alliances*. New York: The Free Press.

Lewis, K. (2008). Small firm owners in New Zealand: Is it for the 'good life' or growth? *Small Enterprise Research*, **16**(1): 61–69.

Lipper III, A. (1985). Remarks at the 2nd Creativity, Innovation and Entrepreneurship Symposium. George Washington University, March 22, 1985.

Lippitt, G. L. and Schmidt, W. H. (1967). Crises in a developing organization. *Harvard Business Review*, **45**(4): 102–114.

Lorenzoni, G. and Ornati, O. A. (1988). Constellations of firms and new ventures. *Journal of Business Venturing*, **3**(1): 41–57.

Luo, Y. and Child, J. (2015). A composition-based view of firm growth. *Management and Organization Review*, **11**, September: 379–411. DOI: 10.1017/mor.2015.29.

Maidique, M. A. (1980). Entrepreneurs, champions and technological innovation. *Sloan Management Review*, **21**(2), Winter: 59–76.

Maidique, M. A. and Hayes, R. H. (1984). The art of high technology management. *Sloan Management Review*, **25**(2), Winter: 17–31.

Mandell, L. and Lundsten, L. L. (1978). Some insights into the under-reporting of financial data by sample survey respondents. *Journal of Marketing Research*, **15**: 294–299.

Manimala, M. J. (1987). Deontic motivation. *The Economic Times*. March 19, 1987.

Manimala, M. J. (1988a). *Managerial Heuristics of Pioneering-innovative (PI) Entrepreneurs: An Exploratory Study*. Unpublished Doctoral Dissertation. Ahmedabad: Indian Institute of Management.

Manimala, M. J. (1988b). Case-survey method in entrepreneurship research. *Graduate Management Research*, **4**(1), Winter: 4–15.

Manimala, M. J. (1992a). Entrepreneurial innovation: Beyond Schumpeter. *Creativity and Innovation Management*, **1**(1): 46–55.

Manimala, M. J. (1992b). Innovative entrepreneurship: Testing the theory of environmental determinism. In Maheshwari, B. L. (Ed.), *Innovations in Management for Development* (pp. 100–118). New Delhi: Tata McGraw-Hill.

Manimala, M. J. (1992c). Entrepreneurial heuristics: A comparison between high PI (pioneering-innovative) and low PI ventures. *Journal of Business Venturing*, **7**(6), November: 477–504.

Manimala, M. J. (1996a). Beyond innovators and imitators: A taxonomy of entrepreneurs. *Creativity and Innovation Management*, **5**(3), September: 179–185.

Manimala, M. J. (1996b). Strategic responses of Indian organizations to economic liberalization. *The Social Engineer*, **5**(2), July: 34–55.

Manimala, M. J. (1998). Networking for innovation: Anecdotal evidence from a large-sample study of innovative enterprises. *Journal of Entrepreneurship* **7**(2), July–December, pp: 153–170.

Manimala, M. J. (1999). *Entrepreneurial Policies and Strategies: The Innovator's Choice*. New Delhi: Sage Publications.

Manimala, M. J. (2002a). *GEM India Report 2002*. Bangalore, India: NS Raghavan Centre for Entrepreneurial Learning, Indian Institute of Management Bangalore.

Manimala, M. J. (2002b). Managing R&D in SMEs: Exploiting the giants' shoulders advantage. *Industry and Higher Education*, **16**(3), June: 177–190.

Manimala, M. J. (2008). Entrepreneurship education in India: An assessment of SME training needs against current practices. *International Journal of Entrepreneurship and Innovation Management*, **8**(6): 624–647.

Manimala, M. J. and Pearson, A. W. (1991). Hoyle Marine Ltd and the T-disc Oil Skimmer. Unpublished case study, Manchester Business School: NIMTECH-LES, Manchester.

Mansfield, E. (1979). *Micro-economics: Theory and Applications*. New York: Norton.

Mansfield, M. (2019). Startup statistics — The numbers you need to know. https://smallbiztrends.com/2019/03/startup-statistics-small-business.html. Accessed 10 May 2020.

Markides, C. C. and Williamson, P. J. (1994). Related diversification, core competences and corporate performance. *Strategic Management Journal*, **15**(5): 149–165.

Maslow, A. H. (1954). *Motivation and Personality*. New York: Harper and Row.

Matlay, H. (1999). Employee relations in small firms. *Employee Relations*, **21**(3): 285–295. https://doi.org/10.1108/01425459910273125.

McClelland, D. C. (1961). *The Achieving Society*. Princeton, NJ: Van Nostrand.

McClelland, D. C. (1986). Characteristics of successful entrepreneurs. In Solomon, G. T. and Whiting, B. G. (Eds.), *Keys to the Future of American Business*. The Ohio State University, National Center for Research in Vocational Education.

McClelland, D. C. (1987). Characteristics of successful entrepreneurs. *Journal of Creative Behaviour*, **21**(3): 219–233.

McClelland, D. C. and Burnham, D. (1976). Power is the great motivator. *Harvard Business Review*, **54**(2): 100–110.

McDaniel, S. W. and Rao, C. P. (1980). The effect of monetary inducement on mailed questionnaire response rate and quality. *Journal of Marketing Research*, **17**: 265–268.

McGregor, D. (1960). *The Human Side of Enterprise*. New York: McGraw-Hill.

McGivern, C. and Overton, D. (1980). A study of small firms and their management development needs. In Gibb, A. and Webb, T. (Eds.), *Policy Issues in Small Business Research* (pp. 128–140). Saxon House.

McGuire, J. W. (1963). *Factors Affecting the Growth of Manufacturing Firms*. Seattle: Bureau of Business Research, University of Washington.

McMahon, R. G. P. (1998). Stage models of SME growth reconsidered. *Small Enterprise Research*, **6**(2): 20–35.

Mill, J. S. (1848). *Principles of Political Economy with Some of Their Applications to Social Philosophy*. London: John W. Parker.

Michel, A. and Shaked, I. (1984). Does business diversification affect performance? *Financial Management*, **13**(4): 18–25. DOI: 10.2307/3665297.

Mintzberg, H. (1976). Planning on the left side and managing on the right. *Harvard Business Review*, **54**, July–August: 49–58.

MoneyControl.com. (2018a). The business of family — The Kirloskars. June 12, 2018. https://www.moneycontrol.com/news/business/companies/podcast-the-business-of-family-the-kirloskars-2588021.html. Accessed 23 Nov 2021.

MoneyControl.com. (2018b). 90% Indian startups fail within 5 years of inception: Study. https://www.moneycontrol.com/news/business/90-indian-startups-fail-within-5-years-of-inception-study-2689671.html. Accessed 10 May 2020.

Moreno, A. M. and Casillas, J. C. (2007). High-growth SMEs versus non-high-growth SMEs: A discriminant analysis. *Entrepreneurship & Regional Development*, **19**(1): 69–88 (Published online on 13 February 2007). https://doi.org/10.1080/08985620601002162.

Morgan, N. (1988). Successful growth by acquisition. *Journal of General Management*, **14**(2): 5–18.

Musso, P. and Schiavo, S. (2008). The impact of financial constraints on firm survival and growth. *Journal of Evolutionary Economics*, **18**: 135–149. https://doi.org/10.1007/s00191-007-0087-z.

Nandy, A. (1973). Motives, modernity, and entrepreneurial competence. *The Journal of Social Psychology*, **91**(1): 127–136. DOI: 10.1080/00224545.1973.9922654.

NDTV. (2020). Mukesh Ambani wins half of 2020 deals in global telecom. https://www.ndtv.com/business/billionaire-mukesh-ambani-wins-half-of-2020-deals-in-global-telecom-jio-platforms-stake-stake-sale-2249059. Accessed 3 Jun 2020.

Nawal, A. (2019). Why is IKEA so cheap? IKEA business model. July 21, 2019. https://www.feedough.com/why-is-ikea-so-cheap-ikea-business-model/. Accessed 8 Feb 2021.

Nielson, S. (2014). Apple's premium pricing strategy and product differentiation. *Yahoo! Finance*. 7 February 2014. https://finance.yahoo.com/news/apple-premium-pricing-strategy-product-191247308.html? Accessed 18 Feb 2021.

O' Farrell, P. N. and Hitchens, D. W. N. (1988). Alternative theories of small-firm growth: A critical review. *Environment and Planning*, **20**: 1365–1382.

Omura, G. S. (1983). Correlates of item non-response. *Journal of the Market Research Society*, **25**: 321–330.

Palich, L. E. and Bagby, D. R. (1995). Entrepreneurial risk-taking: Challenging conventional wisdom. *Journal of Business Venturing*, **10**: 425–438.

Park, S. H., Chen, R. and Gallagher, S. (2002). Firm resources as moderators of the relationship between market growth and strategic alliances in semiconductor start-ups. *Academy of Management Journal*, **45**(3): 527–545.

Park, Y., Shin, J. and Kim, T. (2010). Firm size, age, industrial networking, and growth: A case of the Korean manufacturing industry. *Small Business Economics*, **35**: 153–168. https://doi.org/10.1007/s11187-009-9177-7.

Pedersen, P. O. (1991). A network approach to small enterprise and its environment. In Bergman, E. M., Maier, G. and Todtling, F. (Eds.), *Regions Reconsidered: Economic Networks, Innovation and Local Development in Industrialized Countries*. London: Mansell Publishing Limited.

Penrose, E. T. (1959). *Theory of the Growth of Firms*. New York: Wiley.

Peters, T. J. and Waterman, R. H. (1982). *In Search of Excellence: Lessons from America's Best-Run Companies*. New York: Harper & Row.

Peterson, R. A. and Kerin, R. A. (1981). The quality of self-report data: Review and synthesis. In Enis, B. M. and Roering, K. J. (Eds.), *Review of Marketing 1981* (pp. 5–20). Chicago: American Marketing Association.

Piramal, G. and Herdeck, M. (1985). *India's Industrialists.* Washington, DC: Three Continents Press.

Porter, M. E. (1980). *Competitive Strategy.* New York: Free Press.

Pradhan, S. (2020). Understanding Apple's pricing strategies: Lessons to learn. *Silicon India.* 30 October 2020. https://www.siliconindia.com/news/general/understanding-apples-pricing-strategies-lessons-to-learn-nid-214478-cid-1.html. Accessed 18 Feb 2021.

Ramaswamy, K., Purkayastha, S. and Petitt, B. S. (2017). How do institutional transitions impact the efficacy of related and unrelated diversification strategies used by business groups? *Journal of Business Research*, **72**, March: 1–13. https://doi.org/10.1016/j.jbusres.2016.11.005.

Ramsay, J. E., Pang, J. S., Ho, M. H. R. and Chan, K. Y. (2016). Need for power predicts career intent in university students. *Journal of Career Assessment*, **25**(3): 389–404.

Ramsey, M. (2019). Henry Ford's great-great grandchildren join the family business. *The Wall Street Journal* (India Edition). 23 September 2019.

Ravindranath, S. (1984). Eating into the multinational's markets. *Business India*, March 26–April 8: 100–106.

Reja, U., Manfreda, K. L., Hlebec, V. and Vehovar, V. (2003). Open-ended vs. close-ended questions in web questionnaires. In Ferligoj, A. and Mrvar, A. (Eds.), *Developments in Applied Statistics*, Metodološki zvezki, 19. Ljubljana: FDV.

Reynolds, P. D., Bygrave, W. D., Autio, E., Cox, L. and Hay, M. (2002). *GEM Global 2002 Executive Report.* Kansas, MO: Ewing Marion Kauffman Foundation.

Rindfuss, R. R., Choe, M. K., Tsuya, N. O., Bumpass, L. L. and Tamaki, E. (2015). Do low survey response rates bias results? Evidence from Japan. *Demographic Research*, **32**: 797–828. Article-26 (March). DOI: 10.4054/DemRes.2015.32.26.

Roberts, E. B. and Berry, C. A. (1985). Entering new business: Selecting strategies for success. *Sloan Management Review*, Spring: 3–17.

Robinson, J. B. Jr. and Pearce, J. A. (1984). Research thrusts in small firm strategic planning. *Academy of Management Review*, **9**: 128–137.

Romanelli, E. (1989). Environments and strategies of organization start-up: Effects on early survival. *Administrative Science Quarterly*, **34**(3): 369–387.

Romano, C. A. (1990). Identifying factors which influence product innovation: A case study. *Journal of Management Studies*, **27**(1): 75–95.

Ronstadt, R. (1988). The corridor principle. *Journal of Business Venturing*, **3**(1): 31–40.

Roper, S. (1997). Product innovation and small business growth: A comparison of strategies of German, UK, and Irish companies. *Small Business Economics*, **9**, December: 523–537.

Ross, A. (1975). *The Risk-Takers: The Dreamers Who Build a Business from an Idea.* Toronto: MacLean-Hunter.

Rotter, J. B. (1966). Generalized expectancies for internal versus external control of reinforcement. *Psychological Monographs*, **80**(1): 1–28. http://dx.doi.org/10.1037/h0092976. PMID: 5340840.

Rumelt, R. P. (1974). *Strategy, Structure and Economic Performance.* Cambridge, MA: Harvard Business School, Division of Research.

Rutherford, M. W., O'Boyle, E. H., Miao, C., Goering, D. and Coombs, J. E. (2017). Do response rates matter in entrepreneurship research? *Journal of Business Venturing Insights*, **8**: 93–98. https://doi.org/10.1016/j.jbvi.2017.07.003.

Sadler, P. J. and Barry, B. A. (1970). *Organizational Development.* London: Longman.

Scheinberg, S. and MacMillan, I. C. (1988). An eleven-country study of motivation to start a business. In Kirchhoff, B. A., Long, W., McMullan, W., Vesper, K. H. and Wetzel, W. (Eds.), *Frontiers of Entrepreneurship Research* (pp. 669–687). Wellesley, MA: Babson College.

Schere, J. (1982). Tolerance of ambiguity as a discriminating variable between entrepreneurs and managers. *Proceedings of the National Academy of Management* (New York), pp. 404–408.

Schuler, R. S. and MacMillan, I. C. (1984). Gaining competitive advantage through human resource management. *Human Resource Management*, **23**(3): 241–256.

Schumpeter, J. A. (1934). *The Theory of Economic Development* (Translated by Redvers Opie). Cambridge, Massachusetts: Harvard University Press. 1961 (Originally published in 1934).

Schumpeter, J. A. (1942). *Capitalism, Socialism, and Democracy.* New York: Harper & Bros.

Schwartz, H. S. (1983). A theory of deontic work motivation. *Journal of Applied Behavioral Science*, **19**(2): 203–214.

Sexton, D. L. and Bowman, N. B. (1983). Comparative entrepreneurship characteristics of students: Preliminary results. In Hornaday, J., Timmons, J. and Vesper, K. H. (Eds.), *Frontiers of Entrepreneurship Research* (pp. 213–225). Wellesley, MA: Babson College.

Sexton, D. L. and Bowman, N. B. (1985). The entrepreneur: A capable executive and more. *Journal of Business Venturing*, **1**(1): 129–140.

Sherif, M. (1958). Super-ordinate goals in the reduction of inter-group conflict. *American Journal of Sociology*, **63**: 349–356. DOI: 10.1086/222258.

Shirley, S. (1991). Building an Information Technology Company. Silver Anniversary Lecture, Manchester Business School, January 24.

Siegel, R., Siegel, E. and MacMillan, I. C. (1993). Characteristics distinguishing high-growth ventures. *Journal of Business Venturing*, **8**(2): 169–180. March.

Simon, H. A. (1955). A behavioral model of rational choice. *The Quarterly Journal of Economics*, **69**(1), February: 99–118.

Singh, M. (2012). The story of Colonel Sanders, a man who started at 65 and failed 1,009 times before succeeding. Yourstory.com. 26th July 2012. https://yourstory.com/2012/07/the-story-of-colonel-sanders-a-man-who-started-at-65-and-failed-1009-times-before-succeeding?utm_pageloadtype=scroll. Accessed 1 Mar 2021.

Sjöström, O., Holst, D. and Lind, S. O. (1999). Validity of a questionnaire survey: The role of non-response and incorrect answers. *Acta Odontologica Scandinavica*, **57**(5): 242–246. DOI: 10.1080/000163599428643.

Smallbone, D., Leigh, R. and North, D. (1995). The characteristics and strategies of high growth SMEs. *International Journal of Entrepreneurial Behaviour & Research*, **1**(3): 44–62.

Smith, N. R. (1967). *The Entrepreneur and His Firm: The Relationship between Type of Man and Type of Company*. East Lansing, MI: Michigan State University.

Smith, N. R. and Miner, J. B. (1983). Type of entrepreneur, type of firm, and managerial motivation: Implications for organizational life cycle theory. *Strategic Management Journal*, **4**(4): 325–340.

Smith, C. G. and Cooper, A. C. (1988). Established companies diversifying into young industries: A comparison of firms with different levels of performance. *Strategic Management Journal*, **9**(2): 111–121.

Smith, K. G., Gannon, M. J., Grimm, C. and Mitchell, T. R. (1988). Decision making behavior in smaller entrepreneurial and larger professionally managed firms. *Journal of Business Venturing*, **3**(3): 223–232.

Solomon, G. T. and Winslow, E. K. (1988). Towards a descriptive profile of the entrepreneur. *Journal of Creative Behaviour*, **22**(3): 162–171.

Stam, E. and Wennberg, K. (2009). The roles of R&D in new firm growth. *Small Business Economics*, **33**, August: 77–89. https://doi.org/10.1007/s11187-009-9183-9.

Starbuck, W. H. (1965). Organizational growth and development. In March, J. G. (Ed.), *Handbook of Organizations* (pp. 451–533). Chicago: Rand McNally.

Steinmetz, L. L. (1969). Critical stages of small business growth: When they occur and how to survive them. *Business Horizons*, **12**(1), February: 29–36.

Stevenson, H. H. and Gumpert, D. E. (1985). The heart of entrepreneurship. *Harvard Business Review*, **63**(2): 85–94.

Stevenson, H. H. and Jarillo, J. C. (1986). Preserving entrepreneurship as companies grow. *Journal of Business Strategy*, **7**(1): 10–23.

Stevenson, H. H. and Jarillo, J. C. (1990). A paradigm of entrepreneurship: Entrepreneurial management. *Strategic Management Journal*, **11**(5), Summer: Special Issue on Corporate Entrepreneurship: 17–27.

Tan, W. L., Menkhoff, T. and Chay, Y. W. (2007). The effects of entrepreneurial growth-orientation on organizational change and firm growth. *Small Enterprise Research*, **15**(2): 88–99.

The Economic Times. (2020). One-time billionaire Anil Ambani says he's now worth nothing. https://economictimes.indiatimes.com/news/company/corporate-trends/onetime-billionaire-says-hes-now-worth-nothing/articleshow/74019910.cms?utm_source=contentofinterest&utm_medium=text&utm_campaign=cppst. Accessed 3 Jun 2020.

The Leela Group. (2021). https://en.wikipedia.org/wiki/The_Leela_Group. Accessed 3 Jun 2020.

Thorelli, H. B. (1986). Networks: Between markets and hierarchies. *Strategic Management Journal*, **7**(1): 37–51.

Wall, T. D., Michie, J., Patterson, M., Wood, S. J., Sheehan, M., Clegg, C. W. and West, M. (2004). On the validity of subjective measures of company performance. *Personnel Psychology*, **57**(1), March: 95–118.

Weber, M. (1930). *The Protestant Ethic and the Spirit of Capitalism*. New York: Scribner's.

Weber, M. (1958). *The Religion of India* (reprint). New York: The Free Press.

Weiss, M. (2016). Related diversification: A critical reflection of relatedness and the diversification-performance linkage. In Finkelstein, S. and Cooper, C. L. (Eds.), *Advances in Mergers and Acquisitions* (Vol. 15, pp. 161–180). Bingley: Emerald Group Publishing Ltd. https://doi.org/10.1108/S1479-361X20160000015009.

Wernerfelt, B. (1984). A resource-based view of the firm. *Strategic Management Journal*, **5**(2): 171–180. https://doi.org/10.1002/smj.4250050207.

Wiklund, J., Davidsson, P. and Delmar, F. (2003). What do they think and feel about growth? An expectancy-value approach to small business managers' attitudes towards growth. *Entrepreneurship Theory & Practice*, **27**(3): 247–269.

Wild, R. and Swann, K. (1973). The small company, profitability, management resources and management techniques. *Journal of Business Policy*, **3**: 10–21.

Wilson, P. and Gort, P. (1983). How large and small firms can grow together. *Long Range Planning*, **16**(2): 19–27.

Wikipedia. (2021). Walmart. https://en.wikipedia.org/wiki/Walmart. Accessed 8 Feb 2021.

Womack, B. (2019). Perot used his time at IBM and $1,000 to help change an industry – and DFW. *Dallas Business Journal*. 10 July 2019. https://www.bizjournals.com/dallas/news/2019/07/10/ross-perot-sr.html.

Wotruba, T. R. (1966). Monetary inducements and mail questionnaire response. *Journal of Marketing Research*, **3**, November: 398–400.

Wunder, G. C. and Wynn, G. W. (1988). The effects of address personalization on mailed questionnaire response rate, time and quality. *Journal of the Market Research Society*, **30**(1): 95–101.

Wynarczyk, P. and Watson, R. (2005). Firm growth and supply chain partnerships: An empirical analysis of U.K. SME subcontractors. *Small Business Economics*, **24**(1), February: 39–51. https://doi.org/10.1007/s11187-005-3095-0.

Yu, J. and Cooper, H. (1983). A quantitative review of research design effects on response rates to questionnaires. *Journal of Marketing Research*, **20**(1), February: 36–44.

Zhou, H. and de Wit, G. (2009). Determinants and dimensions of firm-growth. *SCALES EIM Research Reports (H200903)*. Available at SSRN: https://ssrn.com/abstract=1443897 or http://dx.doi.org/10.2139/ssrn.1443897.

Appendix 1: An Illustrative Case-Study[*]

FI Group Plc: Growth from Freelancing to Professionalism

Part I: *A Refugee Girl from Germany*

In 1939, Vera Buchthal crossed over from Germany to the United Kingdom along with about 10,000 other Jewish refugee children. Each of them carried a small backpack and had a number for identification purposes tied around their neck. It was a very traumatic experience, as Vera recalled later: "I remember being sort of dumped at (London's) Liverpool Street Station...we got off that train in silence. Somebody came and looked at my number and said: 'Ah yes, you're mine'. I was taken away. I didn't speak English; they didn't speak German. I was screaming most of the time. It was sheer trauma". Orphanages, rescue homes and foster parents in the UK came forward to house these children, and Vera too had the good fortune of getting shelter and the opportunity to go to school. She even got a new name, Stephanie, given to her by her foster parents, Guy and Ruby Smith.

---

[*]This case is prepared based on an interview conducted with Dame Stephanie Shirley in 1990 and supplemented with information from secondary sources. The case is presented in three parts, where the first two parts end with decision situations, and hence it is possible to use Part-I or Parts I and II together as a separate cases for teaching purposes. Part-I can be used for a session on Entrepreneurship, and Parts I and II together can be used for a session on Enterprise Growth.

Vera (alias Stephanie) was born in 1933 in Dortmund, Germany. Her father, Arnold Buchthal, was a judge in the city, but was removed from his post (because he was a Jew) when the Nazis came to power in Germany. Fearing for the safety of his daughters — Renate (9 years) and Vera (5 years) — he sent them to the UK on the Kindertransport program organized by Jewish and Christian activists and operated by the Quakers (a Christian religious group), which transferred 10,000 children to the UK from Nazi-controlled regions.

After completing her primary education in Staffordshire, she was sent by her foster parents to Oswestry Girls' High School near the Welsh border. As a student, Stephanie recognized that she had special competencies in Mathematics, but the girls' school where she was studying did not teach maths beyond the elementary level. According to the prevailing norms in the UK, the right thing for a girl in those days was to pursue liberal arts and humanities in her studies, as maths and science were not appropriate for girls. The system was obviously unfair to the female students who were gifted in maths and science, but it was difficult for anyone to change the system, particularly for an orphan girl. And yet, Stephanie decided not to give up. She made a special request for permission to attend maths classes in the nearby boys' school, which was a parallel institution run by the same management. Her request was granted, rather surprisingly! Though it was somewhat uncomfortable to be a lone girl student among a class of boys, Stephanie thoroughly enjoyed her hard-won opportunity to learn mathematics.

When she completed 18 years of age, Stephanie applied for and obtained British citizenship under the name, Stephanie Brook, as she preferred to adopt the naturalized British surname of her mother, Margaret Brook. Although her natural parents had survived the holocaust, and Stephanie (Vera) got an opportunity to reunite with them, when the latter came to the UK in search of their daughters after World War II ended, she could not bond well with them after the long years of separation and life in another country with a different language and culture. So, she decided to seek permanent affiliation with her adopted family, country, and culture, and retained a modified version of her adopted name. She became truly British in every sense of the term.

Although Stephanie had the ambition to pursue her studies in Mathematics beyond the school level, it was not possible for her to do so. Botany was the only science course available to girls. Besides, her orphan/refugee status also proved to be an impediment. She, therefore, took up a job with British Telecom (BT). Considering her special competencies in Mathematics, BT offered her the position of a 'Research Mathematician'. The designation sounded great, but the job was thoroughly boring. There was no research in her job. She was nothing more than a "glorified mathematical clerk". The BT job was also one of the lowest-paid among government jobs. Still, it offered her a lot of leisure time and more holidays than a job in the private sector. This extra free time available to her was gainfully utilized. The job at the Post Office Research Station helped her in building computers from scratch (including electronic telephone exchanges and the premium bond computer, ERNIE, the Electronic Random Number Indicator Equipment, used for the random allotment of tax-free prizes to bondholders) and writing codes for them, while her spare time was utilized to support her further studies, which she continued by attending evening classes. Eventually, after 6 years of study in evening classes, she obtained a postgraduate degree in Mathematics at the age of 23. An observation made by Stephanie later in life about not getting the opportunity to continue her studies after school and having to get her degree through evening courses while also working is quite insightful. She said that by the age of 23, she had a degree and six years of work experience, whereas those that had followed full-time studies had to be satisfied with a postgraduate degree and no work experience. As a result, she was able to get a higher-level job as the Chief Programmer at ICL, whereas others had to be satisfied with entry-level jobs.

Stephanie's most important achievements at the personal level during her nine-year period of work with BT were the development of proficiency in computer software and obtaining her postgraduate degree in Mathematics through evening courses. She had thus acquired the qualifications and the confidence to move on to a software development job and was waiting for such an opportunity. The boredom and the low remuneration at BT, however, was not the immediate cause for her to change job. Rather, it was her marriage in 1961 to a colleague, Derek Shirley, who was a physicist at BT. There was a norm in British public sector companies in those days that married couples were not allowed to work together in the same company. She, therefore, took up the post of Chief Programmer at International Computers Limited (ICL), the largest manufacturer of mainframe computers in the UK at that time (which ceased to exist as an independent company in 2002, as it merged with Fujitsu). Even though in her new job she was working for a reputed computer company as a programmer, she felt that her job was peripheral to the company's business, since ICL focused mainly on hardware and practically neglected the software part of the work, which was also the practice of most other hardware manufacturers in those days. In fact, software did not even have the status of an independent product but was treated as something that was given away free of charge with the purchase of the hardware.

Though ICL was "a splendid company" (in the words of Stephanie), the job was not exciting for her, as they placed very little importance on software. For the same reason, the career prospects of the software employees were extremely limited. Moreover, there was the cultural issue of gender discrimination and the resultant 'glass ceiling' for the career progression of women employees. As she was trying to cope with the new job and the organization, she had to take a break because of pregnancy and the birth of her son, Giles. After that break, when she wanted to return to work, apparently nobody wanted her, as they felt she was out of touch with the newer developments in the field! Besides, software was not in great demand in established companies, whose focus was on the 'solid stuff' like the hardware. The software services were provided to customers by the 'unorganized sector' constituted by freelance professionals.

While the software sector was growing very quickly, there were very few organized players in the sector, who could offer employment to others. The large players, with their heavy overheads, found it difficult to compete with freelancers. But the greatest stigma faced by professionals like Stephanie who had taken a break from their careers was that they were perceived as being out of touch with the field. For a field that was changing so rapidly, such career breaks were seen as a sufficient reason to make them obsolete, and they were treated as 'untouchables' by the established organizations. It occurred to Stephanie that this could be a problem more specific to women, who had taken breaks from work for family reasons and that there may be many qualified women like her sitting at home but interested in restarting their work and career. Faced with the difficulties of getting back to work with a large company, Stephanie could visualize the entrepreneurial opportunities available in a growing field like software development and focused her thoughts on creating her own software enterprise. However, she realized that the investment needed to build the infrastructure and meet the cost of professionals required for the work was formidable. She was seriously searching for a way out of her idleness trap.

Part II: *Freelance Programmers — Pioneering the Flexible Organization*

As noted in the first part of this case, Stephanie Shirley (née Vera Buchthal/Stephanie Brook) was at a turning point in her life when she was finding it difficult to get back to employment after she took a career break on account of the birth of her son, Giles. Although she had plans to start a software business, it was stalled by difficulties in finding the necessary capital to invest in infrastructure and pay the initial salaries. She could, however, visualize the kind of opportunities for new business and innovative operations embedded in this new and emerging area of technology.

- The market for software products and services was largely unexploited and growing very rapidly. With the developments in hardware technology, there was correspondingly an increasing need for software to support the new hardware.
- However, the prevailing practice of large computer companies was to focus almost exclusively on the hardware aspects of computers, to the near-total neglect of software development in the organized sector. Hardware companies could have software developed by freelance professionals as and when they needed it.
- Software development was a low-cost operation, which required hardly any physical infrastructure and was based on intellectual capital. It was indeed nothing more than a 'paper-and-pencil' operation of logically organizing the steps involved in the processes. Once the steps were logically arranged on paper, the sequence was entered into the mainframe computer. As there were no desktop or laptop computers at that time, the developer was not required to enter the software into the computer and create a 'digital' version.
- Even though there was enough scope for a few large players in the software segment, if such companies were to be organized in the traditional manner with heavy overheads, they would not be able to compete with the freelance professionals who operated as individuals and with very few overheads.
- Shirley realized that there were many such highly qualified freelance professionals available, especially among women like herself who had taken breaks from work for family reasons. While they were interested in getting back to work, they were not acceptable to the large organizations who saw them as out of touch with new developments in

technology. Besides, such organizations were not able or willing to provide the flexibility that these women required for taking care of their families. Stephanie, therefore, took it up as her mission to do something to help the women in such situations.

- Faced with these problems: on the one hand, the large organizations' reluctance to incur overhead expenses for software development; and, on the other, the freelancers' availability for work while wanting to retain flexibility, coupled with their inability to market themselves, Stephanie was looking for a via-media organizational solution. Her answer to this problematic situation was to create and co-ordinate a consortium of freelance women programmers, each operating from her own home, which eliminated the need for any investment in physical infrastructure. These professionals were registered with her company as 'panel members', not as employees, and therefore they were to be paid only for the specific work done by them, not a regular salary. The company's job was to get software projects from large organizations, partition them into smaller projects and allocate them to the panel members based on their interests, competencies, and availability.

Freelance Programmers was thus founded in 1962 by Stephanie (later, 'Steve') Shirley with an initial investment of just £6 and started operating from her own home in Chesham, Buckinghamshire, UK. The initial size of the company was 12 female freelancers working on a retainership arrangement. Even though they were supposed to be freelancers operating from their own houses, some of them needed a space to sit and work, which was provided at Shirley's own house. It was not a very pleasant existence at all in the initial years, as Shirley recollects: "In our tiny cottage, I had one woman working in a spare bedroom, two more in the living room, with the files piled on top of the piano, and the baby and me at the dining room table. It was pretty much like hell". To add to her woes, by the age of three, her son Giles started showing symptoms of autism (a developmental disorder that impairs the ability to communicate and interact), accompanied by epileptic tendencies with violent seizures and other abnormal behaviors.

The chronic illness of her son had a devastating impact on the personal life and business activities of Stephanie and her husband. The couple would work in shifts to take care of their son and eventually Derek took early retirement. Giles needed constant attention and frequent hospitalization. In one such instance of hospitalization, Stephanie had to run her company for almost nine months from the mothers' unit of the hospital where her son was admitted for treatment. Even when he was at home, his loud cries and violent behavior disturbed the workers and phone callers. In order to conceal her son's cries and shouts from business callers, Stephanie used to play aloud a tape recording of typing noises when answering phone calls.

Those early days were enormously stressful for Stephanie, and she started smoking to relieve her stress. She used to smoke over 60 cigarettes a day, and eventually suffered a nervous breakdown that disabled her for almost 10 months. At one point, she even considered suicide of the entire family as a solution for all their problems, but good sense prevailed over their troubled thoughts and they slowly regained their mental strength to find constructive solutions to their problems. One such considered solution was to build for their son a supervised care home with treatment facilities for autism. Due to financial constraints, they could not undertake this project immediately, but when the company's revenues gradually increased and reached a comfortable level, Stephanie sold 10% of her shares and set up a supervised care home for Giles in 1987. Later, when they realized that such care was also needed for other autistic children, they converted it into a trust (The Kingwood Trust) for the care and treatment of autistic children. This became Stephanie's first step in her journey into philanthropy, which became her full-time activity after the tragic death of her son in 1998 at the age of 35. But this is a much later development, which was to be preceded by troubles and struggles lasting for several years.

In spite of the personal hardships of the founder in the initial years of this new venture, as noted above, Freelance Programmers grew quickly because of its cost-effective and flexible organizational model. Compared to individual freelancers, it had a wide variety of competencies to offer and the capability of taking on larger projects because of the number of professionals it had at its disposal. Since these professionals were retained as panel members operating from their own homes, the company incurred low overhead expenses in terms of office space and equipment. There was also no commitment to pay salaries for the panel members, who were paid only when they were given work. The retention fee for panel members was very low, as the company operated exclusively with female professionals who had become 'unemployable' in the organized sector because of the career breaks they had taken for family reasons.

As Stephanie wanted to help the qualified women sitting idle at home despite their desire to get back to work, she decided to focus solely on the employment of such women in her new venture, which, therefore, became an all-female enterprise. There were only three male employees in the first 300 employees/panelists of the company. This was also her way of protesting against the gender discrimination against women prevailing in corporate organizations and the 'glass ceiling' that routinely hindered their career development options in those days, of which she herself was also a victim. While her motivation to address gender discrimination was appreciated by those in her close circles, it became a constraint for her business operations in a male-dominated industry and society. When she realized that her name, 'Stephanie', failed to elicit much response from potential customers, she started signing her letters with a modified (male-sounding) version of her name, 'Steve' Shirley, which improved the responses from potential (male) customers, and subsequently she became better known by this name rather than Stephanie.

It was undoubtedly the cost advantages associated with the flexible organization that helped the rapid growth of Freelance Programmers. By 1970, it had over 100 people working for it and had operations in two foreign countries, Denmark and the Netherlands. It managed the severe recession of the early 1970s only because of its flexibility and low overhead costs. When the recession eliminated a few other competitors, the company expanded its activities further by offering its products and services to three major sectors: the financial sector, the commercial sector, and the public sector. It also managed to secure prestigious projects such as the programming for Concorde's black box flight recorder. Its operations spread to many more countries including the US. By 1984, the company became the 20th largest computer-consulting firm in the UK with a market share of 1.5% (the largest had a share of 4%), and its annual turnover reached £2.5 million, with a staff of more than 800.

Growth has also brought with it some problems:

- The investment needs of the company were growing fast. While the profitability was good, internal accumulation was not sufficient to meet the expansion needs of the company.
- The name 'Freelance Programmers' was becoming a deterrent to a few large clients, who saw a lack of professionalism implied in the name.
- The all-female employment policy was not helpful in hiring the best talents, especially in areas where there were skill shortages.

- The home-based work of its panel members created barriers to organizing discussions, testing, trouble-shooting, etc., at the customers' premises.
- Working from home had other disadvantages too. There is hardly any spontaneous interaction and knowledge sharing among professionals in such a system. Even when some professionals wanted to hold discussions with others, particularly on complex issues relating to large projects, it was not possible because the relevant people were not available at one place at a fixed time.
- Many professionals had their own career ambitions, even though they had joined the company as panel members. When some were given organizational responsibilities out of the exigencies of work, others became unhappy about it.
- There were also complaints about work allotments. Those who had locational proximity or were keeping in regular contact with the head office were seen to be favored with more prestigious and interesting assignments. Others were given routine and uninteresting work. Since the nature of work also had a bearing on remuneration, there was widespread unhappiness about how work was assigned.

Shirley was concerned about these issues and wanted to find solutions to the problems affecting the organization's smooth functioning. However, many of the solutions proposed militated against the concept of the flexible organization with limited overheads that had given her fledgling venture much of its competitive advantage. Reflecting on these issues, she once responded to a question after her address at the silver anniversary celebrations of Manchester Business School that: "the most critical impediment to an enterprise's growth is the entrepreneur himself/herself". That is why, when she wrote her autobiography later (in association with Richard Askwith), she called it *Let It Go: My Extraordinary Story — From Refugee to Entrepreneur to Philanthropist*. At various stages of the growth of her enterprise, she had to design the right strategies to 'let it go'.

Part III: *From Freelance to Xansa/Steria — Growth through Transformation*

As noted in Part 2 of the case, the rapid growth of Freelance Programmers brought in revenues as well as problems. Many of these problems were in relation to the system of having panel members instead of employees. While this system provided significant cost advantages and flexibility to the company in the initial years, it also became a source of problems for the panel members, the employees, the organization, and its product-market strategies.

A detailed analysis of the feedback from the various stakeholders showed that the growth of the company brought some of these problems into sharp focus, which are briefly outlined below.

- *Freelancer/All-female image*: The name of the company (Freelance Programmers) was giving an image of a less professional organization, which was getting in the way of winning prestigious projects from large companies. Similarly, the all-female image was also not very helpful in getting business from the male-dominated industry of those times, who also had the excuse that the company was using women working from home and so were out of touch with the latest technological developments.
- *Career ambitions*: Although many women joined the company as panel members, they did so because there was no alternative, as the established players in the industry did not recognize them as being acceptable as employees. While working as panel members, they continued to nurse their career ambitions and were often frustrated by not being selected as employees in new positions created through the growth of the organization.
- *Contacts with the administration/other employees*: Since the panel members were working from their homes, they were not able to keep in regular contact with the company administration or the other employees/panel members.
- *Teamwork/Quality of work*: The system of remote working with flexible timings led to difficulties in establishing effective teamwork, which in turn affected the quality of work, especially in cases where it was necessary to collaborate with others, as in the case of partitioned software projects that were allocated to different panel members, all working on different parts of the same project.
- *Work allotments*: Most of the panel members were unhappy about the work allotment system. They complained about irregularities and favoritism in work allotment. The more interesting and high-paying assignments were cornered by a few who were close to the administration, leaving the large majority with trivial and low-paying work. There

were also complaints about the frequency of getting assignments — that some were given more often than others. It was also alleged that the skill sets of the panel members were not properly considered when allotting work to them, which resulted in a gross under-utilization of their skills.

- *Information, feedback & training*: It was felt that information about the developments in the company was not reaching everyone uniformly. This was also the case of feedback on the work done by panel members; and there was no system to collect feedback from them either. There were no initiatives to provide panel members with training in new and emerging technologies.
- *Fees and expenses*: The fees for the work were relatively low and varied across different projects as well as between panel members. Similarly, for time-based work, the norms about compensation for extra hours worked were not clear. There were also issues about the reimbursement of expenses incurred in connection with the work.
- *Lateral recruitment versus internal promotions*: There was a genuine problem that panel members were stagnating in their technical knowledge, as they had limited exposure to the world of practice and were not receiving any training in new technologies. When faced with requirements of new skills, especially in ongoing projects, it was not practical for the company to promote panel members as employees and train them in the required skills. Hence, it was often necessary to engage in lateral recruitment, which was resisted by panel members and existing employees. It was also difficult to find sufficiently qualified female professionals for all project requirements, and hence the company was not able to adhere strictly to its 'only-women' policy.
- *Personal touch and caring culture*: With the growth of the company, it became difficult for the founder to maintain a personal touch with the employees and panel members, which she had done in the early days. It was felt necessary to replace personalized dealings with formal systems and norms to ensure the fair and equitable treatment of all.
- *Work at customer sites*: As the company started taking on more complex projects, there were many occasions when the work had to be done at customer sites. Invariably, such assignments would be given to regular employees, who were available for work at fixed office times and were, therefore, easier and more convenient to form visiting teams.

Panel members would, therefore, miss out on exposure to the corporate setup and the experience of doing more complex tasks with specialist customer groups.

- ***Transition from generalist to specialist projects***: The growth of the business brought about a change in the nature of the projects worked on. The company started to receive more and more specialist projects requiring more advanced technical knowledge and skills, which were difficult to find among the freelancer-panelists.

- ***Expansion/Partnerships beyond the home market***: The low-cost operations of the company attracted customers from outside of the UK. There were also requests for partnerships from similar other operators. Although this provided an opportunity for the company to expand beyond the UK borders, it also necessitated some adjustments in the strategies, systems, and processes of the organization. A strategic issue that came up was whether they should utilize the opportunities for growth through acquisitions, which would involve greater financial risk and cultural non-compatibilities, compared to the organic growth model that had been followed in the initial years.

Growth and Transformation: Actions and Outcomes

The innovative strategies adopted by Stephanie (Steve) Shirley during the start-up phase of her venture helped in significantly reducing infrastructural overheads and employee salaries. However, at the growth stage, many of these innovations turned out to be constraints and impediments to the growth path. The founder had an ideological and emotional attachment to her innovations, but eventually she 'let it go' (at various stages) in the interest of the enterprise and its stakeholders.

- In order to facilitate personal interaction and better teamwork among the panel members, the company created five 'Work Centers' in five different regions of the UK. Although the panel members could go to these work centers to meet their 'virtual' colleagues and discuss work-related issues with them, this was still not a perfect substitute for the free-flowing, spontaneous interactions and discussions happening in the 'conventional' workplace. These interactions had to be pre-planned in advance, with prior appointments with specific individuals, so that they would also be available at the same work center at the same time.

Occasionally, when someone wanted to use a center, it might not be available, as it would be in use by others. So, over a period of time, the entire organization was converted into a more conventional mode. But that is a much later story, before which there were a series of initiatives that gradually led the company to its final transformation.

- A consequence of individual professionals working on different parts of the same project without any real-time interaction among team members, or monitoring of the work by supervisors, was the occasional occurrences of quality problems due to non-conformity with prescribed standards. While they have creditably completed many high-quality programming tasks such as the programming of Concorde's black box flight recorder, there were occasions when customers complained of quality problems — a major issue in this regard, for instance, occurred on a project with Castrol, the motor-oil company. Shirley, therefore, developed a two-pronged strategy to deal with the quality control problems. The first was that she would be available on the telephone at any time her panelists wanted to clarify their doubts about a project. The second was to prepare elaborate quality manuals on more than ten key issues, such as the general quality policy, technical standards for software work, project management, estimating, consulting work, systems design, software documentation, software testing, configuration management, and so on, that panelists could refer to when they had doubts.

- Despite the skill shortages and the business constraints (of achieving acceptance in the industry) caused by the 'only-women' policy of Freelance Programmers in the early years, Shirley tried to adhere to the policy for ideological reasons; (as noted in Part 2 of the case, there were only 3 male employees in the first 300 employees/panel members of the company). However, the policy had to be changed in 1975 when the British Government passed the Sex Discrimination Act, which banned all gender-based discrimination and, rather paradoxically, made illegal even the positive discrimination in favor of women. The company then had to reword its policy as employing only those "people with dependents, unable to work in a conventional environment".

- As the company started getting business from outside of the UK, it was felt that the 'freelance' image was not very conducive for boosting business in Europe. Hence, in 1974, the company was renamed 'F International'. Shirley was particular about retaining 'F' in the company name, which a section of the press interpreted as representing the original concept of the company as a group of 'Freelancing Females', but the official explanation given was that it stood for a 'Flexible' and 'Free' organization. Two European subsidiaries were established with similar names, one in Copenhagen (F International ApS, for taking care of the business in Scandinavian countries) and the other in Amsterdam (F International BV, for the business in the Benelux countries). In addition, they entered into a partnership with Heights Information Technology Services Inc., in the US.

- The original business model did not work as well beyond the UK borders. The home-based, flexible, 'teleworking' system pioneered by Shirley, which was successfully implemented in the UK, did not find much acceptance in other European countries. This was because Continental Europe was far more advanced than the UK in equal opportunity regulations and child-care facilities, and so there were very few qualified women interested in working in the corporate sector sitting idle at home. Eventually, the two European subsidiaries were closed down, and the partnership with the US company was terminated. In 1988, the company was renamed again, as 'FI Group Plc', as it was no longer relevant to highlight the 'International' part of it. The change of name was similar to the previous change, when they suppressed 'freelancers' earlier by abbreviating it to 'F'. This time they additionally abbreviated 'International' to 'I'.

- Changes of various kinds were made possible in the organization, as the founder realized that the innovative ideas that supported the business in its early days may not be relevant in the growth stage and so she adopted a policy of 'let it go'. The process of 'succession planning' was started in the early 1970s, when Shirley divided her business into two parts: Software development (by freelancing professionals) and Consultancy (by its own employees), and appointed Pamela Woodman as the Managing Director of the Freelance Group, while she herself was in charge of the Consultancy Group. Unfortunately, this experiment ended up in failure. Though Pamela was professionally competent, she was not loyal to FI. She instigated underhand dealings with a few of the most important customers of FI and engaged freelancers from the FI panel to create her own venture, Pamela Woodman Associates. This was a major blow to FI Group, and it took a few years for Shirley to recover from the financial and psychological shock.

- The financial shock was aggravated by the recessionary changes in the economy. The UK stock market crashed in early 1973, and the oil prices skyrocketed later in the same year because of the Yom Kippur or the Ramadan War between Israel and the Arab Coalition, which inflamed the feelings of the OPEC countries against the pro-Israel Western world. By 1975, the UK inflation rate was as high as 25%. With some of the major clients being poached by Pamela and many panel members and some employees switching allegiance to the rival company, it was an extremely difficult time for Shirley and FI. One consolation was that Frank Knight, the then Chairman of the Board, whom Pamela had brought onto the Board in 1971, stood firmly with Shirley. His connections in the insurance industry helped in finding new customers for FI.

- As the crisis, both within and outside the company, was deepening, Shirley went into a 'liquidation mode' and started on an asset-reduction drive. She sold off furniture and office equipment that was not in frequent use and moved the head office to a single, cheaper, and self-contained facility away from the sprawling offices spread across two locations. More painfully, she had to reduce the staff by half and carry out all of the clerical and administrative tasks herself, including the sales calls. For calling customers, she used her old crude system of using the cards with details of all her previous contacts to make periodic calls, which occasionally led to new orders. She had no hesitation in taking on the clerical, sales, and administrative jobs even after she re-assumed charge as the Managing Director of the combined entity (merging the software development and consultancy outfits, the former having been under Pamela's stewardship).

- Despite all the financial and personal difficulties caused by the separation of Pamela Woodman and a good number of employees and panel members, Shirley showed a pleasant face in public. In 1972, she even celebrated the 10th anniversary of the founding of her company, with a function held at the Institute of Directors in Pall Mall, which brought in some press coverage as well as a few customers. Slowly, with systematic hard work, the company came out of the red with a nominal profit of £2,000/- in 1973 (from a loss of £3,815/- in the previous financial year), although on a hugely reduced turnover. It was also a pleasant surprise that some of the employees who had joined Pamela started coming back; Shirley received and re-appointed them without any ill-feeling, as she believed that people who have realized their mistakes would not commit them again.

- Having failed in the attempt of succession planning with Pamela Woodman, Shirley was hesitant to revisit this strategic issue and so continued as the Managing Director for more than a decade until 1985, when Hilary Cropper was inducted as the CEO of the UK operations. By that time, the revenues of the company had gone up to £7.6 million, with more than 1,000 employees. Cropper continued in that position till 2000 and then became the Executive Chairperson and the Non-executive Chairperson two years later. She remained the right-hand person for Shirley until her retirement in 2003 due to ill health. During her tenure at the top, the annual revenues of FI grew from £7.6 million to £450 million. She also supervised the transformation of FI into 'Xansa' in 2001, not only in terms of the name change but also in terms of the nature of the organization — from the original home-based working model to the common practice of office-based work. Not surprisingly, the successors of Hilary Cropper as Chairperson of the Board of an originally 'F-only' company were male professionals, Alistair Cox and later, Bill Alexander, which indicated that the transformation of the organization was almost complete.

- With Hilary Cropper firmly in saddle, Shirley could further accelerate her strategy to 'let it go'. She created a non-executive position of 'Life President' for herself and retired from active involvement in the company in 1993 at the age of 60. Another aspect of her 'let it go' policy was to reduce her shareholdings in the company. This process was started as early as 1981, when she created the "F International Shareholders' Trust" to share the ownership. Simultaneously, she started a "Workforce Share Scheme", under which she gifted a small percentage of her shares to employees every year and made a provision for the staff to purchase shares from her personal holdings. Participating in the ownership of the company was a great motivator for the employees, and their holdings started increasing year-on-year. By 1987, the staff ownership of the company had increased to 25%, and by 1991 it became 44%. In March 1996, when the company was listed on the London Stock Exchange, there were about 50 millionaires among the employees of FI Group Plc. Besides gifting shares to employees, Shirley also sold a substantive percentage of her shares and used the money for philanthropic projects (mostly for autism-related assistance schemes), which became her full-time activity after her retirement from executive roles in the company in 1993, although she continued as FI's Life President.

- The changes in the composition of top management (as part of the 'let it go' strategy) and the change of name to FI Group Plc in 1988 were also accompanied by a change of strategy, both in terms of people management and growth management. The company, which had more than 70% of its staff working as panel members in 1985, was slowly moving to a more conventional model in the 1990s. The growth strategy also shifted from organic growth to acquisitions. There were a series of acquisitions in the 1990s: AMP Computer Recruitment (acquired in 1990); the Kernel Group (acquired in 1991) (both of which provided staffing and training services); IIS Infotech Limited, an Indian computer services company based in New Delhi (acquired in 1997), which provided access to low-cost labor and work spaces in India as well as to customers in the US, Singapore, and South Africa; the OSI Group, a London-based project management and IT consultancy group (acquired in 1999); and the Druid group, a Reading (UK)-based software consultancy company (acquired in 2000), which strengthened FI's IT consultancy activities.

- Through these acquisitions, along with internal growth, the company was able to regain its status as an international operator, not confined only to Europe. Clients of these acquired companies were in the east (India, Singapore and South Africa) as well as the west (Continental Europe and North America). By March 2001, it was a truly international operator, with over 6,000 employees (half of whom were working in India). Its market capitalization was £1.2 billion and the projected sales for the following year were £515 million.

- With the change in the nature of its business and the countries of its operations, the company felt that it should get rid of the F-image (which was variously being interpreted as Freelancers, Female, Flexible, Free, etc.). They wanted to be known by a name that either did not mean anything (or meant something in every language — to sound truly international) and chose Xansa Plc. It was also a fact that they couldn't find a suitable word in English, as almost 98% of such English words were already being used for 'dot.com' websites. The company finalized its new name after a 9-month search involving four external consultants and costing around £1.5 million. In the public view, the justification for spending so much of time and money on the name change was that corporate rebranding was fashionable in those days, as was illustrated by several high-profile name changes, such as Arthur Andersen (to *Accenture*), British Steel (to *Corus*), British Gas (to *Centrica*), Thomson-CSF (to *Thales*), and the Post Office (to *Consignia*). The explanation for the choice of the new name, given by the CEO Hilary Cropper, was that Xansa "is easy to say and read in all major market places and has clear phonetic links with 'answer'". She also pointed out that it resonated with the Sanskrit word, *Sanskar* (meaning 'culture'), and indicated a transition from the old (1960s) culture of freelancing women professionals working from home to a new culture of organization-based operations by both men and women.

- Xansa's life as an independent company lasted only for about 6 years (from 2001 to 2007). In 2007, its turnover was £379.7 million, with 8,600 employees, of which more than 50% were working in India. Its financial performance and international operations made it attractive for takeover, and in 2007, a French company, Groupe Steria SCA, acquired it. Xansa became a subsidiary of Steria and was delisted from the London Stock Exchange, thus bringing the 'let it go' policy to its last stage of execution.

- After her retirement in 1993, when she relinquished the post of Chairperson and accepted a titular position as 'Life President', Shirley was engaged almost full-time in philanthropic work, which she started in the mid-1990s, when Hilary Cropper took charge as the CEO. As mentioned above, her entry into philanthropy was occasioned by her own need to find a care home for her autistic son. According to The Sunday Times Rich List 2002, Shirley was among the 100 richest women in the UK and one of the top five most generous donors to philanthropic projects. She has donated more than £67 million of her personal wealth to different projects, besides founding a few charitable organizations. The two main focus areas of her charitable work are to help people with autism and related disorders and to make better use of IT in the voluntary sector. Prominent among the organizations she has created are as follows: The Kingwood Trust (1993) for the long-term care of adults with autism; The Shirley Foundation (1996) to provide funding support for other charitable projects; Prior's Court Foundation (1998), running a school for children with autism; AutismConnect, a web-based user-community to deal with autism spectrum disorders (ASD) and related disability issues; IT Livery Company Charitable Trust, to support the development of IT infrastructure and projects aimed at helping the disadvantaged; and Oxford Internet Institute (2001), which was the world's first multidisciplinary Internet Institute based in a major university. In addition, she has helped several other charitable organizations through the Shirley Foundation and has served on the governing boards of many others. The reason for making such generous donations to philanthropic initiatives is explained in her auto-biography, *Let It Go* (2012), in the following words: "I do it because of my personal history; I need to justify the fact that my life was saved".

- Shirley has been presented with several awards and honors in recognition of her contribution to industry and society. She is the recipient (in 2000) of DBE (Dame Commander of the Order of the British Empire, and has since been known as Dame Stephanie Shirley), the highest civilian award given by the British Government to women. The second highest, OBE (Officer of the Order of the British Empire), had already been awarded to her in 1980. She is also a recipient of fellowships related to her profession, such as FREng (Fellow of the Royal Academy of Engineering) and FBCS (Fellow of the British Computer Society). Paradoxically, but most deservingly, the girl who wanted to attend college to do a degree program after high school but couldn't because of her special circumstances and had to take up a low-paying job at the Post Office and obtained her honors degree in Mathematics by under-taking a six-year-long evening course at Sir John Cass College, London, was later awarded honorary doctorates by as many as 28 universities!

- The pioneering nature of Shirley's achievements in the field of technology entrepreneurship has received commendations from several visionary scholars and analysts, including Alvin Toffler, who characterized FI as the "seed of the future" in his book, *The Third Wave*. In Shirley's own words, she had prophetically pre-created four or five decades before-hand "many features of the gig economy: flexibility, variable remuneration for different modes of working, and a high level of self-reliance". Her brilliant achievements did not come to her as 'unmixed blessings'. They were interspersed with setbacks and failures both in her personal and professional lives. She firmly believed that the real test of an entrepreneur's competence was his or her ability to effectively deal with failures, which was clearly stated by her in unmistakable terms, as follows: "People remember (us) entrepreneurs because of our successes but… it depends far more on how we deal with failures". Her life and career can be summed up as the integration of a series of different phases in life, both positive and negative. She attributed her ability to adjust to changes so quickly and effectively to her childhood experiences, which can be summed up in the following words: She is an entrepreneur in the true sense of the word, a person who can convert constraints into opportunities. The journey as a refugee from Vienna to Liverpool Street, to a "strange country with a strange language, strange people, strange parents, strange food", taught her how to cope with change.

Secondary Sources (Online)

Abbate, J. (2001). Oral History: Dame Stephanie (Steve) Shirley. Interview #627 for the IEEE History Center, The Institute of Electrical and Electronic Engineers, Inc. 20 April. https://ethw.org/Oral-History:Dame_Stephanie_(Steve)_Shirley.

Askwith, R. (1999). Steve. *Financial Times*. 9 October. https://richardaskwith.co.uk/journalism/people/steve/.

BBC Radio-4. (2013). Woman's Hour: Dame Stephanie 'Steve' Shirley. https://www.bbc.co.uk/programmes/profiles/4s0xGFrTYm9GMPD1KD4Tg9S/dame-stephanie-steve-shirley.

Business Standard. (1997/2013). IIS Promoters in Board Seat deal with FI Group. First published on 12 December 1997, and last updated on 27 January 2013. https://www.business-standard.com/article/specials/iis-promoters-in-board-seat-deal-with-fi-group-197121201091_1.html.

Cameron, L. (2021). How a woman named "Steve" became one of Britain's most celebrated IT pioneers, entrepreneurs, and philanthropists. *Computing Edge*. IEEE Computer Society. https://www.computer.org/publications/tech-news/research/dame-stephanie-steve-shirley-computer-pioneer.

Cassy, J. (2001). And the new name for FI Group is .... *The Guardian*. 29 March. https://www.theguardian.com/business/2001/mar/30/6.

Cross, G. (2017). Inspiring Woman: Dame Stephanie Shirley. Runneth London. https://www.runnethlondon.com/2017/03/14/inspiring-woman-dame-stephanie-shirley/.

Daily Mail. (2014). ....Dame Stephanie Shirley .....(had) one heartache that her riches couldn't cure .... *MailOnline*. September/October. https://www.dailymail.co.uk/femail/article-2740146/Pushed-brink-suicide-son-loved-With-150m-fortune-Dame-Stephanie-Shirley-one-Britain-s-women-tycoons-But-one-heartache-riches-couldn-t-cure.html.

Gow, D. (2007). Employees to bank millions as Xansa agrees to takeover. *The Guardian*. 30 July. https://www.theguardian.com/business/2007/jul/31/3.

Murray, A. (2018). Just call me Steve: Dame Stephanie Shirley on a life in tech. *Jobbio.com*. March 29. https://blog.jobbio.com/2018/03/29/just-call-steve-dame-stephanie-shirley-life-tech/.

Pandika, M. (2014). How Dame Shirley Jumped over Tech's Gender Gap in the 1960s. *AllTech Considered: Tech, Culture and Connection*. June 12. https://

www.npr.org/sections/alltechconsidered/2014/06/12/321098728/how-dame-shirley-jumped-over-techs-gender-gap-in-the-1960s.

Refugee Week. (2021). Dame Stephanie Shirley CH: On being a child refugee. Speech delivered at 'Children Displaced by Conflict' Seminar, Ellesmere, Shropshire, 1 April 2020. https://refugeeweek.org.uk/dame-stephanie-shirley-on-being-a-child-refugee/.

Sharpe, R., Hutton, S. and Carter, H. (2017). Interview with Dame Stephanie Shirley. *Archives-IT*. February 20. https://archivesit.org.uk/interviews/dame-stephanie-shirley/.

Shirley, S. and Askwith, R. (2019). *Let It Go: My Extraordinary Story — From Refugee to Entrepreneur to Philanthropist*. London: Penguin. 2019.

Simpson, P. (2020). How Stephanie 'Steve' Shirley changed business. *Management Today*. 6 March. https://www.managementtoday.co.uk/stephanie-steve-shirley-changed-business/reputation-matters/article/1674644.

UNSSC. (2017). Dame Stephanie 'Steve' Shirley. UN System Staff College (Sharing Knowledge Developing Leaders). https://www.unssc.org/about-unssc/speakers-and-collaborators/dame-stephanie-steve-shirley/.

Who's Who. (2002). Dame Stephanie (Steve) Shirley, Life President Xansa plc (previously F.I. Group). http://www.mi2g.com/cgi/mi2g/reports/speeches/dss_profile.pdf.

Wikipedia. (2021). Steve Shirley. October 30. https://en.wikipedia.org/wiki/Steve_Shirley.

Wikipedia. (2021). F International. November 7. https://en.wikipedia.org/wiki/F_International.

Wikipedia. (2021). Xansa. 13 October. https://en.wikipedia.org/wiki/Xansa.

Appendix 2: Entrepreneurial Policies and Strategies — A Questionnaire

We are a team of researchers at the Manchester Business School working on a research project sponsored by the European Foundation for Management Development (EFMD). The major objective of this research is to study the policies and strategies related to venture management. We are approaching you with this questionnaire because of the entrepreneurial initiative shown by you in setting up and managing your enterprise. Needless to say, we need information on a variety of aspects of enterprise management and on a few aspects of an entrepreneur's life and career. The responses you give will be kept confidential and will be used only for aggregate analysis leading to academic generalizations. There are no right or wrong answers to any of the questions given below. It will be a great help to our research if you could freely and frankly indicate those answers that are true about yourself and your enterprise.

This questionnaire is divided into five sections. They are on (1) venture characteristics, (2) management practices of the venture (3) personal policies of the principal promoter, (4) work motives of the principal promoter, and (5) background and early experiences of the principal promoter. Though there are several questions in each part, it is quite easy to complete this questionnaire, as the answers in most cases can be indicated by encircling an appropriate number. The whole questionnaire can be completed within about 30–40 minutes, and we hope you will kindly spare time for this research, which may have important implications for entrepreneurship guidance and counseling in the future.

As may be clear from the titles of some sections, this questionnaire is to be completed by the *principal promoter* of the enterprise. The principal promoter, for the purpose of this research, is the major decision maker in the enterprise, not necessarily the one with the largest financial stakes.

Instructions for answering the questions are given at the beginning of each section. Please return the completed questionnaire to Manchester Business School, in the reply paid envelope enclosed. If you would like to get a summary of the findings, please indicate it by a tick (✓) mark in the margin against this paragraph. We shall be happy to send it to you.

We thank you for your co-operation and look forward to receiving your valuable contribution to this research.

Mathew J. Manimala
EFMD Visiting Fellow
Manchester Business School
Booth Street West
Manchester M15 6PB (UK)

Section 1: Venture Characteristics

There are nine questions in this section. Please write the answers in the space provided on the right-hand side.

1. Name and address of the enterprise:
2. Your name & position:
3. Number of years you have been with the enterprise:
4. Year of venture start-up:
5. Year of commencement of operations:
6. Please give approximate figures on investment, turnover, profits, and employee strength for/as at the years specified in the table below:

	For the first full year of operations	For the year 1985–86	For the last full year of operations
(a) Total investment (Undepreciated)	£	£	£
(b) Sales turnover	£	£	£
(c) Profit before interest & taxes	£	£	£
(d) Employee strength (Number)			

7. Products/services marketed:
   (a) Initial year:
   (please list if more than one)
   (b) Current year:
   (please list if more than one)
8. Average long-term profitability (return on investment) of your enterprise (please tick one):

Not profitable	Less than 10% returns	10–20% returns	20–30% returns	30% or more returns

9. What is your assessment of the growth potential of the industry to which your enterprise belongs? (please tick one).

Declining industry	Stagnating industry	Industry growing at a slow rate	Industry growing at an average rate	Industry growing at a fast rate

Section 2: Management Practices

Given below are a few statements indicating practices related to the start-up and management of business units. You are requested to go through these statements with reference to what you do now and what you did during the start-up of your unit. Record your present practices on the first 7-point scale and start-up practices on the second 7-point scale on the right-hand side of the statements. Encircle 7 if you totally agree with the statement as reflecting your practice and encircle 1 if you totally disagree. Choose any other numbers depending on the degree of your agreement or disagreement about this practice in your organization. It is possible that your practices during start-up were different from what you practice now. In that case, encircle a different number on the second scale or else mark the same number. The meanings of the scale points are given below and are reproduced on top of every page for your convenience.

Very strongly disagree	Strongly disagree	Disagree	Neither agree nor disagree	Agree	Strongly agree		Very strongly agree
1	2	3	4	5	6		7
					Your Organization's		
Statements				Present Practice	Practice during start-up		
1. When starting a new unit/division, we prefer tried and tested product/service ideas to new and off-beat ones.				1 2 3 4 5 6 7	1 2 3 4 5 6 7		
2. We prefer to develop our own new venture ideas rather than borrow from others.				1 2 3 4 5 6 7	1 2 3 4 5 6 7		
3. We do not make any special efforts toward the active search for and development of new ideas.				1 2 3 4 5 6 7	1 2 3 4 5 6 7		
4. If a profitable opportunity presented itself, we do not mind deviating from the professed goals of our enterprise.				1 2 3 4 5 6 7	1 2 3 4 5 6 7		
5. Even though our units are doing well, we keep on looking for new ideas.				1 2 3 4 5 6 7	1 2 3 4 5 6 7		
6. We believe that at least one of the directors should have knowledge of the technology involved in the business.				1 2 3 4 5 6 7	1 2 3 4 5 6 7		
7. We try to recruit the best people for at least a few critical positions.				1 2 3 4 5 6 7	1 2 3 4 5 6 7		
8. We choose partners for the money they can contribute rather than for their special management capabilities.				1 2 3 4 5 6 7	1 2 3 4 5 6 7		
9. We try to subcontract as much of our work as possible.				1 2 3 4 5 6 7	1 2 3 4 5 6 7		
10. We get into technical collaborations with other reputed companies rather than develop our own technology.				1 2 3 4 5 6 7	1 2 3 4 5 6 7		
11. We try to minimize borrowed capital.				1 2 3 4 5 6 7	1 2 3 4 5 6 7		
12. We try to avoid competition by choosing products and markets different from those of competitors.				1 2 3 4 5 6 7	1 2 3 4 5 6 7		
13. When we think of starting new/additional units, we choose areas which are related to our previous work experience/existing operations.				1 2 3 4 5 6 7	1 2 3 4 5 6 7		
14. We try to maintain the quality of our products/services at any cost.				1 2 3 4 5 6 7	1 2 3 4 5 6 7		
15. Our company's image is built primarily through our advertisements and publicity.				1 2 3 4 5 6 7	1 2 3 4 5 6 7		

Very strongly disagree	Strongly disagree	Disagree	Neither agree nor disagree	Agree	Strongly agree		Very strongly agree
1	2	3	4	5	6		7
					Your Organization's		
Statements				Present Practice	Practice during start-up		
16. We make substantial use of professional systems, techniques, and people.				1234567	1 2 3 4 5 6 7		
17. We have strict rules and procedures and will not tolerate much experimentation by our employees.				1 2 3 4 5 6 7	1 2 3 4 5 6 7		
18. We do not launch any of our products/projects/ventures without initially testing their success in the market.				1 2 3 4 5 6 7	1 2 3 4 5 6 7		
19. We believe in the adage: "Don't put all your eggs in one basket".				1 2 3 4 5 6 7	1 2 3 4 5 6 7		
20. We have a decentralized setup with considerable autonomy to the lower levels.				1 2 3 4 5 6 7	1 2 3 4 5 6 7		
21. We collect systematic information on all our new ideas/ projects.				1 2 3 4 5 6 7	1 2 3 4 5 6 7		
22. We closely supervise the work of our employees and take them to task for improper behavior.				1 2 3 4 5 6 7	1 2 3 4 5 6 7		
23. We reward our employees more for loyalty than for their performance.				1 2 3 4 5 6 7	1 2 3 4 5 6 7		
24. We believe in aggressive marketing (that is, we resort to heavy advertising, personal selling, and promotional schemes including discounts, vouchers, gifts, etc.)				1 2 3 4 5 6 7	1 2 3 4 5 6 7		
25. Our strongest selling point is our low prices.				1 2 3 4 5 6 7	1 2 3 4 5 6 7		
26. We are actively involved in industry/professional associations.				1 2 3 4 5 6 7	1 2 3 4 5 6 7		
27. In a crisis, we seek support primarily from friends and relatives rather than from professionals and reputed individuals.				1 2 3 4 5 6 7	1 2 3 4 5 6 7		
28. We grab opportunities to sponsor public-interest activities such as sports and various kinds of campaigns.				1 2 3 4 5 6 7	1 2 3 4 5 6 7		
29. In making decisions, we rely more on our judgment than on professional analysis and expert advice.				1 2 3 4 5 6 7	1 2 3 4 5 6 7		
30. The monetary gains from our business belong entirely to the partners/directors, and so we do not have a practice of sharing them with others such as employees and dealers.				1 2 3 4 5 6 7	1 2 3 4 5 6 7		

(Continued)

(Continued)

Very strongly disagree	Strongly disagree	Disagree	Neither agree nor disagree	Agree	Strongly agree	Very strongly agree
1	2	3	4	5	6	7
					Your Organization's	
Statements					Present Practice	Practice during start-up
31. Information on the various aspects of our business is usually kept confidential, and we do not share it with others such as employees and bankers, unless it is absolutely essential.					1 2 3 4 5 6 7	1 2 3 4 5 6 7
32. We try to minimize investments at all levels including overheads, inventories, etc. and would not mind operating in improvised sheds, or using loaned facilities and/or improvised/second-hand machines.					1 2 3 4 5 6 7	1 2 3 4 5 6 7
33. We prefer to start small and grow big steadily and incrementally relying primarily on internal resources.					1 2 3 4 5 6 7	1 2 3 4 5 6 7

Section 3: Personal Policies of the Principal Promoter

Given below are a few statements. You may please indicate your agreement or disagreement to each by encircling the appropriate numbers on a 7-point scale shown below. On the right-side scale, please mark how you felt about these statements at the time of starting your first venture.

Very strongly disagree	Strongly disagree	Disagree	Neither agree nor disagree	Agree	Strongly agree	Very strongly agree
1	2	3	4	5	6	7
Statements				Now	At the time of starting your first venture	
1. Everything is fair in business as long as it produces results.				1 2 3 4 5 6 7	1 2 3 4 5 6 7	
2. I am confident about my style of managing the enterprise and would not like to experiment with new-fangled ideas.				1 2 3 4 5 6 7	1 2 3 4 5 6 7	
3. I am very clear about the alternatives available to me in any situation and would not like to waste time generating various alternatives.				1 2 3 4 5 6 7	1 2 3 4 5 6 7	

4.	I do not mind selling off my business if I can get an employment which would give me a larger income.	1 2 3 4 5 6 7	1 2 3 4 5 6 7
5.	I like things to be neatly structured and am very uncomfortable with uncertainties of any kind.	1 2 3 4 5 6 7	1 2 3 4 5 6 7
6.	I am confident that I can manage this enterprise very well.	1 2 3 4 5 6 7	1 2 3 4 5 6 7
7.	I have had a few failures in life, and all of them were caused by unforeseen circumstances and not by any mishandling on my part.	1 2 3 4 5 6 7	1 2 3 4 5 6 7
8.	All my successes can be attributed to my own action, and there is very little element of luck contributing to them.	1 2 3 4 5 6 7	1 2 3 4 5 6 7
9.	If I were to predict the future for myself and my enterprise, I see no cause for any worry.	1 2 3 4 5 6 7	1 2 3 4 5 6 7
10.	I think it is essential for people to conform to social norms, and I would not like to employ any social deviants in my enterprise.	1 2 3 4 5 6 7	1 2 3 4 5 6 7
11.	In business, it is not always possible to keep one's promises, and I would not hesitate to break my promises if it brings some business gains.	1 2 3 4 5 6 7	1 2 3 4 5 6 7
12.	The amount of work involved in setting up and managing one's own venture is a little too much for me.	1 2 3 4 5 6 7	1 2 3 4 5 6 7
13.	Business is a gamble. One can never fully understand the risks involved. It is more important to take the plunge than to calculate the risks.	1 2 3 4 5 6 7	1 2 3 4 5 6 7
14.	I find it easier to exercise my authority as a chief executive than to persuade others to do what I want them to.	1 2 3 4 5 6 7	1 2 3 4 5 6 7
15.	I do not like to be told what I am supposed to do.	1 2 3 4 5 6 7	1 2 3 4 5 6 7
16.	If I encounter obstacles to the pursuit of my goals, I would rather change my goals than waste time on repeated efforts.	1 2 3 4 5 6 7	1 2 3 4 5 6 7
17.	It takes time for me to recover from a failure, and therefore, my policy is to avoid failure situations.	1 2 3 4 5 6 7	1 2 3 4 5 6 7
18.	I take pleasure in doing what others consider to be difficult.	1 2 3 4 5 6 7	1 2 3 4 5 6 7
19.	I have a thorough knowledge of what is needed for my business and I do not think there is anything further to learn.	1 2 3 4 5 6 7	1 2 3 4 5 6 7
20.	I feel more comfortable with a legitimate authority structure where things are got done as matter of routine, without any need for influencing, persuasion, and politicking.	1 2 3 4 5 6 7	1 2 3 4 5 6 7
21.	I want to be the best in my field.	1 2 3 4 5 6 7	1 2 3 4 5 6 7
22.	One of my major concerns is that people do not understand me properly.	1 2 3 4 5 6 7	1 2 3 4 5 6 7
23.	I feel more comfortable working alone, than in collaboration with others.	1 2 3 4 5 6 7	1 2 3 4 5 6 7
24.	I have not received much support from others in my entrepreneurial ventures.	1 2 3 4 5 6 7	1 2 3 4 5 6 7

Section 4: Work Motives of the Principal Promoter

The twenty statements that follow are about the reasons why people work. These may apply to different people in different degrees. The statements are worded in such a way that they are applicable also to the employment situation because an entrepreneur may have been working as an employee before launching his/her first venture. You are requested to think about your reasons for work and indicate your agreement or disagreement with the statements on a 7-point scale as shown below, 1 indicating strongest disagreement and 7 indicating strongest agreement. Also, please think about your motives before you started your first venture, and rate those motives on the right-side scale.

Very strongly disagree	Strongly disagree	Disagree	Neither agree nor disagree	Agree	Strongly agree	Very strongly agree
1	2	3	4	5	6	7

	Statements	Now	Before starting your venture	
1.	I work because I get monetary compensation which provides me present and future financial security.	1 2 3 4 5 6 7	1 2 3 4 5 6 7	
2.	I work because it helps me fulfill my family obligations.	1 2 3 4 5 6 7	1 2 3 4 5 6 7	
3.	I work because it is a pleasure interacting with others at work, which gives me a feeling of belongingness.	1 2 3 4 5 6 7	1 2 3 4 5 6 7	
4.	I work because those who control some resources required by me are supportive and understanding. (e.g., a boss in the case of an employee, and governmental or institutional authorities in the case of an entrepreneur).	1 2 3 4 5 6 7	1 2 3 4 5 6 7	
5.	I work because a job well done earns me reputation and recognition within or outside the organization.	1 2 3 4 5 6 7	1 2 3 4 5 6 7	
6.	I work because a good performance will lead me to a top position in the organization (in the case of an employee) or in the industry (in the case of an entrepreneur).	1 2 3 4 5 6 7	1 2 3 4 5 6 7	
7.	I work because my position in the organization enables me to exercise influence on people both within and outside the organization.	1 2 3 4 5 6 7	1 2 3 4 5 6 7	
8.	I work because being in this position helps me attain better status in society.	1 2 3 4 5 6 7	1 2 3 4 5 6 7	
9.	I work because I enjoy my work.	1 2 3 4 5 6 7	1 2 3 4 5 6 7	
10.	I work because it is my duty to do so.	1 2 3 4 5 6 7	1 2 3 4 5 6 7	
11.	I work because it helps me to develop and utilize my skills, knowledge, capabilities, and potentialities.	1 2 3 4 5 6 7	1 2 3 4 5 6 7	

Very strongly disagree	Strongly disagree	Disagree	Neither agree nor disagree	Agree	Strongly agree	Very strongly agree
1	2	3	4	5	6	7

	Statements	Now	Before starting your venture
12.	I work because I want to achieve the targets and standards set for me by myself or by others.	1 2 3 4 5 6 7	1 2 3 4 5 6 7
13.	I work because I want to do something new and path-breaking.	1 2 3 4 5 6 7	1 2 3 4 5 6 7
14.	I work because I consider my work as the best medium to express myself and realize the purpose of my existence.	1 2 3 4 5 6 7	1 2 3 4 5 6 7
15.	I work because my job gives me opportunities for making independent decisions and taking responsibility for them.	1 2 3 4 5 6 7	1 2 3 4 5 6 7
16.	I work because I am a party to the major decisions affecting my job/organization, which gives me a feeling of involvement.	1 2 3 4 5 6 7	1 2 3 4 5 6 7
17.	I work because I get regular, correct, and constructive feedback about my performance.	1 2 3 4 5 6 7	1 2 3 4 5 6 7
18.	I work because there is enough variety in the tasks I perform and so I do not get bored with my work.	1 2 3 4 5 6 7	1 2 3 4 5 6 7
19.	I work because I feel that my work is important and that by doing it well I contribute to the well-being of the society at large.	1 2 3 4 5 6 7	1 2 3 4 5 6 7
20.	I work because the surroundings of my workplace are clean and healthy.	1 2 3 4 5 6 7	1 2 3 4 5 6 7

Section 5: Background and Early Experiences of the Principal Promoter

This section is about your experiences in childhood and early adolescence, say, before the age of 15. We also ask you some questions about your background. Please answer them as instructed.

1. Your age when you started the present venture: _____ years.

2. Have you launched and managed any successful ventures before starting the present venture? (You may have disposed them off before starting the present one or maybe still retaining them). (Please tick one):
   1. No prior successful ventures
   2. One prior successful venture
   3. Two prior successful ventures

    4. Three prior successful ventures
    5. More than three prior successful ventures

3. Did you make any unsuccessful attempts before you started your first successful venture? (Please tick one)
    1. No prior unsuccessful attempt
    2. One prior unsuccessful attempt
    3. Two prior unsuccessful attempts
    4. Three prior unsuccessful attempts
    5. More than three prior unsuccessful attempts

4. How strongly do you support and practice the teachings of your religion? (Please tick one)
    1. Do not believe or practice
    2. Believe in and practice some of the teachings
    3. Generally conforms, but do not take any active interest
    4. Take active interest in some of the religious/community activities
    5. Firmly believe in all teachings and take active part in all religious/community activities

5. Which religion or community do you belong to? (Please tick one)
    1. Protestant
    2. Catholic
    3. Jewish
    4. Other   Please specify _____

6. How would you rate your ancestral family's education level relative to their times? (Please tick one)
    1. Generally not interested in education
    2. Low levels
    3. Average levels (that is, more or less similar to the majority in the country)
    4. High levels
    5. Very high levels

7. What was your ancestral family's preferred occupation? (You may give a generalized opinion based on the preferences of the majority of your family members). (Please tick one)
    1. Unskilled jobs, as employees
    2. Skilled jobs, as employees
    3. Professions, in employment or private practice

    4. Self-employed in trading

    5. Self-employed in service industries

    6. Self-employed in manufacturing

8. What is your educational background? (Please tick one)
   1. Below matriculate
   2. Matriculate
   3. Graduate
   4. Post-graduate
   5. Technical or professional degree holder — including Ph.D.

9. Did you work for someone else (as an employee) before you started your own business? (Please tick one)
   1. Never worked as an employee
   2. Worked for less than two years
   3. Worked for 2–5 years
   4. Worked for 5–10 years
   5. Worked for more than 10 years

10. What is the nature of your employer, if any? (Please tick one)
    1. Government
    2. Services (like educational institutions, banks, accounting firms, etc.)
    3. Trading
    4. Industry, *not* related to the one in which you started your unit later
    5. Industry, similar to the one in which you started your unit later
    6. Industry, the same as the one in which you started your unit later

11. Please rate your childhood experiences on a 7-point scale in terms of the unhappiness or happiness you felt about them.
    Very unhappy   Very happy
              1 2 3 4 5 6 7
              Mixed feelings
    ('4' indicates mixed feelings, movement toward the right-hand side indicates greater degrees of happiness and movement toward the left-hand side indicates greater degrees of unhappiness)

12. Please rate on a 7-point scale the affluence or deprivation you experienced during your childhood.
    Extreme poverty   Extreme affluence
    or deprivation
              1 2 3 4 5 6 7
    Average income and spending habits

13. Did you ever experience in your childhood any psychological deprivations, such as separation from or death of loved ones, etc.? Please rate the intensity of your deprivation on a 7-point scale.

No psychological   Traumatic experience of
deprivation   psychological deprivation
             1 2 3 4 5 6 7
             Psychological deprivations
               of moderate intensity

14. Did you ever feel neglected in your childhood?

Felt totally   Felt totally cared
neglected by elders   for by elders
             1 2 3 4 5 6 7
              Mixed feelings

15. Did your ancestral family or parental family ever have to move from one place to another or from place to place? Please rate on a 7-point scale.

Not shifted in the   Radical shifts (i.e., from one
history you know of   country to another, from one cultural
                 and linguistics area to another, etc.)
             1 2 3 4 5 6 7
               Shifts within the
         same cultural/linguistic boundaries

16. During your childhood, were you used to concentrating your attention on a single task only (e.g., studies) or were you interested in several activities in different fields (e.g., sports and games, literary activities, and hobbies)? Please rate on a 7-point scale.

No special interest   Deep interest in a variety of
in anything   activities in different fields
             1 2 3 4 5 6 7
              Deep interest in the
              main task only

17. Have you experienced many disappointments during your childhood? Please rate.

No significant   Severe disappointment
disappointment at all   in several fields
             1 2 3 4 5 6 7
             Some achievements and
             some disappointments

18. Are you satisfied with the way you had to spend your life up to the start-up of your first venture? Please rate.

Not satisfied at all   Extremely satisfied
                            1 2 3 4 5 6 7
                        Moderately satisfied

19. Would you consider yourself a successful person during the period before the start-up of your venture? Please rate.

Absolute failure   Grand success
                            1 2 3 4 5 6 7
                        Moderate success

20. How will you rate the people around you (colleagues, friends, relatives, etc.) in terms of the encouragement and support you received from them?

Strongly discouraging   Strongly encouraging
and obstructive   and supportive
                        1 2 3 4 5 6 7
                    Support with caution

21. How will you rate the institutions around you (government departments, municipal authorities, banks, etc.) in terms of the support and encouragement you received from them?

Strongly discouraging   Strongly encouraging
and obstructive   and supportive
                        1 2 3 4 5 6 7
                    Support with caution
                      and restraint

22. Is it the result of chance or of purposeful action that you are an entrepreneur today?

Purely due to   Purely due to purposeful
chance   action on your part
                        1 2 3 4 5 6 7
                    Partly due to chance
                    and partly due to the
                    purposeful action

Index

Lightning Source UK Ltd.
Milton Keynes UK
UKHW022300011122
411486UK00003B/84

9 789811 265365